D1571048

LOVE'S AVAILING POWER

LOVE'S AVAILING POWER

IMAGING GOD, IMAGINING THE WORLD

PAUL R. SPONHEIM

Fortress Press
Minneapolis

LOVE'S AVAILING POWER
Imaging God, Imagining the World

Cover design and image: Joe Vaughan
Book design: PerfecType, Nashville, TN

Library of Congress Cataloging-in-Publication Data
Sponheim, Paul R.
  Love's availing power : imaging God, imagining the world / Paul R. Sponheim.
     p. cm.
  Includes bibliographical references and index.
  ISBN 978-0-8006-9821-8 (alk. paper)
 1. God (Christianity) 2. Kierkegaard, Søren, 1813-1855. 3. Whitehead, Alfred North, 1861–1947. I. Title.
  BT103.S688 2011
  231—dc22
                                        2011009202

To the Teachers

CONTENTS

PREFACE

I am dedicating this book "to the teachers."
Likely, I am doing that in some sense because
I am reflecting on nearly five decades in the classroom, now that I find
myself there no longer. But more importantly, the reason for this dedication
is the reason for my writing at all: I believe there is something of value to be
taught. Teaching matters! That has been the conviction animating my previous books. I realize that when I write what I see to be true, both the writing
and the seeing are launched from and located in the particularities of my
personal existence. That humbling recognition has become increasingly clear
to me. But I continue to believe that human beings do exist in a basic sense
together and that truthful insights can be usefully shared even though none
of us has Truth in his or her pocket. I believe this as a human being, and also
as a Christian. I believe that despite/because of our differences, we can help
each other as we try to get some sense of what life on this planet is about.
Thus, it made sense for me to be one of the six perpetrators in a *Christian
Dogmatics*, regarding which the editors said there were at least seven positions represented by the authors. Most recently, this cluster of convictions
came to expression in *Speaking of God*, a sketch or broad summary of basic
Christian teaching. The swath there was perhaps unseemly wide, as was the
work in the *Dogmatics*. In any case, I sense now a need to pare things down
in order to lift up the "one thing needful," so I write here of Love.

This writing is about God. I have long been dissatisfied with systematic theology textbooks that offer an almost endless parade of divine attributes. I have pressed my students to identify a "category proper," a centering affirmation in terms of which other attributes are to be understood. Christians, pastors certainly, need to have a grasp of what is at the heart of things. The biblical witness does speak in such a way in asserting that "God *is* love" (1 John 4:16).[1] Eberhard Jüngel has it right when he writes, "To think God as love is the task of theology."[2] Moreover, on the Christian reading of things, to speak of the love of God is to speak of a God who has created beings in God's image. Thus, in these pages, I am seeking to understand how love "works" for the Creator and the creatures. What power does love have? How does it create effects? These questions are not the private property of people of faith. All of us humans, we who seek love and to love, will be glad for whatever light can be shone on this topic. Accordingly, I hope these pages may make a contribution for people inside and outside of the churches. Inside those churches I direct my writing not only at people with formal theological education. Indeed, I am heartened when Jonathan Strandjord, charged with supervising the work of theological education for a large Lutheran denomination, writes that "first of all, the church, its institutions, and teaching theologians need to shift from acting as if theological education is something primarily for pastors, church professionals, and academics to seeing it as for the whole people of God."[3]

To get some purchase on the nature of love's power, I seek help here from two major voices from the past two centuries: Søren Aabye Kierkegaard and Alfred North Whitehead. They bring us distinctive insights. Kierkegaard will drive us to recognize the stark reality of personal responsibility in the living of a life. Whitehead will unearth the deep fabric of relationships in which the individual faces the chances and choices of life. Another statement my students tired of hearing from me was "Nobody has it all." I have found it so, and in these pages, I make bold to argue that Kierkegaard and Whitehead need each other, and that we need them together. Love's power can be understood only through an exploration of the reality of relational selfhood. I don't want to leave that understanding up in the air of some abstraction. Love has a struggle, a battle, on its hands. Together these "guides" can help us address that challenge as well, so in later chapters, I write of what love must face: finitude and evil.

"To the teachers" because there is something to be taught, yes. Moreover, the *doing* of effective teaching can illumine love's power. If you have been taught well, you have been loved. I will not write specifically here of Kierkegaard's understanding of "indirect communication" and the responsibility of the learner in appropriating the truth.[4] Nor will I address Whitehead's emphasis on the "becoming" character of the educative process of romance, passion, and generalization.[5] But while I write of love without a focus on loving in *teaching*, my dedication reflects my conviction that effective teaching illustrates the power of love for selves in relationship.

I am grateful that I have had many fine faculty members as teachers. Reidar Thomte, Sidney Rand, Niels Thulstrup, Warren Quanbeck, George Aus, Bernard Meland, Jaroslav Pelikan, Paul Tillich, John B. Cobb Jr., Arthur Peacocke—the list lengthens. As I type those names, I am painfully aware of the gender exclusivity represented. Yet as I think of those people who have taught me well, several female names call out for recognition: Kirsten, Mary, Sue, Dorcas, Ann, Ingrid, Jan, Linda, Katherine, Corie, Sharon—*that* list lengthens. Such fuller, fairer remembering reveals the fact that teaching and learning are together in the educational process *and* that they cannot be neatly portioned out. Both teaching and learning take place on both sides of the lectern in a good classroom. My own teaching over the years became, I believe, far more relational. How could I ignore the wonderful lightning that strikes a classroom when students push creatively into the subject at hand, opening up unanticipated avenues of insight? With the gift of teaching by female students come strong male names as well: Curt, Marcus, Darroll, Butch, Jonathan, Tim, Ron, Neal, Tyler. I am grateful to all these former students, who were clearly my teachers. What becomes clear in this interminable business of counting one's pedagogical blessings (let me not begin to mention books) is that education truly is sharing, so these many named and unnamed benefactors join those who have been colleagues with formal faculty status, such as Terry, Lee, John, Lois, Phil, Lloyd, Dan, Marjorie, Bob, Catherine, and Fred. Out beyond the walls of the academy, there are others who have given insight: friends like Lowell and Jim, pastors like Andrew and Anita, and family, the "orienting" one and the one that still provides a nucleus for living. "To the teachers," I said—well, I married one, and Nell has taught me more than I can say in our five and a half decades together. I thank her for her grace and patience, early and late.

For this specific project, I have been particularly helped by three friends who were once my students: Curt Thompson, Kirsten Mebust, and Tyler DeArmond. Curt and Tyler read the manuscript with great care and made a number of helpful suggestions. Curt has been my most persistent and thorough reader of manuscripts in preparation going back to the 1970s. Tyler has a marvelous capacity to connect theological reflection with evangelical passion. Kirsten has influenced the phrasing of the argument in this book in specific ways, as with the notions of imagination and embodiment. My subtitle reflects a phrasing she came up with as part of the title of a course for pastors we co-taught at Luther Seminary in the summer of 2004. I am grateful to these three companions on the way and also for the structure that Luther Seminary represents by which the library staff helped me so generously and faculty secretary Victoria Smith came to teach me patiently as much as I could learn about the wonderful world of computer technology. At Fortress Press, Susan Johnson, Ross Miller, Karen Schenkenfelder, and Marissa Wold have been particularly helpful. Sylvia Ruud closes (and opens) the book marvelously with a detailed set of indexes.

We are beginning to realize that any adequate list of teachers should include the earth. I have often said in class and in writing, "We belong with the creatures." I have been grateful for some participation in the religion-and-science conversation, and I have regretted my relative incompetence in matters scientific. Others speak for the earth as well; surely the ecofeminist voices need to be heard. Sallie McFague is particularly convincing in writing *A New Climate for Theology: God, the World, and Global Warming*.[6] This ecological emphasis expands appropriately the thorough recognition of the essential character of human embodiment long accented by feminist theologians.[7] I touch this topic briefly in chapter 5, but fuller attention awaits further study.

Kierkegaard wrote that God's omnipotence is "in the power of love."[8] Let's see what that might mean.

INTRODUCTION

Looking for Power

We are looking for power, but we have a gnawing sense we might be looking in the wrong place. For that matter, we might ask whether we really know exactly what we are looking for. What is power, after all? We can be attracted to a crude view that says, "The one with the most toys wins." The focus here is on winning and, for sure, not losing. What could be clearer than this—that losing is not winning? Such a quantitative view can easily invade our God-talk as well. And in this view, it is the one with the most power who wins. God is quickly identified as an "all-American" on this playing field. Do not our prayers begin "Almighty God"? But we may have suspicions. Is having power really a zero-sum game? Is power so clearly a commodity, something one can possess quite by oneself? When we think, for example, of the most significant people in our lives, we may sense that this "I win, you lose" emphasis misses something important about power. Those key people—that grandmother, that developmentally or physically disabled friend, that quiet Rock of Gibraltar church member—have power, no doubt. But their power does not seem to be something they hold within themselves. "It" reaches out to others without leaving those people weaker. They are empower*ing*. So we have questions. Just how does power work? If we could locate the source(s) of power, we would claim whatever we could. But where is power to be found? What disciplines can serve us in our search?

We are not without hunches. We suspect power has to do with efficacy, with getting something done, "making a difference," as we say. That suggests that power has to do with a specific person's or group's ability to produce a willed result. Americans speak of their president as "the most powerful person in the world." Thus, if Barack Obama orders a surge of troops for Afghanistan, it will be done. Power seems something a person can possess and use to bring about some state of affairs that corresponds to what the powerful person wills. So we are pointed to the self's desire to assert itself in the mix of things that make up existence—*external* things. Might, say, political science and economics be the fields offering most direct insight into the ways of power? Or is power something more internal, something that speaks of the character, the quality, of the powerful person? We speak of a person's powerful presence in a room, whether or not any explicit action affecting a state of external affairs is involved. Indeed, some events of worldwide significance seem to derive from this kind of personal power. One thinks of the turf trod by Mahatma Gandhi, Nelson Mandela, and Mother Teresa. Thus, we might attend to any source, psychological or philosophical, that would aid in the development of the self.

Or perhaps power does not root in the self in external action or inner identity, but is about realities at work outside the self. I am then led to think of realities that bear on the self relentlessly, powerfully. Perhaps the self's way to power lies in positioning oneself in relation to these forces at work in the world. Human beings might best be seen as essentially passive, at least not to be regarded as originating sources of power but as channels for impersonal energies that do not stay up at night worrying about the human prospect. Might the natural sciences have the most to offer in our search for power? Perhaps they can open us to the powerful forces that really rule our days.

Must we choose among these views? I hope not. A case can be made for each of them. Individual human beings are indeed called by possibilities, sensing they can make choices that do matter for their own intrinsic meaning and for effective life in the world. Yet surely such choosing takes place with resources and within limitations that simply are "given" for the self or community in question. The challenge is to see these factors precisely together. I will outline in these pages a conception of power in which the category of relationship is central. Within relationships, I will identify the self as one essential component in power. To speak truly of power, one must speak of the will that moves to bring about something in the world—indeed, of how the self simply wills to *be* in the world. But I will also want to speak of how the world comes efficaciously to/in that self, making a "worldly" difference in and through the person. These two—self and world, in deep relationship—do seem to be at the heart of the matter. But just how are we to think them together?

Struggling with Self and World: The Modern Framework

This self-and-world framework for the topic of power also helps to locate this venture historically.[1] Stephen Toulmin has suggested that this structure is at the heart of what we call the modern world.[2] He speaks of "the Cartesian dichotomy" as "the chief girder in this framework of Modernity." But these poles, self and world, seem to invite polarization. René Descartes, rightly cited as the proponent of methodological doubt, could not doubt the reality of the doubting self. But he appeals to a nondeceiving God to assure himself that the world does exist.[3] In Descartes's train, we find the intense focus on fathoming the depths of the self, perhaps drawing the psychological disciplines out of shape in the process.[4] Does the road to power run that decisively through the therapist's office?[5] This focus on the self can find expression in a controlling isolation in which the modern self confidently excels in the colonization and conquest of nature.[6]

On the other "modern" hand, we have the empiricist contribution of David Hume reminding us that "our ideas reach no farther than our experience" and cautioning that this reliable "vulgar" experience is simply that of our sense experience.[7] Down that path can lie not science, but a scientism that celebrates the "natural" sciences supposed to be speaking with pure objectivity of what is "out there," innocent of the self's designing and without regard to the self's quandaries. I see Hume's long arm reaching out in Richard Dawkins's scoffing dismissal of any rival to the magisterial role of science.[8] Or in a postmodern twist on the turn from the self, we can find a Richard Rorty holding "the view that human beings are centerless networks of beliefs and desires and that their vocabularies and opinions are determined by historical circumstance."[9]

In such radicalizing of the poles of the self–world relation, we lose the valid elements themselves. Neither pole stays the same without the other. I refuse to accept the notion that in order to understand power, we have to look to worldless selfhood *or* have to grasp the basic nature of a sovereign world in which selves simply exist passively. Perhaps if, resisting the pull of polarization, we can truly find self and world together in relationship, we will garner some insight into what power is. For that effort, a third reality is given as well, for faith's claims about God seem promising turf on which to conduct this effort. On the face of it, God-talk has the needed scope to be a candidate offering genuine integration. Persons of faith do not think of themselves or the world without God being in the picture. More of that third in a moment.

Guides for the Journey

In this fledgling twenty-first century, this late modern if not postmodern time, I think we can get some help from major figures of the previous two centuries: Søren Aabye Kierkegaard and Alfred North Whitehead. These two may seem a strange pairing, but they are alike in refusing to settle for the simplifying clarity of the modern alternatives that Descartes and Hume represent. Their personalities may strike us as indeed disparate, if we think of the tempestuous Dane and the contemplative Englishman. I aim to show that such an oppositional focus can be misleading. I will begin in the nineteenth century with Kierkegaard (1813–1855), who ponders deeply what it is to be, to become, a self. But this enigmatic author will never be found uttering the Cartesian maxim "I think, therefore I am." Then in chapter 2, I will turn to Whitehead (1861–1947), whose multidisciplinary work culminates in a cosmological sketch of the world (the universe). But in that sketch, this transplanted Englishman will be seen to be seeking a deeper experience than his northerly neighbor so fixated on sense experience. In elaborating on what I draw from Kierkegaard and Whitehead, I will add contributions from more contemporary sources, but this pair of giants will dominate these chapters. A vast literature flows from the study of each of these figures, but I do not intend these chapters to be essentially contributions to that literature.[10]

I have long been struck by the fact that in that vast literature, Kierkegaard and Whitehead are seldom brought into conversation with each other.[11] It has seemed strange to the academic world to think of these figures together. Yet my sense is that these two great voices from the modern world need each other. Kierkegaard probes so deeply the reality of the individual—"my reader," as he puts it. But he struggled with human community and had virtually no interest in the natural world in which that solitary self resides.[12] Whitehead, in turn, fathomed the world in its minute becomings, but he found no "continuity of becoming" sufficient to sustain what we would commonsensically call a self.[13] It will not do to settle into camps rhapsodizing over their individual contributions as genuine geniuses. What they have for us reaches us most helpfully within an understanding that truth is finally one, as surely as our common citizenship on this planet must claim priority over polarizing tendencies. They need each other, and *we* need them *together:* the existentialist brooding over the Dane's reading of the self's struggles and the student of science caught up in the Englishman's probing of the microscopic need to come together if we are to face well the challenges of this twenty-first century.

I will make bold to illustrate this conviction by including a paragraph of autobiography.[14] I met Kierkegaard first, through the profound and passionate teaching of my college philosophy professor, Reidar Thomte. As a product of midwestern Lutheran pietism, I was decisively taken by the Dane's fundamental evocation of existence "*before* God." Yet I was left with a problem. My growing-up years had the experience of a family in which some members held to the Christian faith and others did not. Could Kierkegaard give me a way to speak to both sides of the family, to both sides of me? A few years later, I met Whitehead's writing for the first time effectively (though I had read him under Thomte). I was at the University of Chicago in doctoral study. I had gone to Chicago to study with Jaroslav Pelikan (who wrote, of course, *From Luther to Kierkegaard*), and I did so to my great benefit. At Chicago, I also met Bernard Meland and his gentle but challenging rendition of process thought. As I read Whitehead's *Process and Reality* some fifty pages a week, this cosmology of relationship brought forth in me the strong sense that "of course, this is how it is." This Anglican convincingly put God and world together in his rendition of how things are. Yet the nagging sense remained that something was missing here, too, as perhaps suggested by Meland's call to "*re*-mythologize" the biblical message.[15] So it was that Kierkegaard and Whitehead came together in me, as they continue to do in these pages.

We need them together. As we contemplate modern extremes (Descartes, Hume) run amok, we see that. Together they may be able to lead us beyond the roll call of the self (the existentialist in his garret, the therapist looking inward, the self-making man moving on the world) and that of the world (the scientist dismissing any mystical flight within or beyond the sense-perceptible self, the physicist ruling that the other sciences really can be reduced to her realm, the economic man specifying the exchange of goods as the heart of human traffic).

We need them together. So I offer a third chapter, in which I examine how self and world, as delivered to us by Kierkegaard and Whitehead, come together in a hopeful logic of trust. Trust is the call, the challenge, as we face the "other" so powerfully given in our contemporary existence. Our experience is often that we meet the one who is given for us as "other"—different, strange, a dangerous challenge. How am I to understand this other who escapes my categorizing grasp? Moreover, the task is not merely to our understanding. How are we to *live* together on this shrinking planet? What is given *for* us is emphatically other than us. The proposal here is that "the other" (challenging, to be sure) is precisely given "*to*" us—a gift or resource by the Creator's hand. Yet there are genuine threats, actual evil, and real vic-tims. Thus, chapter 4 follows with its call to live powerfully in love, resisting evil, while yet welcoming the stranger and even loving the enemy.

God in the Field

There's that barely disguised God-talk again. Kierkegaard and Whitehead were perhaps not theologians in the strict sense of the word. Christians will search their writings in vain for detailed descriptions of the work of Christ.[16] But they wrote, respectively, of self and world in relation to God. I will seek to do so as well, drawing particularly on my Christian heritage. That heritage faces conceptual challenges, well summarized by Don Cupitt three decades ago: "We need the little interventionist God to give personal qualities to the universal God and to stop him from fading into emptiness and vacuity. Con-versely, the lawlike cosmic God is needed to give breadth and universality to the little interventionist God and stop *him* from declining into a fantasy guardian spirit. But the two deities, the big one and the little one, are quite different from each other. Neither view of God will do on its own. They need each other—and yet they do not go well together."[17] Unless they *do* go well together. I have some difficulty locating "big" and "little" so simply. The word *interventionist* raises a host of problems associated with the implied selectiv-ity of divine action. But Cupitt has put his finger on an important difference in speaking of the "personal" and the "cosmic." The difficulty in thinking these two together brings him in his title to "take leave of God."[18] To the contrary, I believe they come together precisely in their understanding of God's power and our power. These chapters will seek to make that clear. They will sketch a faith in which an intimately loving God is actively present in every moment of the cosmos.

We recognize that our preoccupation with power is not absent when we turn to God-talk. Believers often seem inclined to stress God's power as one of absolute control, a view that can be superimposed on all events so long as we do not remember the Johannine (1 John 4:8, 16) claim that God is love. At least on this view, a loving God could not feelingly experience the world of the creatures. Thus, H. P. Owen writes, "The sorrow and pain that God expe-riences are wholly vicarious; they consist entirely in his imaginative response to the sin and suffering that afflict his creatures. . . . Any suffering that God endures through his love for his creatures is immediately transfigured by the joy that is necessarily his within his uncreated Godhead."[19] A faith with a cross at its center is hard put to locate divine suffering in such a secondary way. Eberhard Jüngel, as mentioned in the preface, well calls us to remember that "to think God as love is the task of theology." He elaborates: "In doing so, it [theology] must accomplish two things. It must, on the one hand, do justice to the essence of love, which as a predicate of God may not contradict what people experience as love. And on the other hand, it must do justice to the being of God which remains so distinctive from the event of *human* love that 'God' does not become a superfluous word."[20] I do want to do justice to that Johannine claim and will do so already in chapter 1 in exploring Kierkegaard's remarkable assertion that God's omnipotence "is in the power of love."[21] Marjorie Suchocki, writing in the Whiteheadian tradition, has observed that the fully-in-control God often seems to arrive on the scene "a bit too late for the victims of this world."[22] Life often enough seems rather out of control. Yet Christians may confess that they have known a certain power in love. Bernard of Clairvaux wrote of this in a twelfth-century sermon pondering the mystery of God's incarnation: "You see how he [Christ] speaks, as though to equals—he who has not equal. He could have said 'me,' but he preferred to say 'us,' for he delights in companionship. What sweetness! What grace! What mighty love! Can it be that the Highest of all is made one with all? Who has brought this about? Love has brought this about, without regard for its own dignity, strong in affection and efficacious in persuasion."[23] Christians will claim that this astounding assertion rings right. But they and other people of faith join skeptical nonbelievers in recognizing challenges to this conviction. A relational view will grant that there is genuine risk in this world—for the creatures and for the Creator. I want to explore Suchocki's bold claim that "paradoxically enough, there is more hope in a riskier world than in that other."[24] What generates hope? From what does hope arise? Well, from love.

Connecting Power and Love

For many in our contemporary culture, connecting power and love is not a self-evident move to make, even (especially?) in speaking of God. My God-talk has to proceed in the face of the many people of faith who would force a choice between love and power as the central attribute to be recognized in our speaking of God. When we turn to human affairs, we also may think of love and power as opposed. Yet when we recall again those key people who have really been powerful for us, we will often find ourselves saying, "I knew they loved me, or at least I know it now. And it made a difference for me; it makes a difference still." I will not claim that all power is an expression of love. We employ vehicles with "horsepower" and agonize over the loss of power when a storm knocks out our electricity. We have heard hard but true words of abusive power.[25] But love also has real power. I resist a conception of love that reduces it to teenagers mooning over each other while the "real" world goes powerfully on, unaffected by their gyrations. Love has to do with how people have to do with each other *and* with how the world runs. The personal, the familial, and the political must all be engaged in any adequate understanding of love. Love seems a many-splendored thing, to be sure. Clarity comes in recognizing the connections among the distinctions.

Thus, I will cite Anders Nygren's classic disjunction between selfless divine agape and selfish human eros.[26] But I have in mind a unitive conception of love where self and other are both benefited. Thomas Jay Oord's definition serves us better: "To love is to act intentionally, in sympathetic response to others (including God), to promote overall well-being."[27] Love and power are together in God—*always*. Thus, I will reject a familiar understanding of God's work of creating that stresses simply power, leaving love to the figure of Jesus. Rather, Michael Lodahl writes wisely of how God "has 'always' been a loving Creator, been everlastingly creating, and 'always' labored with a world by the almighty inflowing of divine love."[28] Following the direction given by Oord and Lodahl, I will argue that this wider reach of love has application for the creatures as well. Surely that must be so of beings created in the image of that Creator.

Love and hope come together in chapters 3 and 4 in a sketch of a truly relational power. That is the kind of power that needs to be attributed to both Creator and creature. We are, after all, truly together in this risky world. Indeed, the connection between Creator and the creatures is precisely what calls for consideration. Thus, in chapter 1, I will explore the reality of the *self's* freedom by using the angle of vision provided by Kierkegaard's insistence that we are created in God's image. Similarly, in chapter 2, I will write of Whitehead imagining the *world* in the relational categories he found insightfully used by church fathers in speaking of the Trinity.[29] That striving for connection between Creator-talk and creature-talk, strengthened, will then be at work in the chapters that follow. I will argue that love is what gives us the power to believe in the face of finitude and to live resisting evil, even while (to the point of) loving the enemy.

There is a pulse in this project. We are emphatically temporal beings, and we know that whatever power means, it has to do with the puzzles of identity and change, with time. So as we seek to live into the image of God, as we seek to imagine a world still being created by that God, we come to the logic of hope that must guide us in our life together. Imagination becomes the instrument by which the human person images God in acting on "propositions" that call us into the future. Thus, in the face of finitude and against the evil around and in us, we hear the challenge to believe and act in *hopeful* love. But we are misled if we are swept into a "no questions to be asked" enthusiasm. We do have questions about how powerful love really is. Moreover, we know that faith's power is a dangerous thing. We have reason to know how much harm faith's frenzy can yield as fruit. People of faith seem often entitled to claim the psalmist's word to "zeal for thy house has consumed me" (Ps. 69:9, RSV). There are questions that must be faced about the mix of the faith, hope, and love, which are said to abide (1 Cor. 13:13). Many of those questions in effect ask whether that mix is so intoxicating that we forget that we live on this earth. So a final chapter explores how we may live creatively even while respecting our limitations and recognizing the power of actual evil. Such creative living becomes the crucible in which faith, hope, and love come to be.

Chapter 1

IMAGING GOD'S LOVE IN FREEDOM: A KIERKEGAARDIAN INVITATION

The self to be found in power is free. He or she wills freely in power to act, to *be*. Of course, any powerful action expresses a confluence of wills, focusing on and in a particular person or group of people. But in any moment of time, the movement in human beings from potentiality to actuality, from indetermination to determination, does not occur without the involvement of will, the wills of individuals. Human will functions in freedom; a choice is made between genuine alternatives. To recognize the reality of choice is not to deny the cumulative efficacy of our choosing. Earlier choices, mine and those of others, shape my freedom in habit's servitude or in character's integrity. But this demonstrates rather than denies the power of will's choosing. Thus, domestic-abuse counselors do not forget this when dealing with the abusive husband who says, "She made me so mad I just couldn't help myself." They speak of a bell curve such that, at some point in the relationship, the man is making choices, freely.[1]

Freedom's Task

If we are to maximize power, we must somehow lay claim to what freedom we can. That is at the heart of what Søren Kierkegaard says about the self. This theme of freedom was there already at the beginning of his authorship.

In his first major publication, *Either/Or*, he asks, "But what is this self of mine? If I were to speak of a first moment, a first expression for it, then my answer is this: It is the most abstract of all, and yet in itself it is also the most concrete of all—it is freedom."[2] How does one claim one's freedom? That calls for decision, bringing actuality out of potentiality. A human being brings about freedom as actuality when that person, in Kierkegaard's language, "wills one thing," "acquiring a history."[3] Those two elements stand out: the individual's choosing (freedom as *means*) and giving that choice continuity in his or her life (freedom as *end*).

So it matters what we choose. In a major work ironically titled *Concluding Unscientific Postscript*, Kierkegaard writes, "The difficulty for an existing person is to give existence the continuity without which everything just disappears."[4] Thus, "for an existing person, the goal of motion is decision and repetition."[5] In effect, the person whose life is constituted by the togetherness of decision in repetition has brought the times of his life together in a willed oneness and so has realized a kind of contemporaneity. Later in the *Postscript*, he uses that term to describe the challenge *uniquely* facing humans: "In the individual the point is to ennoble the successive in contemporaneity. To have been young, then to have grown older, and then finally to die is a mediocre existence, for the animal also has that merit. But to unite the elements of life in contemporaneity, that is precisely the task."[6] The key, we shall see, is to choose oneself in one's "eternal validity."[7] But that will entail concreteness. Earlier, in his ethical second half of *Either/Or*, he provides ample exposition of the theme. When has a person chosen himself ethically? "Not until a person in his choice has taken himself upon himself, has put on himself, has totally interpenetrated himself so that every movement he makes is accompanied by a consciousness of responsibility for himself."[8] Such a person is "sovereign" over himself, "transparent" to himself.[9] Calvin Schragg's summary sentence can serve us: "In Kierkegaard's narrative of the self, it is the act of choosing that centralizes the self and occasions its unity and continuity."[10] That choosing, the exercise of power in freedom's awesome responsibility and the calling to contemporaneity via repetition, will be Kierkegaard's constant drumbeat.

How, then, does a self come to be free, to act freely? What elements come together in any moment in freedom? Kierkegaard provides a tutorial in the coming about of freedom. I will present his understanding of freedom in a human self, drawing particularly on *The Concept of Anxiety* and *The Sickness unto Death*. First, though, I pause for a moment to note the remarkable efficacy of these just-mentioned books. Looking back at them from the perspective of the twenty-first century, it is particularly striking that Kierkegaard's understanding of the human self has influenced a remarkable range

IMAGING GOD'S LOVE IN FREEDOM

of twentieth-century students of selfhood, including both religious writers (e.g., Reinhold Niebuhr[11]) and atheistic authors (e.g., Jean-Paul Sartre[12]). It is the more striking that Niebuhr and Sartre, to take that prominent pair, express indebtedness in precisely the same area of Kierkegaard's thought: the anxious self, finite and free. How is one to account for finding his efficacy in such widely diverse figures? Paul Tillich has suggested this answer: "When Kierkegaard broke away from Hegel's system of essences he did two things: he proclaimed an existential attitude and he instigated a philosophy of existence. He realized that the knowledge of that which concerns us infinitely is possible only in an attitude of infinite concern, in an existential attitude."[13] In contemplating the range of Kierkegaard's influence, one might settle for stressing a shared existential attitude. But I think Tillich is right in emphasizing not only *how* ultimate questions are to be approached, but also *what* we may wisely come to say. Both "how" and "what" matter and have mattered in the reception of Kierkegaard's legacy. We can begin to understand how these are together if we ask from where freedom comes. The answer, it turns out, is from love acting in freedom.

The Art of Power

The range of his influence is rooted in the Dane's own understanding of human life. At bottom, he understands the human self in the light given by his convictions concerning God the Creator. But he recognizes that insight into human selfhood is not the exclusive property of religious types. This is pointedly evident in one of his many journal entries: "Only a wretched and mundane conception of the dialectic of power holds that it is greater and greater in proportion to its ability to compel and to make dependent. No, Socrates had a sounder understanding; he knew that the art of power lies precisely in making another free."[14] In this, as in many other ways, Socrates is his teacher! In *Concluding Unscientific Postscript,* it is clear that, for Kierkegaard, the example of Socrates connects with the content issues of Christian faith:

> Let us consider Socrates. . . . He poses the question objectively, problematically: if there is an immortality. . . . He stakes his whole life on this "if"; he dares to die, and with the passion of the infinite he has so ordered his whole life that it might be acceptable—*if* there is an immortality. . . . The Socratic ignorance was thus the expression, firmly maintained with all the passion of inwardness, of the relation of the eternal truth to an existing person, and therefore it must remain for him a paradox as long as he exists.[15]

I will shortly develop Kierkegaard's *theological* understanding of human self-hood, including explicit critique of Socrates. But it is clear that he understands that human wisdom is not locked up inside the doors of the church. Indeed, at the end of his life, it is Socrates with whom Kierkegaard would speak, even if "for only a half hour."[16] In his praise of Socrates, Kierkegaard perhaps was drawing on his Christian faith that does offer a Creator God who is not anxious about getting explicit credit for wisdom found in the creatures.[17] In the pages to follow, we will spend some half-hours with folks not to be found in our churches, even as I offer this theologically grounded perspective to all comers.

Let us employ the biblical theme of humankind being created in God's image (Gen. 1:26-27) to provide perspective in understanding Kierkegaard's notion of human freedom. God creates freedom in freedom. The powerful work of creation is a work of freedom on God's part. Kierkegaard underscores the freedom of both the Creator and the creatures in a remarkable reflection on the relationship between omnipotence and love: "Oh, what wonderful omnipotence and love! A human being cannot bear to have his 'creations' be something in relation to himself; they are supposed to be nothing, and therefore he calls them, and with disdain, 'creations.' But God, who creates from nothing, omnipotently takes from nothing and says, 'Become'; he lovingly adds, 'Become something even in relation to me.' What wonderful love, even his omnipotence is in the power of love."[18] This loving power wills to have a relationship with the creature that matters to the Creator: "Love also requires something of human beings. Omnipotence does not require anything; it never occurs to omnipotence that a human being is anything other than nothing—for omnipotence he is nothing. . . . But the loving God, who in incomprehensible love made you something for him, lovingly requires something of you."[19] So the Creator God freely ("out of nothing") creates freedom. Is not something about the image of God in the creature suggested by this? In the gift of freedom, we may well find the task of freedom, and would that not have to do with willing, recognizing, receiving the freedom of the other(s)? Joyce Cuff and Curtis Thompson speak of "possibilizing" in these terms: "To possibilize is to expand possibilities, to infinitize, to potentiate. Possibilizing assists the other human being to become free."[20] The freedom of the other finds fulfillment in a loving relationship. As Stephan Post puts it in quite Kierkegaardian fashion, "To be created in God's image means that we are created *for* love *by* love."[21]

Kierkegaard invites us to ponder further where such creative love originates and to what it leads. The rather mind-numbing locution "out of nothing" does underscore that God's initiative "in the beginning" proceeds without any

limitations given in "raw material." But does that initiative reflect a comparable nothing within God? If omnipotence is in the power of love, does not
that reflect back to characterize divine freedom? The freedom caught up positively in love cannot be the unattachment of distance. Moreover, the loving
will to create freedom carries connection as consequence. That we come to
be and what we come to be—both matter to this Creator. *Ex amore* and *ex
nihilo* ("out of love" and "out of nothing") are held together when God creates.[22] Would that not be the calling as well of the creatures imaging that God?
Would we not expect connectedness to matter to the creatures? At the least,
one can say with Kierkegaard that the creature in freedom is called to love.

The appeal to the parallel between Creator and creature does not deny
difference between them. Kierkegaard consistently insists that "God and man
are two qualities separated by an infinite qualitative difference."[23] God is that
different from us as creatures, and—more darkly—there is something more.
The "something" that the creature may become in relation to the Creator may
be opposition, sin. God can do everything possible for the creature, "but he
cannot remove the possibility of offense."[24] The trust this artful God seeks
cannot be coerced. An ominous pair of questions arises: What if faith is not
forthcoming in response to the gift of freedom?[25] Is the relationship itself at
risk?

God's Omnipotent Resolution: Transcendence in Relationship

Central in Kierkegaard's understanding, then, is the assertion that God is
to be distinguished from all that is creaturely by an "infinite qualitative difference." Thus, in *Practice in Christianity*, we hear a withering critique of
"undialectical" rhetoric that "lays out everything, even the paradox, in a direct
superlative so that to be God becomes a direct superlative of what it is to be
a human being."[26] The difference is to be seen in this, that even the use of
creaturely freedom against the Creator does not eradicate the Creator's loving
will to create. To the contrary, it occasions the illustration of the decisiveness, the radicality of the will to create freedom. Again, the freedom in God's
creating is not measured by a capacity to cancel the affair; it is not a matter
of being "free" to pull out of this venture gone wrong. From the outset, the
commitment is firm, rooted in the decisiveness of the divine will. Kierkegaard
expresses this christologically in his use of a beautiful parable of a king who
loved a maiden. The king pretended to be a servant boy to win the maiden's
love on her own level, as it were. But, of course, the king always remained
free to cancel the experiment and reveal his royal identity. Kierkegaard has
used the parable to set up his understanding of God coming in the person

of Jesus of Nazareth. Of this God, he writes, "From the hour when by the omnipotent resolution of his omnipotent love he became a servant he has himself become captive, so to speak, in his resolution and is now obliged to continue (to go on talking loosely) whether he wants to or not. He cannot betray his identity; unlike that noble king, he does not have the possibility of suddenly disclosing that he is, after all, the king."[27]

One notes that Kierkegaard does not abandon the language of omnipotence here. But he proceeds to make the decisive point that the king's having the option to pull back "is no perfection in the king (to have this possibility) but merely manifests his impotence and the impotence of his resolution, that he actually is incapable of becoming what he wanted to become."[28] God's perfection—God's transcendence, we might say—is to be found precisely in God's commitment to the relationship, come what may. He can speak of how by "his will, his free decision," God "has in a certain sense bound himself once and for all."[29] If human beings are to image this God's freedom, they will have to challenge the assumption that it is always best to hold something back, to retain the possibility of abandoning the other.

This transcendence in relationship—that God is so beyond us precisely in being so for us—is not something surfacing only in an early pseudonymous writing (Johannes Climacus, *Philosophical Fragments*, 1844). At the end of his life, preaching on his favorite text, his "only love" (Jas 1:17-21: "Every good and every perfect gift is from above"), Kierkegaard begins with a remarkable prayer to the Changeless God. Here we have the "infinite qualitative difference" clearly located in the love of God: "You are not like a human being. If he is to maintain a mere measure of changelessness, he must not have too much that can move him and must not let himself be moved too much. But everything moves you, and in infinite love."[30] He doubles the dialectic: God's omnipotence is in the power of love; God's changelessness is seen in being moved by all things. Near the end of the discourse, he urges his hearers to allow God's changelessness "to serve you as he wills for your good, your eternal good."[31] And on the discourse's last page, he prays to the changeless God who, unlike a stationary spring, actively seeks the thirsty in spirit: "Thus you are unchanged and everywhere to be found."[32] So the prayer ends with recognition of the relationship, praying that "the one who is praying" may be brought into conformity with God's changeless will.

What becomes clear even in this brief introduction of Kierkegaard's thought is that, for him, God's creating is not an act of sheer power complete in itself. What is revealed is that "omnipotence is in the power of love," a love that entails unbreakable commitment to relationship. To speak rightly of God's power, one must speak of what happens in the give-and-take of life's interaction between the Creator and the creatures. That this is so reveals that God's creating is a matter of grace. That creational grace is confirmed in the coming of the Christ, as explicitly indicated in the parable of the king and the maiden. But the grace that Christians see most clearly in the Christ figure does not begin there.

This point has considerable pastoral importance. If one limits the reality of the decisive divine commitment to the Christ figure, one risks leaving open the possibility that somehow "the real God upstairs" might not be definitively present in Jesus of Nazareth. That hidden God might be otherwise disposed toward the creatures in their sin. Anxious sinners might well harbor such an ominous notion. Happily, there is increasing recognition by contemporary theologians that God does not leave us wondering whether Jesus is on his own in this love for us. Thus, Robert Jenson writes, "God's act to create us and his act of what the tradition calls 'grace' are but two addresses of one word, two utterances in a single conversation of God with his creature."[33] Or again, Ted Peters makes well the point of creation as grace: "Grace is God's favor, and God favors the world. . . . What we know as the temporal creation is a gracious act deriving from God's eternal love."[34]

God Willing One Thing in Creation and Redemption

I have mentioned Kierkegaard's conviction that the human calling is to "will one thing." Such willing would image the Creator, who does will one thing. Part of the secret of God's artful power is this unity of willing. The development of this theme is particularly rich in Kierkegaard's journals. Thus, he clearly makes the point that the love of God does not somehow miraculously originate in the coming of Jesus the Christ. He writes, "They say that God is unchangeable, the Atonement teaches that God has become changed— but the whole thing is an anthropopathetic conception which cannot stand up under reflection. . . . What the Atonement expresses is . . . that God has remained unchanged while men changed, or it *proclaims* to men altered-in-sin that God has remained unchanged."[35] Were Kierkegaard to speak in the Latin of systematic theology, he would say with Lutheran theologian Gustaf Wingren that God's *opus proprium* (God's "proper work"), "which is to give and which is seen most clearly in the Gospel is already operative in Creation and is expressed in the primary fact of life."[36]

But we were just reading Kierkegaard stressing that God actually seeks something from the creatures. Might not our sin somehow qualify God's love then? God's love is indeed affected by human sin; it becomes a suffering love. But it is not qualified. It is again in his journals that Kierkegaard makes this point so strongly: "No, God is not impressed; he changes nothing. Yet believe that it is out of love that he wills what he wills. He himself suffers infinitely in this, but he does not change. Yes, he suffers in love more than you do, but he does not change. . . . In all this he suffers infinitely more than you do, even when it is you who distress him by new sin—but he does not change."[37] Later writers have developed more fully this anchoring of what we see clearly in the Christ back already in the eternal God's gracious will to create temporally. Thus, Jürgen Moltmann has refused to restrict the theme of God's kenosis or self-emptying to what happened in Jesus of Nazareth: "God's creative love is grounded in his humble, self-sacrificing love. This self-restricting love is the beginning of that self-emptying of God which Philippians 2 sees as the divine mystery of the Messiah. Even in order to create heaven and earth, God emptied himself of his all-plenishing omnipotence and as Creator took upon himself the form of a servant."[38] Eberhard Jüngel even pushes that creational grace back into the eternal life of the triune God: "God . . . is overflowing being, and his overflowing being is the expression of his grace, the original image of his covenant with a partner who is not God. . . . In the eternal Son of God, who himself was not created, but comes eternally from God the Father, in this Son of God coming *eternally* from God, God aims at the man [*sic*] who *temporally* comes from God."[39] What opens here is a vision of a God who "has himself only in that he gives himself away. But in giving himself away he has himself. That is how he *is*. His self-having is the event, is the history of giving himself away and thus is the end of all mere self-having."[40]

Kierkegaard affirms strongly the Creator's love willing the freedom of the creature, though in the journal reference with which we began this discussion ("Socrates had a sounder understanding"), he challenges us to think of a creative power that is as much realized as restricted in creating the freedom of the creatures. He seems drawn toward holding God's absolute nature and genuine creaturely independence together: "If in creating man God himself lost a little of his power, then precisely what he could not do would be to make man independent."[41] Here self-having does indeed seem to be precisely self-giving. Yet there is an element of divine limitation present in the commitment entailed in the divine willing.[42] That is clear once again in *The Sickness unto Death*'s reference to "the possibility of offense."[43] The actuality of offense and the resultant divine suffering of this changelessly loving God surely challenges us to think differently about the meaning of an omnipotence actively "willing one thing" in creation and redemption. We are reminded that, with God, "omnipotence is in the power of love." With the creation of genuine freedom comes real risk: "What a rare act of love, what unfathomable grief of love, that even God cannot remove the possibility that this act of love reverses itself for a person, and becomes the most extreme misery—something that in another sense God does not want to do, cannot want to do."[44]

With such real power granted by the Creator, one must ask: How goes it with the creatures?

The Perilous Creation

There is a call here to use our created freedom in the service of the freedom of others. Thus, in the Genesis text, the creation is said to be "good" (Gen 1:10, 12, 18, 25), indeed, "very good" (Gen 1:31). But the creation is not perfect(ed), for there is this call ahead. There is risk in this for the creatures and for the Creator. The Creator risks failure in seeking the love of the creature, who is truly free to respond otherwise. The human creature is called in a way to image the Creator's commitment and risk. But the risk for the creature is not about the response of the Creator, for the divine love is sure. Rather, for the creature, freedom's risk lies precisely in itself, in the unpredictability of freedom's own choices. For the creatures to be, to become, is to be at/in risk. Yet humankind is nonetheless created good, for the path to full imaging of the divine commitment in love is nothing less than a path can be. Indeed, God in Christ can tread that path as the "prototype," "*ahead* beckoning."[45] A path can be made available, but love cannot be coerced to walk that path. Love's power artfully creates freedom. Thus, one might speak of three elements in the image of God: humans are created (1) with an endowment, (2) in relationship, and (3) with a telos.

Let us consider yet another triadic framework for understanding the power of the self: possibility and necessity meeting in the reality of freedom. Kierkegaard's fullest treatment of this triadic understanding is to be found in a book with the cheerful title *The Sickness unto Death*. Part of the melancholy Dane's commitment to concreteness is evident in refusing to offer simply a statement of human selfhood that is abstracted from actual existence. Looking at human life and a state church in Copenhagen in the 1840s, Kierkegaard did not reach a diagnosis of perfect health. But we should begin our anthropological analysis not with a fallen creature but with human nature as created. That distinction is crucial for Kierkegaard. The sinner's fallenness cannot be traced to being a creature. He had made that point through pseudonym Johannes Climacus already in 1844. Climacus asked if the human predicament could be due to an act of God, and his project's "advance on Socrates" provided the unequivocal response: no, "it must therefore have been due to himself."[46] Anti-Climacus, five years later, develops the point fully in writing of the algebra of humans created good and yet coming to despair. Human existence is composed of two elements related to each other dialectically. In the next section, I will write of the third. Taking necessity and possibility as the terms of the relationship (other pairs are available—the finite and the infinite, the temporal and the eternal[47]), they are certainly in recognizable relation to each other. That is true of the One we image. I have just written of how there is something like necessity (love's need and changelessness at least) that meets possibility in the divine willing. Perhaps the human synthesis does indeed image God, potentially if not perfectly.

It is clear to us in our clear-headed moments that what is possible for us is at least in part dependent on what is "given" for us in the constituent elements that flow from our past into any present. I am writing these words in the bicentennial year of Charles Darwin's birth. One might even go beyond Kierkegaard to think of how human possibility "emerges" out of the physical, genetic indebtedness to earlier stages in the evolutionary process. Kierkegaard would applaud the recognition that in such "strong" emergence, novelty is to be found that is neither completely explainable nor entirely predictable in the terms of the antecedent conditions.[48] The closest he himself may come to this developmental understanding is when he writes that the innocent human "self" "is not qualified as spirit but is psychically qualified in immediate unity with his natural condition."[49] Such emergence of humankind would make sense in a creation characterized by what is being called "self-organizing complexity" throughout the process.[50] Stuart Kauffman's work on this theme is well summarized by Ian Barbour, physicist-theologian: "He finds similar patterns in the behavior of complex systems that appear very different—for example, in molecules, cells, neural networks, ecosystems, and technological and economic systems. In each case feedback mechanisms and nonlinear interactions make cooperative activity possible in larger wholes. . . . He finds that *order emerges spontaneously* in complex systems, especially on the border between order and chaos."[51]

Christian faith would speak of such complexity before and in the human called to will one thing as itself a gift of the Creator. Thus, Kierkegaard stresses that this relation is "established by another." It is the Creator's providential will that brings necessity and possibility to be related in the human self. Yet that they are related "dialectically" conveys the fact that there is instability in the relationship. For the emerging self, there is a pull in possibility away from necessity ("In America a child can grow up to be anything she wants to be"), just as there is a drag on possibility given in necessity ("Was that my dad talking in what I just said?"). Poles seem to invite polarization.

But they do not determine the matter, for there is more to be said about the nature of human existence.

The "Positive Third"

In the mix of becoming that is selfhood, there is a third element, the relation between the two constituting elements "relating itself to itself,"[52] a "positive third." Early in his ethical writings, Kierkegaard wrote of "choosing oneself." One might say that here the self's power to "do" something is secondary to and dependent on the self's power to "be" something—itself. Yet that being is always a becoming. This puzzling language of choosing oneself is clarified in his mature (1849) work. Here is the formulation from *Sickness:* "Every moment that a self exists, it is in a process of becoming, for the self κατά δύναμιν [in potentiality] does not actually exist, is simply that which ought to come into existence."[53] Thus, humankind is indeed created "good, but not perfect," to use the formulation just mentioned. Kierkegaard drives home the point: "The condition of man, regarded as spirit . . . is always critical. . . . There is no immediate health of the spirit."[54] So the call to contemporaneity in willing one thing in human existence is for this "positive third," this relating itself to itself, to so choose that an equilibrium exists, and the self is in a posture of dynamic rest.[55] The early pseudonymous writing of the ethicist offers helpful amplification. The person who has chosen himself ethically "then possesses himself as an individual who has these capacities, these passions, these inclinations, these habits, who is subject to these external influences, who is influenced in one direction thus and in another thus. Here he then possesses himself as a task in such a way that it is chiefly to order, shape, temper, inflame, control—in short, to produce an evenness in the soul."[56] Back to that cheerful title: Kierkegaard believed—as earlier noted—that, as "established by another," it was impossible for the human self to accomplish that task, to reach that equilibrium by itself, "but only, in relating itself to itself, by relating itself to that which has established the entire relation."[57] As he looked about himself—and within himself—he saw a multitude of forms of the misrelating that is despair. Again, that misrelation in a person cannot "be something that lies in human nature as such": "If he were not a synthesis, he could not despair at all; nor could he despair if the synthesis in its original state from the hand of God were not in the proper relationship."[58] How does that misrelating come about?

As created, we are anxious. What is that anxiety? Well, it is not guilt: "Just as Adam lost innocence by guilt, so every man loses it in the same way."[59] Rather, "anxiety is freedom's actuality as the possibility of possibility."[60] Here the "positive third" (in the language of *Sickness unto Death*) of the relation relating itself to itself enters crucially. The *Concept of Anxiety* lays claim to the fall narrative in Genesis 3 to identify the spirit, which "is in a sense a hostile power, for it constantly disturbs the relation between soul and body."[61] Yet the dialectic does not collapse, for on the next page we are told. "On the other hand, spirit is a friendly power, since it is precisely that which constitutes the relation."[62] In innocence, "there is peace and repose, but there is simultaneously something else that is not contention and strife, for there is indeed nothing against which to strive. What, then, is it? Nothing."[63] But the nothing begets anxiety. The "dreaming" spirit projects its actuality outside itself, but as unrealized possibility, it is actually nothing. As the prohibition enters the picture, the anxiety is heightened in the sense of "the anxious possibility of *being able*."[64] This possibility does not require an object, for anxiety is at bottom different from specific fears in that respect. The anxiety has as focus the ineluctable risk of sheer possibility. Then the word of judgment ("you shall certainly die") further intensifies the anxiety, for the possibility of being able now "points to a possibility as its sequence."[65] And then, freely, the fall. Kierkegaard draws on the image of dizziness: "Hence anxiety is the dizziness of freedom which emerges when the spirit wants to posit the synthesis and freedom looks down into its own possibility, laying hold of finiteness to support itself."[66]

I have followed here Kierkegaard's "explanation" in *The Concept of Anxiety* of the fall into sin. He describes this as a "psychological" explanation, but he sees the limits of this service: "That which can be the concern of psychology and with which it can occupy itself is not that sin comes into existence, but how it can come into existence."[67] That is, psychology deals with the "real possibility" of sin.[68] Dogmatics, in contrast, deals with the actuality of sin. *The Concept of Anxiety*, looking ahead perhaps to *The Sickness unto Death*, ends with this sentence: "As soon as psychology has finished with anxiety, it is to be delivered to dogmatics."[69] But isn't there a gap in explanation here? Yes, Kierkegaard says, it is called the leap. Thus, "sin does not properly belong in any science, but it is the subject of the sermon."[70]

The preacher properly will have plenty of work to do, for our failing effort to "will one thing" must be interrupted by a time of repentance.[71] Kierkegaard's language is not subtle. One would want one's days to be such that the last would be like the first, the "life of a person who has willed only one thing. But, alas this is not the way it is. Something came in between them: delay, halting, interruption, error, perdition."[72] So repentance has the causality right.[73] *The Concept of Anxiety* constantly drives home the point of the individual's responsibility. Of course, the individual's sin acquires a history, as does the race: "In each subsequent individual, anxiety is more reflective. . . . The nothing that is the object of anxiety becomes, as it were, more and more a something."[74] So Kierkegaard adds the considerable complication that "anxiety is neither a category of necessity, nor a category of freedom; it is entangled freedom."[75] Thus, he can speak of a "predisposition" to sin.[76] There is then a sense in which "sin presupposes itself, obviously not before it is posited (which is predestination), but in that it is posited."[77] So he will not back away from the conviction that, while sin acquires a history, "it *is* only as the single individual himself posits sin by the qualitative leap."[78] Hence, his rejection of an abstract free will is qualified with the word that freedom is entangled "not by necessity but in itself."[79] Kierkegaard will not abandon his recognition of freedom's responsibility by the conventional strategy of retreating to some prior causality. As he puts the matter succinctly in *The Concept of Anxiety*, "Sin presupposes itself." I can trace the causal influences at work in a particular sin, but typically I simply end up positing my earlier sins and sins by others as they bear on me. There is no "explanation" for freedom's fall.

Despair: Sickness and Sin

Despair is a sickness of the human spirit. But this sickness has moral meaning. Kierkegaard explicitly criticizes his beloved Socrates, who is understood to believe that "when someone does not do what is right, then neither has he understood what is right." The "Socratic principle . . . lacks a dialectical determinant appropriate to the transition from having understood something to doing it." But it is "in this transition [that] Christianity begins."[80] In *The Sickness unto Death*, Kierkegaard draws more explicitly on theological categories than in *The Concept of Anxiety*, which is offered by Vigilius Haufniensis, the watchman of Copenhagen, as "a simple psychologically orienting deliberation on the dogmatic issue of hereditary sin."[81] But in his more dogmatic treatment, Kierkegaard does not abandon the emphasis on the individual will's responsibility. Writing as a Christian of "the actual individual person," he stresses how Christianity "arrives at the concept of defiance, and then, to fasten the end very firmly [a sewing image], it adds the doctrine of hereditary sin."[82] To evoke Luther's phrase, "the bondage of the will" is about freedom binding itself, individually and cumulatively.

This emphasis on individual responsibility in the will that sins does not mean that the coming of despair requires a conscious rejection of the Creator. Kierkegaard wrote first of despair as not being conscious of having a self, and then of conscious despair whether in not willing to be oneself or in willing to be a self other than as established by the Creator. No despair, Kierkegaard insists, "is entirely free of defiance," but he makes a famous (or infamous) relative distinction between, "so to speak," "feminine" despair and "masculine" despair.[83] He may skate dangerously close to blaming the victim in claiming defiance in women's "not willing to be oneself," but in another sense, he anticipates feminist challenges to the tendency to identify all sin as conscious and prideful defiance.[84] Moreover, the feminist recognition that cultural stereotyping contributes to loss of self for women does have a Kierkegaardian ring to it. In any case, relative distinctions fade in the face of the fact that we are all sick unto death.[85] How "unto" death? Since despair has to do with something that is wrong in the triadic relation that is the self, the sickness is only "unto" death. The relationship persists, represented in distortion. The despairing person "cannot rid himself of his self . . . because to have a self, to be a self, is the greatest concession, an infinite concession, given to man, but it is also eternity's claim upon him."[86]

I have taught *The Sickness unto Death* more than a dozen times, and each time, I have found the analysis of the forms of despair absolutely convincing. In the middle of the previous century, Paul Tillich found it so as well, for it forms the basis for his much-cited analysis of pathological anxiety in *The Courage to Be*.[87] Tillich is particularly helpful in pointing out the dialectical relationship between "individualization" and "participation." One hears Kierkegaard speaking in his account of this dialectic: "The subject of self-affirmation is the centered self. As centered self it is an individualized self. . . . But the self is self only because it has a world, a structured universe, to which it belongs and from which it is separated at the same time. Self and world are correlated, and so are individualization and participation. For this is just what participation means: being a part of something from which one is separated."[88] Toward the end of the century, Mary Louise Bringle drew on Kierkegaard to offer a penetrating analysis of hopelessness and healing in a book bearing a question for a title: *Despair: Sickness or Sin?*[89] She concludes, "Despair is neither sin nor sickness *per se*, but rather a *symptom* of both."[90] She writes, perhaps more optimistically than Kierkegaard, of how despair can be a "teacher and potential friend . . . schooling us in humility, sensitivity and courage."[91] Kierkegaard can say that "to be aware of this sickness is the Christian's superiority over the natural man"[92] and that conscious despair brings one "dialectically closer to being cured."[93] Yet his concern to connect concretely with his own context permits less of that affirmative sort of talk, though the second half (the "theological" half) of *Sickness* does hold out faith as "the state in which there is no despair at all."[94]

How is that state to be reached? Kierkegaard writes of God's action in ways consistent with what I have termed "transcendence in relationship." Thus, in commenting on the text "And I, when I am lifted up from the earth, will draw all people to myself" (John 12:32), he offers a strong sense of transcendence: "So, then, what truly can be said to draw to itself must be something in itself or something that is in itself. So it is when truth draws to itself, for truth is in itself, is in and for itself—and Christ is the truth." But the creaturely pole of the relationship is not neglected, for Anti-Climacus, the "decidedly Christian" pseudonym[95] of *Practice in Christianity*, continues: "But the human being of whom this discourse speaks is in himself a self. Therefore Christ also first and foremost wants to help every human being to become a self, requires this of him first and foremost, requires that he, by repenting, become a self, in order then to draw him to himself. He wants to draw the human being to himself, but in order truly to draw him to himself he wants to draw him only as a free being to himself, that is, through a choice."[96] Thus, in his final struggle with the state church of Denmark, he picks up again a category from *Practice in Christianity*—Christ as the prototype—and writes that the prototype, Jesus Christ, "does unconditionally place, and unconditionally everyone, under obligation."[97] Verily, relationship as gift and task once again. This God does will one thing.

It is appropriate that this one thing will be received differently in different relational contexts, as Kierkegaard recognizes in his appreciation and critique of Luther's differing reading that could not find a fulsome place for the task. Kierkegaard could be sharply critical of Luther. At the end of his life in that bitter struggle with Christendom, he wrote of Christian existence, even while eschewing that identification for himself, "It is of great importance, to Protestantism in particular, to correct the enormous confusion Luther caused by inverting the relation and actually criticizing Christ by means of Paul, the Master by means of the follower. I, on the contrary, have not criticized the apostle, as if I myself were something. I who am not even a Christian; what I have done is to hold Christ's proclamation alongside the apostles."[98] Yet he could recognize Luther's affirmation of the Christian's responsibility to the neighbor. In *Judge for Yourself*, he writes, "Luther did not therefore abolish imitation, nor did he do away with the voluntary, as pampered sentimentality would like to have us think about Luther. He affirmed imitation in the direction of witness to the truth."[99] A God transcendent in relationship will be appropriately apprehended differently in different contexts. Thus, substituting "pattern" for "task," he writes in his journal of God's willed response to sin:

Luther is entirely right in what he says in the preface to his sermons about the distinction between Christ as pattern [*Exempel*] and as gift. I am quite conscious of the fact that I have moved in the direction of Christ as pattern. But something must be kept in mind in this regard. Luther was confronted by the exaggerated misuse of Christ as pattern; therefore he accentuates the opposite. But Luther has long since been victorious in Protestantism and Christ has been completely forgotten as the pattern, and the whole thing actually has become pretence in hidden inwardness.[100]

Pretense is possible in hidden inwardness. Kierkegaard will insist that "the inner is not the outer." Who, then, can really judge? Further, his resilient emphasis on subjectivity leads us to put a related question to him: In my living the task, will I be alone?

The Self and the Other(s)

Søren Kierkegaard is particularly relentless in stressing how the call to become oneself confronts each person as an individual. He often speaks of writing for "my reader"—singular. His edifying discourses are often dedicated to *hiin Enkelte* ("that solitary individual"). If one accepts one's truly individual identity, one cannot hide in "the public," the press, or "what the age demands." In *The Sickness unto Death*, casting the matter theologically with evangelical fervor, he writes in part 2, "That Christianity is proclaimed to you means that you shall have an opinion about Christ; He is, or the fact that He exists and that He has existed is the decision about all existence. If Christ is proclaimed to you, then it is offense to say: I do not want to have an opinion about it."[101] One may ask whether there is adequate recognition here of the more than individual dimension of human existence. What of the social connectedness of individuals? The other(s) surely can be seen to function for me as both necessity and possibility. Early in his authorship (the *Or* of *Either/Or*, 1843), he wrote ethically and expansively of marriage as the greatest end or ideal of human existence. Kierkegaard's pseudonym distinguishes married love from "first love": "What does the wedding ceremony do, then? 'It halts the lover.' Not at all—but it allows what was already in motion to appear in the external world. It affirms the universally human. . . . Marital love has the possibility of an inner history and is as different from first love as the historical is from the unhistorical."[102] Does a sense of "made for relationships" as entailed in the universally human make it into his mature theological writings? Many a college sophomore has memorized the *Postscript*'s theme that "subjectivity is the truth."[103] Such facile readers have tended to ignore strong claims to the objective, to "something historical . . . which can become historical only against its nature."[104] Yet subjectivity remains the truth. Perhaps our best candidate for a sense of the relationality of the self is *Works of Love* (1847), with its insistent emphasis on the universality of the duty to love. A strong statement of this call is found in Kierkegaard's "like for like" formulation: "But the Christian like for like is: God will do unto you exactly as you do unto others. . . . The direction is inward; essentially you have to do only with yourself before God. . . . In the Christian sense, to love people is to love God, and to love God is to love people—what you do unto people, you do unto God, and therefore what you do unto people, God does unto you."[105] But one may wonder if that task is supported adequately by a gift of relatedness to/with other human beings. He can write in a promising way of God as the "middle term" between persons. But one hungers for a recognition of a more direct connectedness with the neighbor. Kierkegaard italicizes this summary: *"To love God is to love oneself truly; to help another person to love God is to love another person; to be helped by another person to love God is to be loved."*[106] He can also write of the neighbor as the middle term questioning the conscientiousness of preferential love.[107] One senses that his conviction that the relationship to God ("the Christian like for like . . . will turn you upward or inward"[108]) was in such a severe state of neglect in his Denmark that it holds him back from developing a more fully "horizontal" sense of relatedness.[109] I have suggested earlier in this chapter that something of that sense would seem to follow from the conviction that the art of power is to create freedom with consequence. At least that seems to be the case with God, who has "bound himself" to the creatures. Would not a comparable connectedness be called for in creatures imaging this God?

May it be that whatever insufficiency one senses regarding relations between humans is tied into Kierkegaard's radical severing of human nature from the environing nature we inhabit with all the other creatures?[110] Do we not walk together on this planet Earth? Moreover, if we walk, we do so with our bodies. Kierkegaard's view of the human synthesis also uses the body and psyche positioned together with and in the positive third of spirit. But in *The Concept of Anxiety*, the body seems compromised. He writes of how the fall has two consequences: "that sin came into the world and that sexuality was posited; the one is inseparable from the other."[111] It follows that "sinfulness is by no means sensuousness, but without sin there is no sexuality, and without sexuality, no history."[112] But if we were created good, not perfect, and if creational anxiety is a task as well as a gift, would not sinless embodied life with the others bring about a history?[113] A century later, Dietrich Bonhoeffer thought so: "Humankind is derived from a piece of earth. Its bond with the earth belongs to its essential being. . . . The body is not the prison, the shell, the exterior, of a human being; instead a human being is a human body. A human being does not 'have' a body—or 'have' a soul; instead a human being 'is' body and soul. . . . What is to be taken seriously about human existence is its bond with mother earth, its being as body."[114]

Many people in Kierkegaard's train are active in resisting a scientism that loses sight of the responsible self. A striking literary example is Walker Percy, the Mississippi novelist. Percy read Kierkegaard while recovering from the tuberculosis that interrupted (and, it turned out, ended) his medical studies. In his aggressively titled *Lost in the Cosmos: The Last Self-Help Book*, he wonders why "it is possible to learn more in ten minutes about the Crab Nebula in Taurus, which is 6,000 light years away, than you presently know about yourself, even though you've been stuck with yourself all your life."[115] Percy has described his meeting Kierkegaard's critique of Hegel's system as "the great bombshell."[116] Percy had been looking for something that was missing in his studies at Columbia University Medical School, "almost the quintessential institution of scientific humanism." In Kierkegaard, he came to see that what had been "left out by any kind of synthesis, by scientific synthesis or a philosophical synthesis . . . is nothing less than the individual himself."[117] Staying simply within the field of literature, one could add discussions of Kierkegaard's emphasis on the individual influencing such figures as William Styron, John Updike, and Flannery O'Connor.[118] With some cause, existentialism is often targeted as one of the leading contributors to the tendency to collapse the world into the regnant self—a tendency people such as Alasdair MacIntyre and Robert Bellah have lamented.[119] In a sense, the modern synthesis of self and world Stephen Toulmin identified for us in the introduction is under great pressure as the world fails to find its place sustaining and challenging the self. A test for the reality of "world" may be found in the capacity to communicate.

Making Sense for Self and Other(s)

In worrying about the individual's connectedness socially, there arises the issue of the intelligibility of human existence. Should one perhaps give up on claiming a shared human reason to make sense of human existence? Can something as deeply personal as words really offer us a shared world? Richard Rorty, in espousing an "edifying" philosophy that does not seek to provide a mirror of nature, claims Kierkegaard as member of a tribe (Goethe, Santayana, William James, Dewey, the later Wittgenstein, and the later Heidegger) united in "their distrust of the notion that man's essence is to be a knower of essences."[120] If one leaves "essence" aside as ambitiously abstract, one still must simply ask whether one can make sense for others of what one believes to be true about oneself. If not, does one in any meaningful sense "understand" oneself? The charge of irrationalism is often launched at Kierkegaard's view of God's response to the human predicament, with particular attention to his christological formulations.[121] But our subject in this chapter—his analysis of the human situation with the emphasis on entangled freedom—is certainly a candidate for such critique as well. Here the category of the "leap" is crucial. Can one understand the leap into sin, the leap into faith? The enigmatic Dane locates both questions in the logic of paradox: "First of all, Christianity proceeds to establish sin so firmly as a position that the human understanding can never comprehend it; and then it is this same Christian teaching that again undertakes to eliminate this position in such a way that the human understanding can never comprehend it."[122]

Kierkegaard's pseudonym Johannes Climacus does suggest that human reason can serve the faith it cannot understand:

> Consequently the believing Christian both has and uses his understanding, respects the universally human, does not explain someone's not becoming a Christian as a lack of understanding, but believes Christianity against the understanding and here uses the understanding—in order to see to it that he believes against the understanding. Therefore he cannot believe nonsense against the understanding, which one might fear, because the understanding will penetratingly perceive that it is nonsense and hinder him in believing it, but he uses the understanding so much that through it he becomes aware of the incomprehensible, and now, believing, he relates himself to it against the understanding.[123]

Very well, with the fading of the modernity that Kierkegaard challenged so decisively, we will not be so rationalistic that we seek to serve "speculation, which talks itself out of the paradoxes."[124] But will it suffice for a postmodern faith seeking understanding to "locate" the leap(s) in the logic of paradox and leave it at that?[125] Can one say more? Could one make sense of paradox as truth that is *para-doxa*, "against the (conventional?) opinion?" Will not the Christian message of sin and forgiveness necessarily be quite precisely paradoxical, if the prevailing cultural opinion is George Bernard Shaw's "Forgiveness is a beggar's refuge; we must pay our debts"? Shall one instead claim Martin Luther's last word of confession: "We are beggars; that is true"?[126]

Kierkegaard's call for "indirect communication" comes into play here as regards his understanding of both what is being communicated and to whom the message is directed. In *Practice in Christianity*, he writes of the God-man as "the sign of contradiction": "To justify the name of 'sign,' there must be something by which it draws attention to itself or to the contradiction. But the contradictory parts must not annul each other in such a way that the sign comes to mean nothing or in such a way that it becomes the opposite of a sign, an unconditional concealment. . . . A communication that is the unity of jest and earnestness is thus a sign of contradiction."[127] Moreover, the one who would make Christian sense for others must be mindful of the recipient's freedom and responsibility in receiving the truth.[128] We have seen that Kierkegaard will not accept an "explanation" of freedom that explains away freedom. Thus, we saw that anxiety does not "explain" sin. Anxiety is the natural human condition as created. As such, it is "no troublesome burden," and he is relentless in his critique of what he sees about him as spiritless lack of anxiety.[129] If anxiety were the cause of sin, then the Creator would be the perpetrator. Instead, Kierkegaard will speak of "sin presupposing itself," for "*Sin came into the world by a sin.*"[130] The leap must not be forgotten. In chapter 3, this challenging Dane will have more to say to us of the leap into faith when we speak of imagination as crucial in the call into the future. Of the leap into sin, he speaks of anxiety as a "*sympathetic antipathy* and *an antipathetic sympathy*" and readily grants, "There is nothing in the world more ambiguous."[131] Here we can at least comment: the leap into faith is not less ambiguous. The leap stands, also in the speaking and receiving of the Christian message.

Summing up, we can say that in our analysis of power for or in the self, we will not want to say less than Kierkegaard does of individual responsibility in the action of the will. His profound analysis of human freedom invites or indeed urges us to recognize this element in trying to understand power. Power does not simply pass through a self functioning as an inert channel. In creation and redemption, God does give the individual a solitary challenge.[132] Kierkegaard will keep us mindful of the anxious, somewhat dizzy individual pondering her freedom in the face of a call to choose herself. But we may be wise to look across to England and the United States for a deeper sense of the constitutive character of the embodied relationships in and through which that individual does exist.

Chapter 2

IMAGINING THE WORLD IN RELATION: A WHITEHEADIAN INCLUSION

Kierkegaard brought us a view of the self as freedom: created in love and anxiously poised over possibility, dizzy and falling, despairing and caught in consequences, claimed by grace and called to discipleship. That picture demands attention in our attempt to understand what power is and what, specifically, is the power of love. But with Kierkegaard, we found ourselves struggling to recognize a full connectedness—of mind (or the "third" of spirit, for that matter) with body, of the individual with other humans, of humans with nature. That struggle for connection is addressed if we look to Alfred North Whitehead and his work at Cambridge (1880–1910) and London (1910–1924) and at the "American Cambridge" (1924–1947).[1] His work in England in mathematics, natural science, and education already speaks to what we may have been missing in Kierkegaard. But the inclusive character of his vision is most evident in his mature work at Harvard in cosmology and philosophy of religion.

Whitehead's description of religion has an element that resembles Kierkegaard's conviction about the solitary individual before God: "Religion is the art and theory of the internal life of man, so far as it depends on the man himself and on what is permanent in the nature of things. . . . Religion is what the individual does with his own solitariness."[2] Moreover, the Kierkegaardian emphasis on being held by God in a loving relationship is suggested as well. Religion "runs through three stages, if it evolves to its final satisfaction. It is the transition from God the void to God the enemy, and from God the enemy to God the companion."[3] But that God is present does not distinguish the human creature from all the other creatures. In *Religion in the Making*, Whitehead cites an Egyptian papyrus from the early Christian centuries: "Cleave the wood and I am there."[4] God is purposefully present in all of creation. In his magnum opus, *Process and Reality* (1929), he offers a full cosmological sketch in which "each temporal occasion embodies God, and is embodied in God."[5] Without any question, this philosophical theologian belongs in the diverse crowd of "panentheists" gathered by Philip Clayton and Arthur Peacocke in their book *In Whom We Live and Move and Have Our Being*.[6] They take their title from the apostle Paul's sermon to the philosophers on Mars Hill in Athens (Acts 17:28). Paul's missionary emphasis is on all human beings as created. With Whitehead, all created beings are explicitly included. Thus, God's presence in the whole creation is the framework in which God's presence with the human individual must be understood. Similarly, that questing individual will not be satisfied with a solitariness that becomes isolation: "In its solitariness the spirit asks, What, in the way of value, is the attainment of life? And it can find no such value till it has merged its individual claim with that of the objective universe. Religion is world-loyalty."[7]

Worldly Wisdom

Thus, at the outset, in listening to Whitehead's voice, we come to be clear that if we are to find God, we do well to study the world. People of faith claiming to know God should have motives aplenty for that study. What is a "world," after all? A world provides a "universe of meaning" in which our speaking and our acting can make sense.[8] A commitment to claiming such a "cosmos" can be found in Whitehead's work well before his explicitly cosmological ventures at Harvard. Thus his biographer, Victor Lowe, points to his concern to "save causation" in his responses to David Hume and Bertrand Russell already in his 1922 presidential lecture to the Aristotelian Society.[9] More to our point about inclusion, Whitehead's contention is that if we truly understand the world, we will find ourselves speaking of God within that world.[10] Christian theologians should not be surprised by that, if they do mean what they say when they speak of God's omnipresence. It follows that any accurate sketch of how the world works should be of interest to those theologians. People of faith simply seeking to serve their God in this world may expect to acquire some tactical wisdom from such a sketch. Thus, if we aim to bring positive change in human relationships, we will want to know what a relationship is. How does it "work"? Moreover, the claims faith regularly makes about God's action—for example, "God acts in history"—will become materially meaningful as they are understood within the frame of a sketch of reality in which "history" makes explicit sense.

To suggest such a sketch is the point of the metaphysical venture, "the science which seeks to discover the general ideas which are indispensably relevant to the analysis of everything that happens."[11] In addition to such analytical assistance, a metaphysical contribution to theology could be constructive in the critical sense. In *Adventures of Ideas*, Whitehead suggests such a role in balancing the contributions to be had in religion and metaphysics having to do with each other: "Religion lends a driving force to philosophy. But in turn, speculative philosophy guards our higher intuitions from base alliances by its suggestions of ultimate meanings, disengaged from the facts of current modes of behavior."[12]

Of course, there is the risk that the servant stages a coup and deposes the queen of the sciences.[13] Faith speaks with a particularity that resists reduction to the recital of universals. But a theologian who speaks of the hiddenness of an omnipresent God would be well advised to be slow to dismiss any truly persistent element in how the world works. I will construct this discussion somewhat in the mode of a conversation between faith-based prescriptive claims and the descriptive sketch offered by Whitehead, recognizing that God-talk was necessarily part of that sketch for him.[14] In any case, as one unpacks the work of theologians, one finds implicitly or explicitly some sketch of the way things are. In *Adventures of Ideas*, Whitehead identifies several metaphysical questions we can paraphrase thusly: How are the many actually one? More personally, Who really am I through all the changes over the course of my life? and, How are the truly "persuasive elements in the creative advance" grounded in the nature of things?[15] To address these theologically pressing questions, we need a broad sketch of how things are. I have been citing Whitehead's argument from his mature works, but he saw the danger of narrowness early on. In *Religion in the Making* (1926), he wrote, "You cannot shelter theology from science, or science from theology; nor can you shelter either of them from metaphysics, or metaphysics from either of them. There is no short cut to truth."[16]

Alternatives are available, of course: Aristotle, Spinoza, Hegel—the list goes on. Whitehead is helpful because he is so explicit and thorough in his sketch, as well as being persistent in his appeal to experience as known prior to and apart from the development of the categories. To get fully into the conversation, we turn to Whitehead's conviction that the nature of the presence of God in the world is clarified and confirmed by an understanding of the *internality* of relationships in the nature of all that is actual.

Direct Immanence

We begin with God, as we did with Kierkegaard. In *Adventures of Ideas*, Whitehead offers a remarkable discussion of the early Christian theologians of Antioch and Alexandria. What Whitehead is seeking in his metaphysical vision is to draw on his own specific wording, an understanding "exhibiting the plurality of individuals as consistent with the unity of the Universe."[17] If that can be found, we can make sense of "the mystery of personal identity, the mystery of the immanence of the past in the present, the mystery of tran-science [*sic*]."[18] Whitehead traces an adventure of this unitive idea in three phases, from Plato through the emergence of the Christian religion to these early theologians. Plato, "the greatest metaphysician, the poorest systematic thinker,"[19] toward the end of his life made the revelatory discovery that "the divine element in the world is to be conceived as a persuasive agency and not as a coercive agency."[20] In the second phase, this discovery is "exemplified": "The Mother, the Child, and the bare manger: the lowly man, homeless and self-forgetful, with his message of peace, love, and sympathy: the suffering, the agony, the tender words as life ebbed, the final despair: and the whole with the authority of supreme victory."[21] The revelation Plato "divined in theory" Christianity brings with the power of incarnating action.

But how is that revelation to be related to the whole realm of particulars?[22] Can the actual unity of the many in the one be comprehended through this discovery and exemplification? Not with Plato, Whitehead laments: "When Plato is faced with the problem of expressing the relationship of God to the World, and of the relation to the World of those Ideas which it is in God's nature to contemplate, Plato's answer is invariably framed in terms of mere dramatic imitation."[23] He grants that Platonic influence on Christian theology was considerable. But "it is also true that Plato is the originator of the heresies and of the feeblest side of Christian Theology."[24] Enter phase three, those theologians from Antioch and Alexandria.

Whitehead argues that the answer to the challenge of the one and the many requires tackling the relationship of the world and God. He observes, "The Arian solution [compromising the eternity of the Son, as in the hymn line the Arians sang, "There was when he was not"], involving a derivative Image, is orthodox Platonism, though it be heterodox Christianity." What the orthodox alternative gives us instead is "a multiplicity in the nature of God, each component being unqualifiedly Divine."[25] This entails the crucial point, "a doctrine of mutual immanence in the divine nature." He holds back from unqualified praise: "I am not in any way venturing upon a decision upon the correctness of the original assumption of this multiplicity." But he drives home what he understands these theologians to have found: "The point is the doctrine of mutual immanence."[26] Accordingly, he finds that doctrine crucially present in what the church came to say of the persons of the Trinity. Thus, regarding the person of Christ, "they rejected the doctrine of an association of the human individual with a divine individual, involving responsive imitations in the human person. They decided for the direct immanence of God in the one person of Christ."[27] So, too, they came to speak of the Third Person of the Trinity in terms of "the direct immanence of God in the World."[28]

Throughout this programmatic discussion, Whitehead more than once cautions, "I am not making any judgment about the details of their theology, for example, about the Trinitarian doctrine."[29] But he finds in that doctrine the key to answering the metaphysical question about reconciling the many and the one. Understanding how relationship works with God serves the inclusive commitment to understanding how relationship works with all of creation. Hence his summary: "My point is that in the place of Plato's solution of secondary images and imitations, they demanded a direct doctrine of immanence. It is in this respect that they made a metaphysical discovery. They point out the way in which Platonic metaphysics should develop, if it was to give a rational account of the role of the persuasive agency of God."[30] Whitehead's praise for this discovery is followed by a lament: "Unfortunately, the theologians never made this advance into general metaphysics."[31] Thus, "they made no effort to conceive the world in terms of the metaphysical categories by means of which they interpreted God, and they made no effort to conceive God in terms of the metaphysical categories which they applied to the World." I have subtitled this chapter "A Whiteheadian Inclusion." The point is precisely that God *and* all that is not God are to be identified and described *within* any adequate metaphysical sketch. In Whitehead's wide-ranging sketch (*Process and Reality* being the fullest statement), in addressing the theme "God and the World," he drives the point home famously: "In the first place, God is not to be treated as an exception to all metaphysical principles, invoked to save their collapse. He is their chief exemplification."[32]

This inclusiveness may seem boldness verging on arrogance, but I use the modest term *sketch* to reflect Whitehead's recognition that what he is up to is "an experiential adventure": "Rationalism is an adventure in the clarification of thought, progressive and never final. But it is an adventure in which even partial success has importance."[33] Readers of *Process and Reality* are often struck by the vast sweep of Whitehead's speculative work. Yet even in that work, replete with categories, he can write, "The ultimate test is always widespread, recurrent experience, and the more general the rationalistic scheme, the more important is this final appeal."[34] His cosmological flight was in the service of life on the ground, and an argument can be made that his later works, especially *Adventures of Ideas* (1933) and *Modes of Thought* (1938), carry that empirical feel more palpably.[35] Thus, *Adventures of Ideas* begins with a "sociological" first part in which this student of the microscopic devotes a hundred pages to the historical adventures of the idea of divine persuasion in *human* affairs.

With Whitehead, as in chapter 1 with Kierkegaard, we will attempt locating his thought in relationship to more recent developments. If Whitehead had been able to witness such developments in Trinitarian thinking, he might particularly appreciate the theme that the economic Trinity (the triune God acting in the world) *is* the immanent Trinity (God in God's self). Robert Jenson nicely summarizes the range of this development, citing the agreement between "the most important contemporary Catholic Trinitarian theorist and the most important Protestant, Karl Rahner and Eberhard Jüngel."[36] Whitehead's concern for inclusion could in principle have reached back to a Kierkegaard who found God's transcendence precisely in the decisiveness of God's relating to the creation.[37]

But does this commitment to inclusiveness squander any notion of God's qualitative superiority? I believe it does not, and later in this chapter, I will write of such distinction in discussing what Whitehead calls "the reversal of the poles." Even here, I note that in this stark statement of inclusion, there is a hint of difference in the little word *chief*. This discussion of Whitehead's reading of the theologians of Antioch and Alexandria can lead us toward that fuller discussion of how God is to be understood within this inclusive metaphysical vision and to a better understanding of power, God's or our own. But a question lingers: Why did these theologians fail to make the categorical connections between God and the world?

The Galilean Vision: The Poet of the World

The fault for the lack of metaphysical follow-through lies with the traditional notion of God's power. God "became the one absolute, omnipotent source of all being, for his own existence requiring no relations to anything beyond himself. He was internally complete." So this "general concept of the Deity stopped all further generalization."[38] Here we confront the schema termed, by friends and foes, classical theism. A representative of this tradition, H. P. Owen, is particularly insistent that "God's transcendence means that he is

incomprehensible. . . . Since his nature (being infinite and self-existent) differs in kind from all other natures we cannot conceive it at all. Although we
can apprehend God we cannot comprehend him."[39] Whitehead notes that the
consequences of holding this notion of God are considerable. The believer
is left with lack of clarity and certainty about what lies on the other side of
the metaphysical gulf. Do we really know this God we claim to "apprehend"?
Moreover, "the worst of unqualified omnipotence is that it is accompanied by
responsibility for every detail of every happening."[40] But what can we say of
a God no longer beyond that gulf but rather fully with us?

Theologians often address the problem of moral evil by appealing in
the freewill defense to creaturely agency. We get credit at least for our sins.
Unlike many process theologians, I believe Whitehead can be employed
in a variant of that defense. It will be essential in that appropriation to
understand God's self-limiting in creating as truly decisive for God. If God
can (does?) cancel the limitation(s) on occasion, we are back behind that
metaphysical gulf. Then troubling questions arise. How can one fathom such
inscrutable decisions in the selectivity of such canceling? How can one trust
such divine unpredictability? Most concretely in this post-twentieth-century
world, what about the Holocaust? I am concerned as well with the implications of the metaphysical gulf for an understanding of *creaturely* power in
any action, evil or good. Of what are we creatures capable? I pause to note
that Whitehead's trenchant critique of traditional theology need not find a
Kierkegaard among its numerous targets. Recall the Dane's emphasis that
"omnipotence is in the power of love" so that the Creator calls on the creature to "become something even in relation to me."[41] With the recognition
that that "something" may well be the taking of offense, the gulf is bridged,
decisively.

In the final part of *Process and Reality*, Whitehead turns from the highly
abstract cosmological discussion of the preceding sections to write of "the
brief Galilean vision of humility."[42] In his reading, Christianity "does not
emphasize the ruling Caesar, or the ruthless moralist, or the unmoved mover."
Rather, "it dwells upon the tender elements in the world, which slowly and
in quietness operate by love; . . . Love neither rules, nor is it unmoved; also
it is a little oblivious as to morals."[43] Four pages later, this passage is followed
by Whitehead's own rendering of the Platonic discovery of the persuasive:
"God's role is not the combat of productive force with productive force, of
destructive force with destructive force; it lies in the patient operation of
the over-powering rationality of this conceptual harmonization. . . . He is
the poet of the world, with tender patience leading it by his vision of truth,
beauty, and goodness."[44]

The ellipsis in my quotation contains a sentence that will catch the concerned attention of Christian theologians: "He does not create the world, he saves it." Does God not create—indeed, do so *ex nihilo*, out of nothing?[45] We have heard Kierkegaard's testimony on this matter. Is there, with Whitehead, enough God? Whitehead would have us address that question by reflecting on our actual religious experience. We do well to resist reaching an answer too quickly. Religious passion can tempt us to say that there is simply no limit to God's power. But what of our choices? Do they not matter at all? Can God have all the power, if we have some? Whatever speaking about creation out of nothing may say about the absolute origin of things, are we *now* nothing? Is God *now* creating out of nothing?

In assessing what might be seen as Whitehead's disregard for a creating God, we should remember that he is writing from the middle of things. As an empirical philosopher, he is looking around, trying to make a cosmological sketch of how things now are. He finds a God working with other realities that share this world with God. Presumably, the Christian will want to say something of that sort. A familiar tactic is to work with a distinction between primary and secondary causation, as Ted Peters notes: "Through this distinction traditional theologians found a way to affirm that everything is universally dependent on God but that human beings still have an influence on determining the shape of particular events. Omnipotence does not mean omnicausality. Theologians did not for the most part confuse omnipotence with blind power, with a lifeless force."[46] What remains unclarified in such distinctions is often precisely the key causal link between primary and secondary causality. I will shortly introduce Whitehead's helpful locating of the link in the combination of "efficient" and "final" causality.

I delay further treatment of this "size of God" issue for a few pages, but I do so noting that the reader of this poetic final part of *Process and Reality* will find Whitehead speaking of a God who "at once exemplifies and establishes the categoreal conditions."[47] Both verbs matter, and they qualify each other. This "establishing" God is here uniquely identified, even as this "exemplifying" God acts in genuine relationship with other realities. How this cosmological point bears on the meaning of power is nicely summarized by Tyron Inbody: "Power, even in the context of creation, is a relational concept. Power as a social concept means that nothing whatsoever not even God can wholly determine something else. Power no longer means the capacity coercively to impose one's will on a totally powerless object; it means the power to affect another free center of power through persuasion."[48] A theologian speaking of the will of God for relationship will enhance that cosmologically given relatedness in speaking of God's love for the creatures seeking a more intimate connectedness. Here we approach the Whiteheadian recognition of God's suffering reception of all other reality. Again in part 5 of *Process and Reality*, he writes that God "shares with every new creation its actual world; and the concrescent creature is objectified in God as a novel element in God's objectification of that actual world."[49] And on that work's last page, we have his much-cited sentence "God is the great companion—the fellow-sufferer who understands."[50]

Some people of faith may wonder if we miss here a Kierekgaardian sense of God's "infinite qualitative difference" from us. But why must we assume that relationship denies such difference? A relationship that entails mutuality need not require equality. Here Whitehead may connect with reformist feminist thought. Elizabeth Johnson has said succinctly, "Sophia–God and the historical world exist in mutual, if asymmetrical, relation. Insofar as each is directed toward the other with reciprocal interest and intimacy, the relation is mutual. Insofar as the world is dependent on God in a way that God is not on the world, the relation is not strictly symmetrical."[51] In Whiteheadian terms, that distinctive dependence will be seen shortly in a discussion of God's role in the coming about of every other entity in the universe. In any case, implications of this relationship between unequals are readily available: love has power, but love does not coerce. God's love does not.[52] Created in the image of that God, our lives should not. But how does that non-coercing love work?

The Time of Internal Relations

We are back to the task of generalizing that metaphysical discovery of the theologians of Antioch and Alexandria. Whitehead spoke of these theologians making a claim of "direct" and "mutual" immanence regarding the persons of the Trinity. In rejecting the gulf between God and all that is not God, he comes to speak of how relations are internal to the becoming and being of anything at all. He is explicit about rejecting what he understands to be Aristotle's notion of a substance as requiring nothing but itself in order to exist.[53] He is also countering a popular notion that relationships are accidental to our selfhood, optional as it were. His understanding, to the contrary, is that "the actual entity, in virtue of being *what* it is, is also *where* it is. It is somewhere because it is some actual thing with its correlated actual world."[54] We can broaden this point, reaching to the human level. Liberation theologians have worked to make us acknowledge that crucial "spatial" character of our speaking, so we talk about the "social location" of our locutions. Similarly, we seem called to say that all theology—not just feminist or liberation or (!) process theology—is "adjectival."

In speaking of the spatial, we are actually talking about our experience of time. Wherever the entity is, it is doing something. Looking about
him as he seeks to construct his cosmological sketch, Whitehead is driven
to recognize that "all things flow": "Without doubt, if we are to go back to
that ultimate integral experience, unwarped by the sophistications of theory,
that experience whose elucidation is the final aim of philosophy, the flux
of things is one ultimate generalization around which we must weave our
philosophical system."[55] He did not think philosophers and other folks who
do not emphasize change were dunces. He recognized that in some ways,
this processive universe seems counterintuitive. He will find a place for "a
rival notion" that "dwells on permanences of things—the solid earth, the
mountains, the stones, the Egyptian Pyramids, the spirit of man, God."[56] But
the dominant emphasis is on a deep recognition of the pervasive reality of
change, constituted by the process of internal relations. Thus, he opens his
discussion of "the categoreal scheme" by writing of "the category of the
ultimate," which is "Creativity": " 'Creativity' is the universal of universals
characterizing ultimate matter of fact. It is that ultimate principle by which
the many, which are the universe disjunctively, become the one actual occasion, which is the universe conjunctively. It lies in the nature of things that
the many enter into complex unity."[57]

This recognition of the time-full character of existence is not merely a
matter of speculative theory. In *Modes of Thought* (1938), he wrote, "Apart
from time there is no meaning for purpose, hope, fear, energy. If there be no
historic process, then everything is what it is, namely a mere fact. Life and
motion are lost."[58] But there *is* process in reality, for the past is not dead and
gone but flows into the present constitutively. His language can be vivid,
speaking of creativity as "the throbbing emotion of the past hurling itself into
a new transcendent fact."[59] I must somehow deal with the stuff that time's
flow brings (in)to me. That "efficient" causality will include "done deeds," but
also the subjective purposing of those beings with whom I share this world.
Well below the human level, Whitehead speaks of the category of "subjective
intensity" to indicate how in the temporal process there is an aim of feeling
for the immediate present and the relevant future.[60]

As we carry the past with us, we do lean into the future purposively
(the "final" causality of the becoming moment) with fear and/or hope. This
leaning makes sense of purpose and the other realities Whitehead links
with time, and I will argue that it very much does so for the power of love
as well. Whitehead explicitly employs the conventional terms "efficient"
and "final" causality to identify the power of the past and the power of our
anticipatory aiming at the future. Thus, time's inflowing power is vitally

important, but there is a limitation to be recognized. The past has a constitutive role, but not an exhaustive one. We have some choices to make with respect to what we do with what is inexorably given to us. Here something resembling a Kierkegaardian note of freedom asserts itself, paired with the recognition of the internality of relationships: "The creative process is rhythmic: it swings from the publicity of many things to the individual privacy; and it swings back from the private individual to the publicity of the objectified individual. The former swing is dominated by the final cause, which is the ideal; and the latter swing is dominated by the efficient cause, which is actual."[61] In describing this rhythmic process, he calls the reader to recognize that things may not be just as they seem to be. That recognition can open us to a crucial level of experience that reveals much about our knowing, and indeed our becoming.

A Deeper Experience

I have twice referred to Whitehead as an empirical philosopher. He proposes for philosophy something analogous to science, where "the ultimate test is always widespread, recurrent experience."[62] But he casts his net more widely than many philosophers identified as empiricists: "Nothing can be omitted, experience drunk and experience sober, experience sleeping and experience awake, experience self-conscious and experience self-forgetful, experience intellectual and experience physical, experience anxious and experience carefree, experience anticipatory and experience retrospective, experience happy and experience grieving, experience dominated by emotion and experience under self-restraint, experience in the light and experience in the dark, experience normal and experience abnormal."[63] In introducing this book, I referred to David Hume and his reduction of reliable experience to sense perception. Whitehead does not simply reject Hume's reduction. He offers an understanding of two different kinds of experience and of the relationship between them, such that Hume's emphasis finds a prominent specific place in understanding how we come to know without ruling out a deeper experience. The terminology ("presentational immediacy," "causal efficacy," and "symbolic reference") can become irksome, but the novel character of the unfamiliar language choices can keep us alert to the distinctions he is making.

Whitehead argues that "Hume neglected the primary experiences of bodily intimacy."[64] In that experience, our sense of being time-full beings is accentuated. Thus, we have experience "derived from antecedent fact, enjoyed in the personal unity of present fact, and conditioning future fact."[65] In this threefold experience, we sense "our essential connection with the world without, and also . . . our own individual existence now."[66] In this primary experience, the body is basic: "My brain, my heart, my bowels, my lungs, are mine, with an intimacy of mutual adjustment. The sunrise is a message from the world beyond such directness of relation."[67] I have quoted extensively here from *Modes of Thought*, perhaps the most accessible of Whitehead's discussions of this primary experience, "causal efficacy." This account may still seem pretty vague, but that is how it is with this deeper experience itself: "The main characteristic of such experience is complexity, vagueness, and compulsive intensity."[68] I believe this primary experience, for all its vagueness, is decisive in our experience of the power of love. How do I know that my wife loves me? A verifiable bill of objective particulars will not convince. Yet we can know love and its power. The beloved experiences love that calls forth a trusting response. In the next chapter, I will say more of that call to trust, despite the vagueness.

But, of course, we do have experience with much greater precision: sharpness of shape, definiteness of location. Here we are on Hume's ground, the turf of the senses "such as shades of blue, and tones of sound."[69] But Whitehead makes a radical move in accommodating Hume's emphasis on sense perception: he finds such experience to be a "triumph of abstraction" from the more primary experience. His understanding of this distinction is best developed in earlier works, *Symbolism: Its Meaning and Effect* (1927) and *Process and Reality* (1929). In sense perception, we experience typically something in our environment immediately presented to us with definiteness regarding its spatial shape and its spatial relation to us. Here space seems to rule, rather than time, the conformation of present to past in causal efficacy. His response to Hume further involves the third category, "symbolic reference." Almost all our ordinary experience of sense perception involves a process by which what we call time and space come together, in effect, to yield the sensation experienced. How can this occur? Whitehead recognizes a certain "unison of becoming" by which a particular pattern of connectedness (he terms this an "eternal object," a form of relatedness) can be pried out of the vague primary experience and projected out onto the environment shared in that becoming. In summary, we can say "the sense-data, required for immediate sense-perception, enter into experience in virtue of the efficacy of the environment."[70] Our bodies function in a primary way in that environment. Whitehead speaks often of perception through the "*withness* of the body": "We see *with* our eyes, we taste *with* our palates, we touch *with* our hands."[71] Or as he puts the point in one of his more colorful phrasings, "A traveler, who has lost his way, should not ask, Where am I? What he really wants to know is, Where are the other places? He has got his own body, but he has lost them."[72]

I have stressed that in speaking of this primary, deeper experience, Whitehead emphasizes the power of the past flowing into the present. The past functions effectively, causally, in our knowing. We know because we are caused to do so. The "stuff" of the past is not dead but living in us. But as that past is received, we are leaning into the future. God is at work in the becoming moment purposefully, "aiming" or calling for something that serves God's vision.[73] Even as we act in the present, we anticipate the future. Whitehead speaks of this leaning into the future as acting on "propositions"—that is, one may say, on proposals. He gets our concerned attention when he says, "In the real world it is more important that a proposition be interesting than that it be true."[74] As propositions create interest in us, they draw us into the future. In responding to this call to the future, the human imagination may image the still-creating God.

Imagining God's World

Whitehead understands God to be present in the becoming of every moment in all of creation—quite literally, with an aim, that is, with what he terms the "initial aim" for how the many moving together in this moment can well be one. Traditional theologians have regularly affirmed the omnipresence of God but have failed to draw on that very fully in their understanding of how the world works. Whitehead will fill that gap. As I put my world together, God is there with a purpose. And what may that be? Whitehead argues that "the teleology of the universe is directed to the production of beauty."[75] "Novel order" marks out the boundaries of beauty. What, then, is beauty? Whitehead traces the nisus toward novel order to the ordering initiative of God. In triviality, as experienced in boredom on the human level, we lack the intensity needed for true novelty. We could use some genuine chaos. In discord, however, we lack the harmony needed for order, as two or more elements clash so there is a feeling of mutual destructiveness.[76] It is easy enough to type thus the sentences carrying the criteria. But bringing harmony and intensity together in actual life is challenging. For example, growing intensity requires an incorporation of complexity, which can trouble the calm waters of concord. But Langdon Gilkey, quite able—as noted in "Worldly Wisdom" above—to criticize aspects of process theology, wisely remarks, "Part of the elegance of this philosophy is the way these two usually antithetical aspects of existence here interweave and cooperate to form actuality and value."[77] Those aspects form actuality, for order and novelty are together in every coming together to constitute an actual entity. In each such instance, possibility is realized and created anew.[78] Again Whitehead's summary sentence serves us: "The many become one and are increased by one."[79] Value through the increase of novel order becomes possible as that entity, now one of the many, offers itself to the dawning future.

One might say at this point, "Stop the process; I want to get off." The imagining that is an imaging can be daunting. Yet God is at work, patiently if not dramatically. One can well say that this "great companion—the fellow-sufferer who understands" shares the challenge we experience.[80] That human beings experience God's "aiming" or calling the emerging occasion does not imply that they are conscious of God's activity. Rather, Whitehead calls for "the secularization of the concept of God's function in the world." Thus, while "the concept of God is certainly one essential element in religious feeling, . . . the converse is not true: the concept of religious feeling is not an essential element in the concept of God's function in the universe."[81] Marjorie Suchocki has linked this absence of God-consciousness with the point of God's purpose in the world: "The content of God's touch upon each concrescent occasion is toward an optimum mode of existence in the world. Thus God's aim directs us toward the world, not necessarily toward God, and again, God is present in a mode of hiddenness."[82]

What kind of power is this that does not require conscious acknowledgment? Clearly, it is not the greedy power seeking fawning creaturely self-denigration. The Godward side of such denigration can be a notion of unlimited power. Whitehead finds the notion of absolute divine control prominently present in the history of Christianity: "When the Western world accepted Christianity, Caesar conquered; and the received text of Western theology was edited by his lawyers."[83] He continues in unstinting critique of the notion of a God "aboriginal, eminently real, transcendent, . . . whose imposed will it [the world] obeys."[84] In *Religion in the Making*, he offers his lament: "On the whole, the Gospel of love was turned into a gospel of fear. The Christian world was composed of terrified populations."[85] He can apply this critique to particular attributes regularly assigned to God. Take "infinite," for example: "The limitation of God is his goodness. . . . It is not true that God is in all respects infinite. If He were, He would be evil as well as good."[86] We will want to consider what "good" means, materially. Can a God working incessantly for the togetherness of intensity and harmony that is beauty be properly termed good? Has an aesthetic category usurped the place of religious or moral talk? Within that question lies another we must now consider: Is this limited God simply not enough God to sustain the claims religion places on the human spirit?

Some pieces of that consideration are in place already. God is clearly omnipresent, if not omnipotent, in the sense classical theism espouses. Omni-

presence can serve to point us toward a redefinition of omnipotence. Kierkegaard certainly seemed to be pointing toward some such redefinition in writing of how God's omnipotence is in the power of love. He had us look to
Socrates, who knew that the art of power is to make free. Here, too, God
does not hoard all the power, but has the power of active presence in all situations. In any case, God is known here in the middle of things not as creating
out of nothing but as working with the creaturely to advance God's purposes.
Yet we have noted that, even in the middle, this philosopher's drive to get at
the base of things leads him to speak of God not simply "exemplifying" but
also "establishing" the "categoreal conditions."[87] Again, even in the exemplifying, we recall that God is, tantalizingly, "chief." To clarify this further, it is
necessary to introduce how in God the poles that characterize every instance
of becoming are reversed.

For convenience's sake, we may speak of both God and human beings
as involving two poles: that of being acted upon and that of acting. For all
entities except God, the first mentioned pole is primary. Whitehead calls this
the "physical" pole, and we may agree that our bodies, dramatically at birth
and perhaps especially as we age, remind us of our dependence. The other
pole, that of acting, Whitehead terms the "mental" pole, and again we can
understand how our minds through language and otherwise can open up a
world in which we can act, we can exercise initiative. Here is the decisive
point: in God, the order of the poles is reversed, so the "mental" pole is primary. Whitehead terms this the "primordial" nature of God, distinguishing it
from the "consequent" nature in which God is acted upon by the nondivine.
We might find Whitehead's favorite Gospel, the Gospel of John, making this a
point of priority for us in speaking of God as Spirit (John 4:24). Is this reversal of the poles a difference of kind or of degree? That is a difficult question
to answer. God, like every other reality, is dipolar; there is no metaphysical
exception here. Yet in speaking of the "subjective intensity" of an actual entity,
he writes, "The absolute standard of such intensity is that of the primordial
[i.e., the "mental"] nature of God, which is neither great nor small because it
arises out of no actual world. . . . It has within it no components which are
standards of comparison."[88] Here is a longer statement of this point: "In the
case of the primordial actual entity, which is God, there is no past. Thus the
ideal realization of conceptual feeling takes the precedence. God differs from
other actual entities in the fact that Hume's principle, of the derivate character
of conceptual feelings, does not hold for him."[89]

This surely feels like a difference of kind, something Kierkegaard might
call "an infinite qualitative difference." In this primordial character, would
there not be the grounds for a moral claim on us? Whitehead does speak

of it cosmologically as the ground of the novel becoming that characterizes every actual entity: "Apart from God, there could be no relevant novelty."[90] The universe's teleology of beauty is based in God's primordial envisioning of the ideal. Whitehead was critical of an understanding of law as imposed externally, a notion he linked with "the correlative doctrine of a transcendent imposing Deity."[91] He reached for an understanding of the laws of nature that emphasized "identities of pattern in the mutual relations" that make up "the essential interdependence of things."[92] But the ideal to be sought in that flowing mix is grounded in the primordial pole of God in which a divine decision functions in freedom. He can speak of this as *causa sui* ("cause of itself"), meaning "that the process of concrescence is its own reason for the decision."[93] Of course, people of faith, while living in the "middle," reach for words to speak of absolute beginning and end, and Whitehead would not challenge that search. At the end of the "cosmological" section of *Adventures of Ideas*, he writes, "The task of Theology is to show how the World is founded on something beyond mere transient fact, and how it issues in something beyond the perishing of occasions." Thus, "we ask of Theology to express that element in perishing lives which is undying by reason of its expression of perfections proper to our finite natures."[94] It seems fair to say that he, working as a cosmologist in the middle of this cosmos, has rendered service to religious faith even on the questions of ultimate boundary. I will take this up for further consideration in chapter 5 in asking, "What more may come?"

Perhaps this, the unity of God's creative purpose, is part of the secret of genuine power. God is not simply present and active in every situation. God is that with a unity of purpose that calls each entity toward a form that represents God's singular purpose. In the preceding section, I wrote of God "aiming" the becoming entity. As that entity leans into the future, it does so with a "subjective aim" that yields the unity attained in the coming together ("concrescence" is Whitehead's neologism) of the causal flow of the past into that particular moment. Whitehead proceeds to speak of the "initial phase" of that aim as "a direct derivate from God's primordial nature."[95] This is surely a distinctive feature of the God notion in his thought. This omnipresent—that is to say, omniactive—God is at work in the beginning of every becoming. Not at work *on*, but at work *within*. Isn't there a power here that can persuasively *influence* the life choices made on the human level, as surely as there is a steadfast aiming of what "flows into" each emerging moment?[96]

The imagination is a crucial capacity as human beings ponder the "propositions," the proposals, encountered in the process of becoming. As these possibilities are entertained with interest, Whitehead speaks of how feelings of "horror, relief and purpose" may be involved.[97] Life certainly brings the "harvest of tragedy" as much as "the dream of youth."[98] Ultimately, the hope is for "peace," which "comes as a gift." But in the middle of things, one is advised that "the deliberate aim at Peace very easily passes into its bastard substitute, Anaesthesia."[99] The call for our purposing is to join "the teleology of the universe" in the production of beauty. In the next chapter, I will speak primarily of the call to respond to these possibilities with purposeful hope.

That there is power in the hopeful imagination is a point biblical scholar Walter Brueggemann has made repeatedly in his analysis, particularly of the prophetic materials. He writes, "Prophecy is not in any overt concrete sense political or social action. It is rather *an assault on public imagination*, aimed at showing that the present presumed world is not absolute, but that a think-able alternative can be imagined, characterized, and lived in. The destabi-lization is, then, not revolutionary overthrow, but it is making available an alternative imagination that makes one aware that the presumed world is imagined, not given."[100] Brueggemann finds important the delicate combina-tion of the "now" and the "not yet": "Hope requires a very careful symboliza-tion. . . . It must not be expressed too fully in the present tense because hope one can touch and handle is not likely to retain its promissory call to a new future. Hope expressed only in the present tense will no doubt be co-opted by the managers of this age."[101] Whitehead's writing on propositions offers a parallel balancing in the notion of "real potentiality," which is always "relative to some actual entity," just as terms like *actual world, yesterday*, and *tomor-row* are.[102] On the human level, Brueggemann offers a helpful analysis of the roles played by memory, pain, hope, and discourse. What a Whiteheadian approach would add is the cosmological understanding that locates human becoming deeply in the actuality of the becoming universe. That does seem to be available biblically as well, as Terence Fretheim emphasizes in writing of "the vocation of the Nonhuman."[103] For example, he writes of how in Gen-esis 1–2, "several times God invites the earth and the waters to be involved in creative acts."[104]

In the next chapter, I will turn more fully to possible process contribu-tions to the what and the how of such prophetic imagining. But here I will reach back to appropriate a category employed in the preceding chapter: the image of God. If, as earlier suggested, we speak of the image as an endow-ment in relationship for a telos, we get the needed mix of tenses. As—enter-tained by and "interested" in the propositions of possibility—we imagine the future, do we not see in this something of the imaging of God? We reach back here once again to the primordial nature of God. Whitehead speaks of the primordial nature as involving a decision by which all possible forms of becoming are ordered in their relationships.[105] Out of what does that divine decision emerge? After considering and rejecting "vision" as expressing God primordially (lacks God's "yearning after concrete fact"), Whitehead settles on the term "envisagement."[106] My dictionary uses "imagine" as one of the synonyms of that term. Indeed, there are explicit references throughout his writings to the role of imagination in the human creature. Thus, he writes of how "self-determination is always imaginative in its origin."[107] Simply to get to the deeper dimensions of *present* reality, imagination is needed. We can get there, satisfying our "thirst" after the real.[108] We ordinarily "observe by the method of difference," with the result that universals, as by definition omnipresent, will escape our grasp. However, we can imagine what we do not notice. With "the play of a free imagination, controlled by the requirements of coherence and logic," we can discover those "metaphysical first principles [that] can never fail of exemplification."[109] In such creative use of the imagination, do we not image God, derivatively? In chapter 3, I will seek to harvest constructively some of Whitehead's writing on the imagination as we look to live with courage facing finitude.

Lost in the Cosmos?

I take the phrase "lost in the cosmos" from Walker Percy, whom I cited in the preceding chapter as worrying about how an ambitious science (scientism?) seduces the reader to "learn more about the Crab Nebula in Taurus, which is 6,000 light years away, than you presently know about yourself, even though you've been stuck with yourself all your life."[110] The phrase may remind readers of the process literature of an often-discussed issue that challenges us now in our effort to appropriate Whiteheadian thought in understanding power. We have just been occupied with the question of whether there is "enough God" in Whitehead's scheme. I have argued that his recognition of God's power is sufficient for a morally acceptable God in a world no better than this. But that response lays claim to nondivine agents in the case of moral evil. Hence, a new question presses: Is there enough self here? *Human* self?

Some theologians might try to turn a weaker self into a virtue. Does not God call us to die to the self? A relational-world theological view can certainly speak of *aspects* of self that must die—specific distortions of creational intention. But one must be wary of talk of total dying. To speak of a genuinely relational understanding of our selves before God does require something like the gathered Kierkegaardian self, "willing one thing." Edith Wyschogrod makes this point in responding to such continental figures as Jacques Derrida,

Michel Foucault, and Julia Kristeva. She discerns in these writers a "henopho-bia," a fear of the one. She wonders what happens to a category like "saint-hood" in such an environment: "There can be saints only if there is singularity, if each and every time there is compassion there are more than disseminated drops of desire, if each and every time there is suffering there is more than unanchored affliction."[111] Process theologian Catherine Keller agrees but is concerned to avoid the lifeless opposite extreme as well: "Some of us will go on working and playing at an alternative sense of self, one quicksilvery enough to elude the fixed centers of essence, one firm enough to stand its ground. Standing one's ground: this allows the persistence needed not to remain self-identical, which only blocks the flow of relation and energy; but to face difference, conflict, loss, reality, future. And a grounded self, unlike a fixed ego, thrives in its dependence on earth and only as earthling, on the matrix of relations to all the other earthlings."[112]

The issue in Whitehead's thought has to do with the fact that his scope is so wide, and his focus so small. His scope is incredibly wide in this cos-mological sketch that even stands on tiptoe to speak of cosmic epochs other than the one in which we exist.[113] The contrast to typical theological emphasis on the "God and man" narrowing concentration is striking and enlightening. But there is risk in this width. Our human adventure seems on the verge of getting lost in this cosmos. In one sense, this aspect of Whitehead's thought might be claimed as a strength, actually, for we are beginning to realize that theology centering on the human (even in energetic denunciation) is far too narrow when we realize that we appear at 11:59 on the evolutionary clock in a world that would well go on without us.[114] But this cosmology focuses so intently on the microscopic character of becoming that efforts to reach a credible account of the organization of process that we know as human life are uphill going. Robert Neville summarizes my concern nicely in his well-titled book *The Cosmology of Freedom*, contending that while Whitehead gave thorough attention to matters of microcosmology (elementary particles) and macrocosmology (the cosmic origin of matter and energy), he "skimped" on "mesocosmology," cosmology arising from attention focused on things of a human scale.[115] In the introduction, I cited Whitehead's provocative remark that "there is a becoming of continuity, but no continuity of becoming." He is not reluctant to apply that distinction to human life:

> It is obvious that we must not demand another mentality presiding over these other actualities (a kind of Uncle Sam over and above all the U.S. citizens). All the life in the body is the life of the individual cells. There are thus millions upon millions of centres of life in each animal

body. So what needs to be explained is not dissociation of personality but unifying control, by reason of which we not only have unified behavior, which can be observed by others, but also consciousness of a unified experience.[116]

Precisely! That is what needs to be explained. Whitehead's response to the challenge he states so clearly is to appeal to a set of organizational distinctions in the grouping of occasions. Hence, "in nature we find four types of aggregations of actualities": the inorganic, the vegetable, the animal, and then the human. In the human, the function of one centering reality has been "immensely" extended through the introduction of novelty of functioning.[117] He explicitly states that the distinction between the nonhuman and the human "is in one sense only a difference in degree. But the extent of the degree makes all the difference. The Rubicon has been crossed."[118] Will this do? Whitehead clearly intends to account for human responsibility. Thus, concerning "our experience of responsibility, of approbation or of disapprobation, of self-approval or of self-reproach, of freedom, of emphasis," he writes, "this element in experience is too large to be put aside merely as misconstruction. It governs the whole tone of human life."[119] He himself was active in matters of social concern, writing and lecturing on, for example, issues of education (*Aims of Education*, 1928). It is striking that the process theologians who have done the most detailed exposition of the cosmology have in later career turned vigorously to such social concerns.[120] But the question remains as to whether Whitehead's cosmological analysis adequately supports such ethical efforts.

Several scholars who work with the process literature have made suggestions looking to a fuller anthropology; they include Robert Neville (the "discursive individual"), Joseph Bracken (the collective field of nested occasions), and Lewis Ford ("inclusive occasions"). Whitehead seems to invite such moves toward some kind of "top-down causality" in writing, "The concrete enduring entities are organisms, so that the plan of the *whole* influences the very characters of the various subordinate organisms which enter into it."[121] But there remains the nagging sense that his account of the human self is inadequate. Ian Barbour, process-friendly physicist and theologian, voices the view of many in writing that he believes "that Whitehead himself overemphasized the momentary and episodic character of the self."[122] Here we need to return to the profound reflections of Kierkegaard on the individual as "the relation relating itself to itself." There is a sense in which we will not leave Whitehead altogether behind in doing so. He has not only the recognition of religious solitariness with which we opened this chapter but also a cosmological parallel of sorts. There is a sense in which the universe closes on the individual in the causal flow of the past. Thus, process-relational and feminist author Catherine Keller, knowing that one needs "a room of one's own," writes of "the vast causal independence of contemporary occasions."[123] But transferring descriptions of the microscopic occasion to the self still leaves one uneasy.[124]

This mathematician-philosopher-theologian knows about being alone before (or for him, perhaps better, "with") God.[125] His notion of a softer self helps us sense the power of relation and the importance of the body, even if the companion notion of a smaller self calls for strengthening. His appreciation of the body's relational power brings an important qualification of Kierkegaard's narrowing emphasis on consciousness.[126] But is conscious choice given sufficient place in his understanding of human life?

Now, how are we to understand power if we let both Kierkegaard and Whitehead teach us? How would we then live?

Chapter 3

TO BELIEVE, FACING FINITUDE: TRUSTING TOGETHER IN HOPE

Faith's Challenges

If our understanding of power is going to be real for us, it is going to have to connect with the living out of our days. In this, we have two problems to face. On the one hand, we need to recognize our finitude, our limits. We run up against our limits all the time: we aren't smart enough or strong enough to accomplish a desired objective. This frustrating finitude does not always wear dramatic garb. There are the husband and wife, genuinely devoted to each other, "talking past" each other. There are those good and earnest parents discovering that they cannot meet all the needs of their children. One size does not fit all, and, besides, there isn't time enough. Verily! So often, there isn't time enough to do what we earnestly desire to do. Looking (a little?) further down the road, we see the dark specter of our death; there isn't time enough. How much time would be enough? Well, more than that child had dying of inoperable cancer of the throat. Indeed, back in the middle of things, we sense the passing of precious moments all too quickly. Those grandkids grow up too fast, don't they? Honeymoons fade, as do the phases of the moon. If we are to live lives of genuine power, we need to find a way to face up to our finitude. We are not going to stop being finite, but we want to be able to look our limitedness in the eyes and still live powerfully.

Then there is something more. As we try to get somewhere in this business of living, something else gets in our way: evil. I am not thinking of earthquakes and the like. They travel on the territory of finitude, though many "natural" disasters certainly have a human element in their causality, at least as an exacerbating factor. But there is plenty more to talk about: Jews being marched into gas chambers, Native Americans being marched down the Trail of Tears.[1] We can switch to a smaller scale. The news readily provided by the daily paper and the ever-present tube and Internet server tell of the latest domestic homicide or the rape of displaced persons. An empowered life will be a life that has a battle on its hands.

There is little dispute in this: finitude is there to be faced; evil is there to be fought. In these next two chapters, I treat the two problems in turn, though I recognize that they often combine to trouble us in a given situation. I believe there is pastoral, practical wisdom in distinguishing the travail of finitude from the tragedy of moral evil. At least with the distinction in place, we will be less apt to assign guilt to finitude. We don't need an extra burden to bear, such as trying to locate the hidden sin carrying the consequences of being a creature. In contrast, we do bear the burden of genuine guilt. I will not offer an apology for moral evil, such as seeing it as simply evidence of evolution's choppy course. Covering for evil enhances its power. Confronting it openly, we have some chance to diminish its power. Naming evil for what it is is part of the work of overcoming it.

In the dark light of these challenges, we struggle to believe. Collum McCann, a National Book Award winner for *Let the Great World Spin*, was asked in a reader's guide interview if one of his novel's most challenged characters was a person of faith. Tillie, a prostitute in the Bronx and a mother and grandmother, pleads guilty to a robbery charge in a plea deal that lets her prostitute daughter, Jazzlyn, off. Jazzlyn is killed in an automobile accident on the way home from the court appearance. Tillie eventually hangs herself in the shower in prison. The question to McCann: "Does Tillie somehow still believe?" His response: "She has to believe. Otherwise it's completely hopeless. Even in suicide there's a belief that she will see her daughter once more. . . . In the deep dark end, there's no point unless we have at least a modicum of hope. We trawl our way through the darkness hoping to find a pinpoint of light."[2] McCann knows that "it's more difficult to have hope than it is to embrace cynicism." He is surely right in that. We must ask if faith in the face of finitude and evil occurs only in a fictional world. Can one actually believe in such a way that hope becomes possible? Moreover, there is real-world risk *in* faith, and in chapter 5, I will recognize the troubling tendency for faith's ambitious gambling on the absolute to become violent arrogance against the nonbeliever. But for now, two challenges *to* faith: finitude and evil. In this chapter, I will begin, as does our creaturely life, with finitude. We'll need to talk about time.

A Timely Faith

Our guides in the previous chapters both have much to say about time. Kierkegaard and Whitehead can both be characterized as offering a "timely faith." By this, I do not mean keeping our interpretation of faith's claims applicable in human life. One seeking such relevance might simply settle for focusing on our talk *about* the faith, as if such "second-order" stuff were the target.[3] But the timeliness I have in mind has to do with the very content of the faith. Kierkegaard calls the Christian to recall that particular temporal happenings are central to faith's claims. In *The Concept of Anxiety*, he explicitly critiques an understanding of time that flattens matters into a single, continuous, linear thing. The consequences of such a view are devastating: "One does not get the past by itself but in a simple continuity with the future (with this the concepts of conversion, atonement, and redemption are lost in the world-historical significance and lost in the individual historical development). The future is not by itself but in a simple continuity with the present (thereby the concepts of resurrection and judgment are destroyed)."[4] Christian faith is timely in that it is "about time." Such faith identifies particular events as having a distinctive, life-changing significance. In that sense, Kierkegaard's pseudonym Johannes Climacus could devote two major works to the proposition that an "eternal happiness" can be built on "a historical point of departure."[5]

Whitehead may appear to illustrate the view Kierkegaard is attacking, for with him, the approach to understanding time is certainly cast more broadly. We have already seen how he attaches himself cosmologically to the proposition that "all things flow."[6] But in that cosmology, he bids us to understand that what we call time is an abstraction from the primary reality of our experience of the past flowing into us. In *Symbolism*, he writes of how "the immediate present has to conform to what the past is for it, and the mere lapse of time is an abstraction from the more concrete relatedness of 'conformation.'"[7] Thus, John Cobb has warned us that with Whitehead, "we are not to think of four-dimensional space-time as a fixed reality into which all entities are placed. Space-time is a structure abstracted from the extensive relationships of actual entities."[8] In recent decades, this recognition that actual happenings must claim pride of place has been gaining wider recognition. Thus, in this twenty-first century, Ted Peters has made this point by contrasting Einstein's understanding with the Newtonian worldview in which "the natural world exists within a container of time and space, so to speak. In the Newtonian world we can start with calendar and map and then locate material objects within an otherwise empty container of time and space."[9]

If we give up a Newtonian notion of an empty "absolute time" and recognize with Peters that "natural events have an ontological priority, that time is event-dependent," perhaps we will no longer speak of ourselves as existing "in time." But we may be prepared to say that "time is in us," in the sense that the abstraction we call time finds its concreteness in the life flow of conformation to the past.[10] This will surely make us more attentive to events in their particularity and distinctiveness. That can perhaps be seen as a cosmological preparation for Kierkegaard's comparable critique of a flat linearity. But if time is normed by conformation, we will not lose our sense of time's irreversibility. We remember the past and anticipate the future; not the other way around. This seems not merely to be the way we humans function. Ian Barbour writes of the physical world: "Astrophysics adds its testimony to that of evolutionary biology and other fields of science. Time is irreversible and genuine novelty appears in cosmic history. It is a dynamic world with a long story of change and development."[11] The study of "open" systems into which energy is flowing has made clear that the sequence and history of a particular phenomenon becomes critical, even in disciplines like physics and chemistry. One could speak of this as "lawful unpredictability."[12]

So our creaturely condition is one of "flowing time." Moreover, the reality of irreversibility does not require a flat "calendar yet to be filled with events" understanding. Natural history speaks of "punctuated equilibrium" with "long periods of stasis interspersed with bursts of rapid speciation in relatively short periods."[13] But with all its variety granted, the arrow of time does point from the past into our present. We do remember the past. Indeed, in particular, our bodies remember.[14] There's that incredible way in which our sense of smell carries us back to the goodies—and the goods—of holidays past. It's not all sweetness and light. There's that pain, that ache, the body remembers all too well.

The irreversibility of flowing time does incline, if not require, us to look to the future. Each day, we give our deeds to the future. Our guides, Kierkegaard and Whitehead, seem to understand that well. The calm Englishman spoke of our being "interested" in the "propositions," the proposals, emerging in each moment of time. And the frenetic Dane, focusing on the despairing human, put it more vividly in writing of the "battle of *faith*, battling, madly, if you will, for possibility, because possibility is the only salvation. . . . For without possibility a person seems unable to breathe."[15]

This focus on the future is not a matter of theologians and philosophers leaning into the future while locked safely in their musty studies. Barack Obama in his remarkable memoir *Dreams from My Father* writes of a break-through bus trip to a government office with a small group of Chicago South Siders during his community-organizing days: "I changed as a result of that bus trip, in a fundamental way. It was the sort of change that's important not because it alters your concrete circumstances in some way (wealth, security, fame) but because it hints at what might be possible and therefore spurs you on, beyond the immediate exhilaration, beyond any subsequent disappoint-ments, to retrieve that thing that you once, ever so briefly, held in your hand. That bus ride kept me going, I think. Maybe it still does."[16] Obama's dreams may have arisen "*from* his father," but they functioned *for* the future. His ability to dream led him to this land's highest office. Other examples come to mind outside academia. Social historians have pondered the power of the frontier for Americans.[17] The lure of new land just to the west may have provided the power of possibility for immigrants. Thus, Sydney Mead can write of the "lively experiment" in which American settlers could "confront all traditional institutions with tolerance, with amusement, with anger . . . with impatience, but never with submissiveness."[18] Those settlers were what I call "horizontal" people, people on the move. But what if we have reached the Pacific? Space exploration will not likely serve as a frontier for most earth dwellers. But here again the temporalization of space may apply. We do live in the information age, and Bill Gates cheerfully points us to *The Road Ahead*.[19] Or perhaps the forecast is not unambiguous. In the next section, I will write of the looming "singularity" promised by the world of artificial intelligence. We may man-age more than a little anxiety in sensing that the significance and standing of human life may soon be altered decisively. Leaning into the future joins remembering the past in not being all sweetness and light.

There may well be risk out ahead, but Christians need not yield to the temptation of a Plotinian view where "the separation of moments in the flow of time is due . . . to a 'fall' of the soul from the original unity."[20] Christian faith does not call believers back to Eden, to some real or imagined golden age. We have written in these pages of how the Genesis accounts imply that humankind was created "good," but not perfect. Claus Westermann speaks of it in this way: "The creation of man in God's image is directed to some-thing happening between God and man. The Creator created a creature that corresponds to him, to whom he can speak, and who can hear him."[21] Ter-ence Fretheim emphasizes that "God's creation is a dynamic reality and is going somewhere; it is a long-term project, ever in the process of becom-ing."[22] Perhaps what God and we are to do together is to write a story. Paul

Ricoeur seems to think so: "Time becomes human time to the extent that it is organized after the manner of a narrative; narrative, in turn, is meaningful to the extent that it portrays the features of temporal experience."[23] If we are going to understand the power of love, we must not neglect the liberating potential of story. Native American author Leslie Marmon Silko has written of how "you don't have anything if you don't have the stories."[24] Theorists have pondered the power of story in therapy[25] and social criticism.[26]

This emphasis on story may seem to be describing a fairy tale. Am I supposing optimism, celebrating the onward and upward pull of *The Universe Story?*[27] Faith in that pull requires a too-selective reading of things. Christians should be able to resist such cheery optimism, for they know of evil in this wide world and in themselves. Thus, Barack Obama can write of how sacred stories "helped me bind my world together . . . they gave me the sense of place and purpose I'd been looking for."[28] But as a black community organizer, he came to know that he "couldn't separate that strength from the hurt and distortions that lingered inside us." The stories "had arisen out of a very particular experience with hate. That hate hadn't gone away; it formed a counter-narrative buried deep within each person and at the center of which stood white people."[29] Yes, two issues: finitude *and evil.* In any case, when we face the timefulness of finitude, terror is possible. Less dramatically, perhaps many people live without any sense of a story knitting their lives together. They tell a tale of neither tragedy nor comedy, but of pointless chaos. And for all of us, Shakespeare's sixty-fifth sonnet holds:

> O, how shall summer's honey breath hold out
> Against the wrackful siege of battering days,
> When rocks impregnable are not so stout,
> Nor gates of steel so strong, but Time decays.[30]

How, indeed? Kierkegaard and Whitehead both could ask that question in very personal ways—the Dane through the dying of three sisters, two brothers, and his mother before he was twenty-two years old; the Englishman through the death of his son Eric in World War I, after which his wife wrote to Bertrand Russell: "I cannot tell you about Alfred, he looks much older."[31]

Ambiguity and Audacity

There are things that are not clear to us that we might like to know with certainty. The future, for example. We lean into the future, anticipating as much as we can—perhaps more than we can. But we do know that we do not at present know much of what that anxiously attended time ahead holds for us. We may try to hang on to what we think is stable in our present life, but we can read the futurists and know that the pace of change is accelerating. Our teenagers teach us that the social networking system of texting, tweeting, commenting, and the like can move into the center of human life. Does/will the relentless rise of new technology necessarily serve human life?[32] Computer scientists have been working for years toward the goal of creating lower-level systems called "seed AI" that can write code themselves. Given continuing cybernetic progress, this stage may be only a few decades away.[33] If the neural networks of the computers accomplish everything done by the neurons in the human brain, has the distinctiveness of human intelligence been vanquished? If so, what will happen for human life when that rapidly approaching "singularity" arrives? There are important dissenting voices in this debate, but the discussion certainly poses anxious questions to us.[34] Philip Clayton states the matter plainly: "We are in the midst of the most rapid social and technological change that our species has ever undergone. When you look at predictions for the future, the curves that describe the rate of change just keep getting steeper and steeper."[35]

For that matter, even the present seems to harbor ambiguity aplenty, keeping company with the uncertain future. After all, much of that future seems to come out of what we now call the present. We are uncertain just how what is now happening will affect us in the future, but we quite surely expect it to do so. Some of this not-knowing seems a function of spatial distance. I am dimly aware that there are powerful forces at work out of my sight and beyond my ken. I am writing this early in 2009, as I hear President Obama and his economic advisers warn me that they don't really know whether the economic recovery plan is going to work. The point about the uncertain present can be put in more personal terms. What is happening right now for that child away at the university? I recall in the days before cell phones when our son Scott was "biking for peace" to Hiroshima and Nagasaki. My wife and I could not know what was happening to him on what seemed to us a valuable but perilous journey.

Some of our uncertainty about "right now" is even about matters spatially present. What does that nonverbal gesture of my partner mean? Or what is behind and in those words that she speaks to me in this very moment? About even these very personal matters, I am not clear. The French Jewish philosopher Emmanuel Levinas has written in powerful ways of the "otherness" of the "Stranger, who disturbs the being at home with oneself. . . . He escapes my grasp by an essential dimension, even if I have him at my disposal. He is not wholly in my site."[36] There are moments of disclosure when we discover that folks who look like us or even live with us seem more than a little strange to us. We have heard the calling to exercise hospitality, but we may worry with Richard Kearney that "it seems to preclude our need to differentiate between good and evil aliens, between benign and malign strangers, between saints and psychopaths."[37] This lack of certainty about the present is, of course, exacerbated by the fact that we don't know the past fully. That's where the present in large part comes from, after all—the past. The flow of time functions for us, *in* us. We may want to claim the past as sure footing for our present lives; at least what's done is done![38] But many of the questions we have identified can be raised at another level about the present efficacy of the past. I know Scott made it to Japan and back, but I do not know what that experience means to him now. What difference does it now make that he witnessed then those incredible scenes of destruction? What difference will those experiences of my young adult son make as he now sets about teaching his three teenage sons?

There is a tone of concern in my writing of these uncertainties. That is the case because, among the many things we do not know, there are some that are indeed important for us.[39] Morally so. The distinction between good and evil may seem a muddled mess sometimes, but we are not prepared to relinquish the notion. However, not much comes to us with the labels convincingly attached. Or perhaps we will banish our doubt about the identification of the good, but we face ineluctable ambiguity when the question is what we ourselves will *do* in the choices to come. Kierkegaard's pseudonym Vigilius Haufniensis speaks of this in making note of the anxiety associated with our sense of "being able."[40] We are perhaps not less unsure about the others. Will "the right thing" be done, individually and overall? A scan of past record and current experience does not remove all doubt.[41] We have reason to agree with Douglas John Hall, who makes this critical point emphatically in writing that a theology of the cross "is not able to shut its eyes to all the things that are wrong with the world—and with ourselves, our human selves, our *Christian* selves."[42]

This talk of good and evil is not far from God-talk. There, too, we have questions—two at least: Is God real? And is God (if real) good? Ambiguity abounds. On the first question, the great deniers Marx, Freud, and Nietzsche have descendents in their train: for example, Richard Dawkins, Sam Harris, and Daniel Dennett.[43] Trading on credentials in science and philosophy, this new trio and their compatriots invite us to abandon "the God delusion" and welcome the "end of faith." The second question has to face moral outrage over a God allegedly in absolute control over a universe no better than this. That theodicy question presses on us most keenly perhaps in connection with "natural evil." There surely, the Creator God is to be indicted. I am making revisions in the spring of 2010, when whoever is in charge of nature seems to favor earthquakes. Ask the people of Haiti (or China, Chile, or Japan) if the Creator God is good. I will have a word of response later in this section, but I want to note here that a familiar line of response to these theodicy challenges leads us to a third question: Will this God avail? To retreat (?) to the notion of a limited God by recognizing creaturely freedom as active in moral evil may leave us with renewed uncertainty as to whether faith can reasonably look to the future with hope.

In sum, David Hume's reappropriation of Epicurus's old questions about God serves us: "Is he willing to prevent evil, but not able? Then is he impotent. Is he able, but not willing? Then is he malevolent. Is he both able and willing? Whence then is evil?"[44] To opt for the "finitely perfect Deity" of Hume's Cleanthes[45] will not suffice, unless we can reach a new understanding of power. Such a new understanding is the point of these pages. I will argue that a powerfully loving God avails potently (if not omnipotently) against evil. In the face of our challenging finitude, such a faith claim can be sufficient to sustain us.

The key emphasis to get right is power in relationship. Here two things need to be said: First, relationship entails some element of mutual freedom. Second, ambiguity in our knowing is entailed in that freedom in our choosing. Let us fill out the argument at least a little. We will grant the first point rather readily in reflecting on human relationships. Anyone who has lived with a spouse or raised a child will have had experience that testifies to the freedom of the other, for good or ill. But some Christians may hesitate to use the word *mutual* of their relationship with God. Is not God, the transcendent One, in absolute control of all things? Did not this God create out of nothing?[46] Ah, but that's the point: God did create creatures to whom these Kierkegaardian words are spoken: "Become something even in relation to me."[47] We can speculate over whether God could create robots with merely the illusion of freedom. But such a scenario would actually entail the defeat of any divine purpose seeking real relationship. Chapter 1's development of Kierkegaard's understanding of God's will for relationship should underline dramatically the Socratic truth that "the art of power is to make free."

I have been stressing the creaturely character of human life. "We belong with the creatures." And all of us creatures belong in a creation that has been granted some independence by the Creator. There is uncertainty in the gift and task of freedom. And there is an analogous randomness in the creation in which human life emerges. Anglican theologian-physicist John Polkinghorne states well the risk given in creation: "The created order looks like a package deal. Exactly the same biochemical processes that enable cells to mutate, making evolution possible, are those that enable cells to become cancerous and generate tumors. You can't have one without the other. In other words, the possibility of disease is not gratuitous. It's the necessary consequence of life."[48] Polkinghorne speaks thus of pairing the "free process defense" with the "free will defense": "I do not believe that God directly wills either the act of a murderer or the incidence of a cancer. I believe God allows both to happen in a creation that has been given the gift of being itself."[49] He ties this argument to his conviction that God is both faithful and loving: "The natural gift of the faithful God will be reliability in the operation of creation . . . and the natural gift of the loving God will be an independence granted to creation."[50] The pairing of the causalities involved in the suffering of human beings and the other creatures does not eliminate differences. We will not be about the task of assigning guilt to the tectonic plates. Perhaps earthquakes and the like do not qualify as natural "evil," though the suffering caused is real enough. But in any case the point is that we do belong with creatures in this: the various creational elements come together to position correctly the question of guilt: the Creator God faces indictment.

The claim that the Creator of such independence is truly to be trusted cannot be made unambiguously. Even the more dualistic Whiteheadians present a God who "lures" the creatures toward greater freedom. If one retains the *ex nihilo* formulation, one still must ask whether an irreversibly self-limited Creator has the power we need. Moreover, how good is such a God? Even if one abandons the notion of God's absolute foreknowledge, could not the Creator have anticipated at least the *possibility* of the suffering that would ensue through the willing of such genuine relationship?[51]

What about the claim that ambiguity follows from freedom? Can such created ambiguity for the creatures be fairly called "good" by the Creator (Gen 1:31)? We face here the fundamental sense that new "unlived life" is ahead for the one who is free. One need not see this as special pleading for a person of faith. Simone de Beauvoir, the atheistic novelist and existentialist philosopher of the mid-twentieth century, expresses my point clearly in her well-titled book *The Ethics of Ambiguity*. She writes of how the future that freedom intends necessarily lacks being: "Man makes himself this lack of being *in order that* there might be being." De Beauvoir juxtaposes this human leaning into the future in freedom with a God idea of "a being who, from the very start, would be an exact co-incidence with himself, in a perfect plenitude."[52] No ambiguity would exist for such a being; no newness could threaten. But suppose it is not so with God. Suppose there is a freedom in relationship and so a future also for God. With that unknown element in that future comes genuine risk for a "God of the possible."[53] Such a God in faith ventures toward something genuinely new.

If that ambiguity is there for the Creator, *a fortiori*, it is given for the creatures. John Hick developed the notion of "epistemic distance" to speak of what obtains for the creatures in their knowing of God. His formulation nicely connects freedom and ambiguity:

> In creating finite persons to love and be loved by Him God must endow them with a certain relative autonomy over against Himself. . . . God must set man at a distance from Himself, from which he can then voluntarily come to God. . . . The kind of distance between God and man that would make room for a degree of human autonomy is epistemic distance. . . . God must be a hidden deity, veiled by his creation. He must be knowable, but only by a mode of knowledge that involves free response on man's part.[54]

The apostle Paul makes our point succinctly in Rom. 8:24: "Now hope that is seen is not hope. For who hopes for what is seen?" Yet here arises a question that is not to be ignored. *Shall* we hope? There remains the possibility of living without hope. One can simply despair, either quietly settling into the pedestrian run of days or dramatically rising up to curse the heavens. To hope takes energy. In Barack Obama's word, it takes "audacity."[55] Such courage is possible for us as human beings. Simone de Beauvoir writes of this, again without any appeal to a theological grounding for hope: "The notion of ambiguity must not be confused with that of absurdity. To declare that existence is absurd is to deny that it can ever be given a meaning; to say that it is ambiguous is to assert that its meaning is never fixed, that it must be constantly won."[56]

Her courage is admirable. I believe it is a testimony to how the Creator has endowed human beings with a capacity for hope without requiring, as it were, a "footnote" acknowledging the gift.[57] Analysts of the human scene have differed here, with some arguing that meaningful human creativity depends on a sense of the transcendent. George Steiner "proposes that any coherent understanding of what language is and how language performs, that any coherent account of the capacity of human speech to communicate meaning and feeling is, in the final analysis, underwritten by the assumption of God's presence."[58] In contrast, this century's "new atheists" join—indeed exceed—de Beauvoir in the Godlessness of their looking to the future. We all look to the future. Shall we do so with fear or with hope? Christians have claimed to find in God a grounding for hope. The writer of 1 Peter knows that such grounding can be questioned. He exhorts his readers, "Always be prepared to make a defense to any one who calls you to account for the hope that is in you" (1 Peter 3:15, RSV).

How might one respond to that exhortation? What case can be made for audacity in the face of ambiguity? What defense does the Christian have for her faith in God? One level of response is to critique the atheistic arguments, old or new.[59] A second is to offer a positive argument for exercising our capacity to hope for such audacity. Regarding the first, one must face the fact that the new atheists muster the massive reputation of "science" in their attack. Back in 1927, Sigmund Freud offered these last lines in *The Future of an Illusion*: "No, our science is no illusion. But an illusion it would be to suppose that what science cannot give us we can get elsewhere."[60] Eight decades later, Richard Dawkins, the most celebrated of the new atheists, has the same emphasis, even if it takes him far more pages to express it. Dawkins can write that "the presence or absence of a creative super-intelligence is unequivocally a scientific question." What about Stephen Jay Gould's notion of religion and science representing "non-overlapping magisteria"? Shall we not learn from both teachers? Why, "the very idea is a joke."[61] I quite agree that it would be a mistake to wall off religion and science from each other, but on what grounds are we to conclude that it is science that is to rule on all questions?[62] Dawkins distracts the reader from that question by constantly raising up varieties of extreme fundamentalism as the religious candidate. As options he offers theism, deism, pantheism, and atheism, but one waits in vain for a consideration of pan-en-theism.[63] The view that all things exist in a God who acts in all things carries impressive historical credentials.[64] Things may appear to be simpler if, disregarding scientific dissent, we can refer all questions of meaning and value to the sovereign scientist. But how is it to be determined that "the simplest explanation is to be preferred"? Must we shave with Occam's razor?

Dawkins drives us to that second question of evidence, the question of evidence supporting faith. The Christian has reason to be interested in that question.[65] We may be speaking here of audacity in faith, but we know with Aristotle that courage is not foolhardiness.[66] About evidence, there actually are *two* subordinate questions: What counts as evidence? And how much is enough? On the first question, both Kierkegaard and Whitehead can help us. Both call us away from a "flatland" rule of evidence in which only that which can be observed and measured truly counts. Kierkegaard's writing was done in the shadow of the Hegelian system, which he found to be a leveling of key distinctions. The very first sentence in his first major work, *Either/Or*, responded to such tyranny in this way: "It may at times have occurred to you, dear reader, to doubt somewhat the accuracy of the familiar philosophical thesis that the outer is the inner and the inner is the outer."[67] He was merciless in his criticism of "outer" arguments for the faith, such as the "the Evidence of the Centuries for the Truth of Christianity."[68] We have followed Whitehead's guidance in reaching for that "other," deeper experience. Breaking through Hume's sovereignty of sense impressions, he can speak of "our own individual existence now" in almost Kierkegaardian terms, while also affirming that we receive the world through the intimate "withness" of the body.[69] This move to depth is not special pleading for things religious. As I put the matter in an earlier book:

> Consider the deepest connections we have in life. For example I claim to know my wife. I could write on a chalkboard a list of descriptions that could be empirically verified. (She is 5'5" tall, weighs a determinate amount, has hair of one color and not another, etc.) But the woman I know is not adequately conveyed by that list. That matters as I come to talk about our life together. . . . My [further] claim that she loves me is much more important than the claims about her that could be objectively proven on a sense-perceptible basis.[70]

Very well, let us accept a more complicated criterion for what counts as evidence. The second subordinate question still presses: How much evidence—shallow or deep—is enough? Recall that we are speaking here of trusting together in hope. We lean into the future in this timely hope, but we do seek whatever empirical support may be forthcoming. As we look ahead, we face options that the intellect alone cannot resolve, options William James called "living" options. James argues that the option of faith is living, and it is "momentous," for "we are supposed to gain, even now, by our belief, and to lose by our non-belief, a certain vital good."[71] He evaluates the choices facing him:

> When I look at the religious question as it really puts itself to concrete men [sic], and when I think of all the possibilities which both practically and theoretically it involves, then this command that we shall put a stopper on our heart, instincts, and courage, and wait—acting of course meanwhile more or less as if religion were not true—till doomsday, or till such time as our intellect and sense working together may have raked in evidence enough,—this command, I say, seems to me the queerest idol ever manufactured in the philosophic cave. Were we scholastic absolutists, there might be more excuse. If we had an

infallible intellect with its objective certitudes, we might feel ourselves disloyal to such a perfect organ of knowledge in not trusting to it exclusively, in not waiting for its releasing word. But if we are empiricists, if we believe that no bell in us tolls to let us know for certain when truth is in our grasp, then it seems a piece of idle fantasticality to preach so solemnly our duty of waiting for the bell.[72]

James is talking about possibilities in an "unfinished universe."[73] He understood how deep and relentless is the pulse of change. In an appendix to *A Pluralistic Universe*, he conveys that understanding in a passage strikingly anticipatory of Whitehead: "Novelty, as empirically found, doesn't arrive by jumps and jolts, it leaks in insensibly, for adjacents in experience are always interfused, the smallest real datum being both a coming and a going."[74] Thus, the temporal passings "deflect us from the original paths of direction, and all the old identities at last give out, for the fatally continuous infiltration of otherness warps things out of every original rut."[75] Bob Dylan got it right: "The times they are a-changin'."

I leave to the final portion of this chapter the question as to whether there are *sufficient* "reasons for hope," given that the empiricist in us is looking to the future. My task here has been to clarify what it means that we are talking about the audacity of believing in the light of the ambiguity with which finite creatures are faced. Specifying what counts as evidence in a situation of ambiguity and exploring how much evidence is enough prepares the way for assessing whether one can claim sufficient reasons for a faith that hopes. But before considering grounds for hope, it makes sense to ask how such hope can function. What is the engine that serves hope? It is time to speak of the power of the imagination.

Imagination's Twin Tasks

In chapter 2 I made reference to the very considerable importance imagination plays in Whitehead's understanding of leaning into the future. I raised then the possibility that in our use of imagination, we might be acting in the image of God. If anything, Kierkegaard gives imagination an even greater place in his thought. It is "the capacity *instar omnium* [for all capacities]." He elaborates: "When all is said and done, whatever of feeling, knowing, and willing a person has depends upon what imagination he has, upon how that person reflects himself—that is, upon imagination."[76] Imagination will be a key faculty as surely as we must "live forward," even as we seek to understand life "backward."[77] Other writers have similarly placed a high value on imagination. To add just another pair: from England, Samuel Taylor Coleridge, and across the waters, American John Dewey.

So what role does imagination play? First of all, imagination can serve us by locating us as real selves in a real world. Thus, Coleridge can write of "the primary Imagination" as "the living power and prime agent of all human perception" and even hold it to be "a repetition in the finite mind of the eternal act of creation."[78] Coleridge grasps for the divine element in human imagination. Dewey will not let us forget the human, asserting "that human experience is made human through the existence of associations and recollections, which are strained through the mesh of imagination so as to suit the demands of the emotions."[79] One can see Dewey speaking of the service imagination renders to bring the self into being; Coleridge finds imagination locating that self in a real world.

Whitehead recognized the role of the imagination in thus orienting the self. We spoke of Whitehead emphasizing how, in ordinary perception, "we habitually observe by the method of difference," taking note of that which stands out by its occasional presence, but missing the constants in reality. But thought "can play with inconsistency; and can thus throw light on the consistent, and persistent, elements in experience by comparison with what in imagination is inconsistent with them."[80] Perhaps the poet William Stafford gets at this capacity in the following lines:

So, the world happens twice—
once what we see it as;
second it legends itself
deep, the way it is.[81]

Similarly, Coleridge suggests such a deeper knowing in eerily Whiteheadian terms by speaking of imagination as "the power by which one image or feeling is made to modify many others, and by a sort of *fusion to force many into one.*"[82]

There is a critical function in the imagination's service in locating the self in a present world. But as the future looms, we encounter a more fully critical role as the imagination functions to *dis*locate the person. It does that in order to *re*orient the person toward a time yet to be. So the imagination faces two tasks: deconstruction and reconstruction. To speak of the second task as *con*struction serves us better, for the imagination voices a call to something involving possibility, sensing something new that can come to be. The deconstructive is needed to make the way clear for the constructive. This coming of the new will be unsettling. Thus, Whitehead wrote, "If there is to be progress beyond limited ideals, the course of history by way of escape must venture along the borders of chaos in its substitution of higher for lower types of order."[83] Dewey as well called for deconstruction first, for of promising new conceptions, he wrote: "Until they have displaced from *imagination* the heritage of the immutable and the once-for-all ordered and systematized, the ideas of mechanism and matter will lie like a dead weight upon the emotions, paralyzing religion and distorting art."[84] His hesitant praise of the imagination suggests the importance of tests, a matter to which I will turn in a moment. But he would very much second what Coleridge writes of the "secondary Imagination": "It dissolves, diffuses, dissipates, in order to re-create."[85]

To move to matters explicitly religious, Walter Brueggemann can easily devote an entire chapter to the decisive criticism of the dominant consciousness that Jesus brought: his birth, his eating with outcasts, his healing on the Sabbath, his attitude toward the temple, his solidarity with the marginal, and above all, his crucifixion. But he is clear that the focus of the work of Jesus "was not dismantling, but the inauguration of a new thing."[86] So cross, yes, but most assuredly also resurrection, "the ultimate energizing for the new future."[87] Brueggemann is stressing the transformative power of specific events. How does this happen for the one undergoing transformation? Craig Dykstra writes of how it occurs "in the form of a new patterning of the imagination": "Often this is a pictorial image in the mind, but it may also present itself as a gesture, as a new way of saying something, or in a new pattern of action. Whatever the form of the insight, it is a creative reorganization of the imagination, in which all of the elements of the conflict are related in a new gestalt."[88] Kierkegaard locates the twin moments of deconstruction and construction in more dramatic fashion in *Practice in Christianity*. In "The Moral," he asks:

> "But if the essentially Christian is something so terrifying and appalling, how in the world can anyone think of accepting Christianity?" Very simply and, if you wish that also, very Lutheranly: only the consciousness of sin can force one, if I dare to put it that way (from the other side grace is the force), into this horror. And at that very same moment, the essentially Christian transforms itself into and is sheer leniency, grace, love, mercy. Considered in any other way Christianity is and must be a kind of madness or the greatest horror.[89]

In such life-changing transformation there is an element of volition that cannot be reduced to imagination. But imagination plays a crucial role, for in the words of Kierkegaard scholar Arnold Come, "I cannot choose what

I do not 'see' and recognize."[90] Jamie Ferreira has emphasized the role of imagination in the Kierkegaardian seeing. She ponders Iris Murdoch's claim that "imagination transcends the dichotomy between active and passive."[91] In imaginative attraction, there is a qualitative change "with the surrender constituted by captivating yet free engagement."[92] That dialectic would locate Kierkegaard solidly in the Lutheran tradition. Ekkehard Muhlenberg notes the Lutheran insistence that conversion is not a human doing: "Conversion . . . occurs when the human will follows the knowledge of God's mercy and the affection of the love of God. Human will does not materially add anything to the process, because object and objective are given in reason's knowledge and the movement or locomotion in the affection." But he can quickly add, "The human self must *recognize* itself in the new knowledge and in the new affection and not in other affections."[93] In Kierkegaard's rendering of this divine–human dialectic, the human will is not jettisoned, for the One who "from on high will draw all to Himself" wants "every human being to become a self" and so "wants to draw him only as a free being to himself, that is, through a choice."[94] Perhaps will and imagination keep close company in this, as Ferreira's reference to the experience of falling in love suggests in asserting that in this "the spontaneous, non-deliberate surrender is nevertheless active and free."[95] Flowing power finds its way in, calling a self to freely receive it.

Clearly, there is power in imagination. But in that power is risk as well. Kierkegaard persistently pleads that imagination is not fantasy. He was well aware of the human capacity for self-deception.[96] One form of despair he recognized is becoming bewitched by sheer possibility, neglecting the necessity that co-constitutes the human synthesis.[97] Yet there is genuine originality offered in imagination. David Gouwens stresses this in his study *Kierkegaard's Dialectic of the Imagination*: "The ethical life is never mere conformity to external norms; it requires originality to envision an ideal and make it real in one's own existence. And . . . Christian discipleship for Kierkegaard is never . . . an automatic, unreflective imitation of Christ. Rather, discipleship requires imagination to determine how one can follow Christ as Pattern in one's own time and place."[98] We recall Whitehead's provocative assertion that it is more important that a "proposition" (proposal or possibility) be "interesting than true."[99] But Brueggemann surely has it right in stressing that the prophetic imagination for Israel "means to move back into the deepest memories of this community and activate those very symbols that have always been the basis for contradicting the regnant consciousness."[100] So, too, Whitehead warns that the flight of imaginative generalization needs to land "for renewed observation rendered acute by rational interpretation."[101] We lean into the future, but as we do so, we remember the past and live in the present.

Given the risks entailed in the exercise of the imagination, one may surely hesitate. One may not be satisfied by the old certainties, but they are comfortably familiar.[102] Struggling to believe, we do lean into the future in *hope*. But we may well ask whether there are reasons, *sufficient* reasons, for hope.

Reasons for Hope

What, then, might legitimately function as reasons for hope?[103] For *Christian* hope? Well, I would not so orient myself if that-to-be-hoped did not connect deeply with me. I may have an impressive laundry list of problems, but I am not going to abandon myself to chase after a will-o'-the-wisp fantasy. But we have learned of one reality that is no such fairy tale: "the other." Our lives are lives *with* others. Who those others are makes a constituting difference in what I am, in *who* I am. We are indeed known by the company we keep. Kierkegaard understood this when he wrote, "The criterion for the self is always: that directly before which it is a self."[104] Now suppose there is one Other with whom my existence is always to be calibrated. Such a One, who never comes into being or ceases to be, will condition all the conditions of my life. The psalmist knows this:

> Whither shall I go from thy Spirit?
>   Or whither shall I flee from they presence?
> If I ascend to heaven, thou art there!
>   If I make my bed in Sheol, thou art there! (Ps 139:7-8, RSV)

Indeed, he knows this One is emphatically for him:

> If I take the wings of the morning
>   And dwell in the uttermost parts of the sea,
> Even there thy hand shall lead me,
>   And thy right hand shall hold me. (Ps 139:9-10, RSV)

Kierkegaard knew this too. He writes of how the human self "takes on a new quality and qualification by being a self directly before God. . . . What infinite reality the self gains by being conscious of existing before God, by becoming a human self whose criterion is God!"[105] As we turn to "face" God consciously and cry out, "I believe; help my unbelief!" (Mark 9:24), our lives take on new qualitative meaning. Imagine living "before," in direct, conscious relationship with, the God who formed the cosmic seas. Each person of such a faith has a Psalm 139 to write.

Is this intensification of the self a reason for hope? Perhaps, but Kierkegaard does not permit the reader to rest in romantic reverie at this point. He has no sooner written of the "staggering reality" a self has "directly before Christ" than he writes, "But the more self there is, the more intense is sin."[106] He is on solid Lutheran ground here in taking the measure of the sinner. This book, cheerfully titled *The Sickness unto Death*, takes its first half to diagnose the depth and variety of human brokenness. To exist before God is to be claimed, called into the intensifying ethical life. But many of us will know with another of Kierkegaard's pseudonyms, Vigilius Haufniensis, that our ethical striving regularly is "shipwrecked with the aid of repentance."[107] Perhaps in a quiet moment of self-awareness, I might say that if "sinner" is what I am, I want to know that truly, to come to terms with that judgment. Still, if that kind of intensification—"Guilty!"—is all there is to this religion game, I may join the many who say, "Count me out." But there is more, decisively so. That was the point of the passage from Anti-Climacus, cited in the previous section. It is precisely the sinner who is a candidate to hear the gospel of grace. "Only the consciousness of sin can force one . . . into this horror. And at that very same moment the essentially Christian transforms itself into and is sheer leniency, grace, love, mercy."[108] Is this faith an entrance ticket to a club where one only feels good when one feels bad? The self-denigrating religious practice of some Christians may suggest that. Masochism is available, if the diagnosis of sin lacks specificity certainly. Yet the dizzying Christian reversals this troublesome Dane rehearses for us, while puzzling, do touch us at points deep in our experience. We have known sin—our sin and the sin of others. And our faith declares that God would have us know much of love.

For many of us, there is a larger question: Does this scheme of things make sense? If the verdict the faith receives is "nonsense," that surely would be a reason for *not* hoping. Do these intense permutations of the self find their place within a world of meaning at all? Or do the passionate pyrotechnics familiar to us in the company of the religious self-destruct in incoherence? For example, it is easy enough to find mind-numbing assertions about a timeless God entering time.[109] Or to strike at the center of things Christian, how can two natures be present in Jesus "without confusion without change, without division without separation"?[110] I have addressed these questions in some detail elsewhere.[111] Here I will simply suggest that the one who seeks to believe in the face of finitude can find here a world, a sketch of ordered meaning that makes sense of her experience. There is a world*view* here. Indeed, I will claim that our lives make more sense, so understood. There is a singularity here—in the decisiveness and universality of this God-talk. In such faith, life comes together in a kind of integration.

Let's listen again to our principal guides. Kierkegaard would tell us of the consistency of a loving Creator who says to the creature, "Become something even in relation to me," and that Creator stays by that word with the sinner, saying, "You distress him by new sin—but he does not change."[112] This truth penetrated even his troubled relationship with his father: "I learned from him what fatherly love is, and through this I gained a conception of divine fatherly love, the one single unshakable thing in life, the true Archimedean point."[113] And Whitehead will tell us of how the theologians of Antioch and Alexandria discovered in the Trinitarian reality of internal relations a basis for "a rational understanding of the rise of civilization, and of the tenderness of mere life itself, in a world which superficially is founded upon the clashing of senseless compulsion."[114] Despite all the aberrations of *Homo religiosis*, these two prophets of the modern world have a coherent offering for folk poised on the cusp of the postmodern. The brooding student of the inner life and the mathematician making flights launched from the microscopic come together to testify: here is a God worthy of worship.

Sufficient, Together

Is that sufficient? Are these truly reasons for hope—such offerings of intensification, reconciliation, and integration?[115] Well, it is tempting to say that is for the individual alone to decide. But such a conclusion would stand in contradiction to the message itself, which asserts that the individual is precisely not alone. These reasons function for hope to human beings who, on message, are *not* alone. Christians have reason to know that, for they have read an ancient book that speaks of the unbeliever being "consecrated through" the believing spouse (1 Cor 7:14, RSV). We are carried by the faith of our sisters and brothers, as surely as they are disturbed in any easy rest by our turbulent doubts.[116] Lament (possibly as protest) and praise come together in community.[117] As surely as relations are constitutive but not exhaustive of identity, there will be individual responsibility to be recognized in matters of faith. But the individual is not alone in her struggle with/for faith.

Why is that? Is it not because that is where power flows, in the living relationships between individuals? Dietrich Bonhoeffer was reaching for that in trying to understand what freedom is. In *Creation and Fall*, he wrote, "Anyone who scrutinizes human beings in order to find freedom finds nothing of it. Why? Because freedom is not a quality that can be uncovered; it is not a possession, something to hand, an object; nor is it a form of something to hand; instead it is a relation between two persons."[118] That is the descriptive truth of the matter, metaphysically. Power is in the flow of one person into the responsive and responsible freedom of the other, and on and on. Bonhoeffer was a theologian, and in pondering freedom, he found reason aplenty to speak of God:

> It is the message of the gospel itself that God's freedom has bound itself to us, that God's free grace becomes real with us alone, that God wills not to be free for God's self but for humankind. Because God in Christ is free for humankind, because God does not keep God's freedom to God's self, we can think of freedom only as a "being free for. . . ." For us in the middle who exist through Christ and who know what it means to be human through Christ's resurrection, the fact that God is free means nothing else than that we are free for God.[119]

The Christian tale has it that we are created in the image of that God. So Bonhoeffer will write of the human being, "To be more precise, freedom is a relation between two persons. Being free means 'being free for the other' because I am bound to the other. Only by being in relation with the other am I free."[120] He was not without a human world, writing much of community.[121] Moreover, he did not find humankind isolated in this relatedness: "I belong wholly to this world. It bears me, nourishes me, and holds me. . . . God, our brother and sister, and the earth belong together."[122] It sounds as if all of us creatures are in this together. Most assuredly, each of us faces finitude. But we are not alone.[123] The ethics of believing is not to be excluded from the reality of relationship. Thus, Jonathan Strandjord, drawing on Levinas's recognition of the disturbing presence of the other, writes of how "the speaker's discontent is hope's incandescence."[124]

As we lean into the future, we come to see that finitude is not the only challenge for humankind. We know of something that darkens the face of the earth and works powerfully against a finite but truly good life. Perhaps the calling to believe in the face of finitude is answered positively only if we can live against the grain of the evil we know around us and in us. What can be said of the prospect of such a life?

Chapter 4

TO LIVE, AGAINST EVIL:
THE POWER OF LOVE FOR
AND WITH THE OTHER(S)

In the previous chapter, we focused on how the believer might well *view* life with regard to the reality of power. We wrote of how the person of faith with a logic of hope might "look out" at/to the environing world, how she might look upon her own self. We called for the courage to believe, for faith in the face of our finitude. I will not abandon that call in what I write here. But I am aware of something that is missing in that call to believe and even in the earnest effort to follow that call, as we look out from our position in the middle of things. Something is missing because life in the middle won't hold still; the middle is life on the move. Faith calls us to be part of making a difference in the minutes and decades that propel the one-looking-out into some kind of future. So the call is not simply to "look" at the self and the world from the best viewing distance, as it were. We are not comfortably seated in a theater, watching from a distance the action featuring the performers on the stage before us. *We* are called to "perform," to act. The call is to live into that world, as surely as self and world refuse to stay neatly apart and unrelated.

The call cannot be to "live into" without any more specific direction. Following such a general imperative could yield simply a weary (and weary*ing*) activist who settles for a sort of cumulative or quantitative presence without definition. Without further specificity, the frenetic actions might simply cancel each other out. But specific direction is hard to come by. Given the

complexity and plurality of the condition(s) in which we find ourselves, a unifying direction seems available only in safely abstract terms. But is our principle to be only as materially uninformative as, say, that the principle of our
acting must be universalizable? If the calling into the world does not always
itself yield clarifying definition, there is nonetheless something in the world
and in the self that calls for action quite urgently and specifically. I write now
not of finitude, but of moral evil. Looking back to the nineteenth century, we
know with and from Native Americans something of the Trail of Tears on this
continent. Wounded Knee follows quickly on December 19, 1890. Europe's
twentieth century has the enduring witness to the Holocaust, despite desper-
ate, literally incredible, denials. And the twenty-first century has candidates
of contemporary horror: the name Darfur takes its place alongside Auschwitz
and Wounded Knee in the legacy of evil these last centuries have generated.
We have written of how viewing finitude calls for a significant measure of
acceptance of the limitations that come part and parcel with creaturely life.
But these names—Auschwitz, Wounded Knee, Darfur—surely do not call
for acceptance. Ambiguities can be found even here, of course, but we are
driven to ask: Is there not something that we can *do* so that such realities
never happen again? These names carry concrete meaning and fail to fade
into abstractions. We sense a call to *live against* evil.

Seeing things better, more clearly, does not necessarily yield making
things better. We need to move from seeing to changing what is there to
be seen. That movement is spurred also by the frustrations we experience
even in the work of seeing better. There is a keen sense that the call to trust
and faith runs up against difficulties that resist resolution. We have already
pondered in the preceding chapter's reflections on "Ambiguity and Audacity" what one might call the "whence" of evil. We have tried to understand
how things are with the Creator and the creatures such that the limitations of
finitude and the aberrations of evil come to be. In that pondering, we have
repaired to the freewill defense and paired that with a free-process defense,
in which the universe joins the human creature in being granted a certain
independence. But there are unsatisfied questions. Many of them cluster
around the peril of human freedom. How free are we, really? How is it that I
know the good quite clearly at times yet do not do it? As for the free-process
part of the pairing, what of all the immense suffering of animals before
humankind arrived at 11:59 on the evolutionary clock? How can it be just
that all these other creatures get to suffer in the evolutionary drama so that
we humans can emerge with our splendid freedom? Taking free will and free
process together, we question the value of the vaunted independence. Most
radically, is that purposed freedom granted by the Creator all that precious?

Yes, freedom seems required for and in a genuine relationship. But does the prized genuine relationship merit the price paid by so many victims in this logic of relationship? We cannot "answer" these questions, and we cannot stop asking them. Must we be paralyzed by them? Is there something positive we can do in response to the evil that does not merely challenge our intellects? Without setting such whence questions aside—indeed, while still agonizing over them—we turn to the whither question: What can be done to alleviate, to reduce, suffering?[1]

Is that move a cop-out? I think it is not, though one must grant that formulations (freewill and free-process defenses) that seem most promising for whence concerns seem least helpful on whither questions and vice versa. Therefore, I do need to keep the questions together, checking on each other as it were. I see the connection working both ways. Whatever clarity we can muster on the whence will inform our energetic living to affect the whither. It will help to know what causes lurk in what we are combating. Yet some clarity may come the other way around as well. As we experience the struggle of living against evil, we may gain some purchase on the issues of causality. That may be Emmanuel Levinas's point in writing that "first philosophy is an ethics."[2] So we do bring this whither concern of living against evil into conversation with faith agonizing over the whence. Those two foci, together, fit folk who live in the middle. Thus positioned, we take up our lives with much that is given and in turn give our choices to the future. The ravaging reality of evil calls us to a battle that seems overwhelming. With none-too-quiet desperation, we ask if something more is there for us in the given. As we seek to complete our elliptical sketch, we have cause to learn from both faith and experience that we are not alone in our effort.

God at Work Here

Faith in God the Creator connects our experience of this world with the work of God. Some believers will make that connection by asserting that God created this world "out of nothing" (*ex nihilo*). That assertion traditionally reaches back to emphasize the absolute origin of things. That is certainly one way of making the essential point that God is qualitatively different from the creatures who create only nothing from nothing. But Christians certainly will seek to make that point of qualitative difference regarding God as it bears on our *present* experience of the world as well. "Original" creation aside, faith in a Creator God has a point to make about God's presence and action right here in the middle of things, which is where we happen to find ourselves and where we do not seem to be nothing. When Jesus was criticized for healing on the Sabbath, he responded by saying, "My Father is still working" (John 5:17). He goes on to speak of the Father raising the dead. God is still creating life, new life. So when we set about to size up our situation in which we hear a call to live transformatively, a reassuring prior word to hear would be that in all that is given for us, to us, God is at work.

Our principal guides, Kierkegaard and Whitehead, can help us hear this—differently. Actually, in their differences, there is a common theme: God works through order and novelty. Those terms are drawn from Whitehead's very explicit references to how God is to be understood as "the foundation of order and as the goad towards novelty."[3] The God claim is essential for Whitehead: "Apart from the intervention of God, there could be nothing new in the world, and no order in the world."[4] The term *intervention* is often employed in theological formulations that identify an apparently capricious God's on-again, off-again behavior in the world. But that is not Whitehead's understanding. Without God in the system, we cannot explain order and novelty in the world. But his point leaves no question of divine selectivity. He is making his point cosmologically, that "'Order' and 'novelty' are but the instruments" of God's aim in *every* moment of creation.[5] But he can write in more specific ways quite movingly of how order and novelty are to be sought together in large-scale social change: "The art of progress is to preserve order amid change and to preserve change amid order. Life refuses to be embalmed alive. The more prolonged the halt in some unrelieved system of order, the greater the crash of the dead society."[6] What we are looking for is "order entering upon novelty, so that the massiveness of order does not degenerate into mere repetition, and so that the novelty is always reflected upon a background of system."[7]

Whitehead's quest seems to have been taken up in recent decades by those in the religion-and-science conversation stressing the "emergence" of the "self-organizing complexity" mentioned earlier.[8] That same conversation offers further detail on how God may operate toward ordered novelty, novel order, through "top-down" and "bottom-up" causalities and, notably, in chaotic systems.[9] One need not master the details of the several options identified in this conversation in order to catch a sense of the how of God's continuing creativity. It is crucial to recognize that this is not a matter of special pleading for theology. "The loose causal weave" of order and indeterminacy provides access for the intentional actions of personal agents, divine or human.[10]

Can Kierkegaard be read well with these categories in mind? The terms themselves do not leap out from his pages, but I believe they can identify major themes in his thought. Some, reading him as a Lutheran, might expect a valuing of order over novelty. That would be a misreading twice over, distorting Kierkegaard *and* Lutheran ethics. A static "orders of creation" is not set in the Lutheran DNA. Nobody shows that better than Dietrich Bonhoeffer. This Lutheran martyr certainly valued "formed life," arguing, "If life severs itself from this form, if it tries to assert itself in freedom from this form, if it will not allow itself to be served by the form of the natural, then it destroys itself down to its roots."[11] But he was alert to distortion and wrote of "mandates" rather than "orders," intending to keep the emphasis on the One who mandates.[12] So he sees that "in the concrete case, persistent, arbitrary violation of this task through concrete forms of work, marriage, government, and church extinguishes the divine mandate."[13] More explicitly, he identifies a criterial test: "Where *being-over-against-one-another* is no longer present, God's mandate no longer exists."[14]

Here another Lutheran, Kierkegaard, enters the scene. From his last turbulent years, consider the criticism of a state church that filled issues of *The Moment*.[15] That final battle with the church was the culmination of an authorship marked by a relentless restiveness with the structures of Danish life. Could any "over-againstness" survive in a Copenhagen where to be a Dane was to be a Christian? Against such blurring of categories, Kierkegaard actually recognizes the destabilizing promise of the new within God's ordering. So he can write of God that "at every moment he holds all actuality as possibility in his omnipotent hand."[16] As *possibility*! In a similar vein, contemporary Lutheran ethicists revisit the two kingdoms doctrine with a keen sense of the "over-against" and "the possible." Vitor Westhelle writes, "Luther's insight brings into question the relation between revelation and the regimes that control knowledge, establish rationalities, norm the market and rule the church (the visible church is an earthly regime, just like the state or 'economy'). This reading of the two kingdoms doctrine suggests that knowledge of Christ can emerge only when we understand that it is in the fissures and ruptures in the order of things that a new justice can be shaped."[17] This critical perspective can be claimed by both feminists and process thinkers in their appropriation of Luther. Thus Deanna Thompson writes of how "feminist theologians set forth a theological vision from the underside of society, of history, an approach not unlike Luther's destabilizing move to the cross of Christ."[18]

Discerning which order serves God's creative purpose will not be a simple matter. Indeed, many say they simply do not see the presence of this challenging God. Kierkegaard offers a reason for that. You say, "I see no evidence of God." Well that fits the hypothesis, for "God's invisibility is his omnipresence."[19] That nicely specifies Whitehead's oft-cited point that when we observe by the "method of difference," we fail to see that which is universally present. Moreover, the Creator values freedom. Thus, a moral point may be involved in the difficulty we experience in seeing God at work here. Our seeing is not neatly separated from our willing. If sin turns the will in on itself, as Luther liked to say, it is not surprising that our seeing is distorted. Thus, twice over, given that we are finite *and* fallen, it is not strange that God is not obvious. But the Creator's work for human flourishing does not depend on the creatures' conscious acknowledgment.

But there is one who is visibly present, in the flesh of history and in the texts of faith's tradition: Jesus of Nazareth. After all, in that circumstance where he was criticized for healing on the Sabbath, he followed "My Father is still working" with "and I also am working" (John 5:17 again). So in any effort to "live against evil," the believer has cause to consider the Christ. Whitehead's focus on the cosmological might seem to swallow up such historical particularity, but he knew that "philosophy may not neglect the multifariousness of the world—the fairies dance, and Christ is nailed to the cross."[20] Thus, in *Adventures of Ideas,* in surveying the adventures of the idea of divine persuasive agency, he writes vividly of "the life of Christ as a revelation of the nature of God and of his agency in the world." The concreteness with which this cosmologist writes is striking in his description of "what elements in the record have evoked a response from all that is best in human nature. The Mother, the Child, and the bare manger: the lowly man, homeless and self-forgetful, with his message of peace, love, and sympathy: the suffering, the agony, the tender words as life ebbed, the final despair: and the whole with the authority of supreme victory."[21]

He is not writing these moving words to make a detailed theological point, but because the reality of Jesus of Nazareth makes "in act" the decisive cosmological point about divine persuasion.[22] Here Kierkegaard will keep us focused longer on the theological significance of the very particular story of Jesus. That is particularly the contribution of Anti-Climacus, the pseudonym he described as "a Christian on an extraordinary level," "in contrast to Climacus, who said he was not a Christian."[23] We have two works from the hand of Anti-Climacus. In *The Sickness unto Death,* he writes that Christianity "by means of the Atonement wants to eliminate sin as completely as if it were drowned in the sea."[24] How does that work? In a way, Kierkegaard seems to anticipate Whitehead's "Christ nailed to the cross," for Anti-Climacus's other work, *Practice in Christianity,* will speak of "the infinite importance his death has as a death of Atonement."[25] But Anti-Climacus will not leave *us* unchanged. Calling for the "imitation" not the "admiration" of Christ, he writes of what he calls the *prototype*: "Thus in one sense the prototype is *behind,* more deeply pressed down into abasement and lowliness than any human being has ever been, and in another sense, *ahead,* infinitely lifted up."[26]

One might leap here to a link with Thomas à Kempis. Kierkegaard did own *The Imitation of Christ*. But I hear in Anti-Climacus a remarkable expression of what Martin Luther called "two kinds of righteousness." In the Reformer's understanding, both forms of righteousness are "alien," deriving from God's gracious action. The first "swallows up all sins in a moment" and suggests God's decisive act of forgiveness, as Anti-Climacus does in speaking of the "done deed" of atonement. But the second speaks of how "Christ daily drives out the old Adam more and more in accordance with the extent to which faith and knowledge of Christ grow." This "is not instilled all at once, but begins, makes progress, and is finally perfected at the end through death."[27] Here we anticipate Anti-Climacus's reference to Christ "the prototype," who—from behind and ahead—would draw all to himself.

What Luther and Kierkegaard enunciate here about the Christ as part of the given is a theme being developed by contemporary theologians. So Mark Thomsen, a Lutheran who has given much of his life to missionary concerns, writes of a broader and deep appreciation of the meaning of the Christ: "The Abba of Jesus actually comes in a gigantic 'box,' inclusive of a multitude of cultures and universes and addressed to a multiplicity of people and intelligent life forms. Placing the finality of Jesus within the meta-cosmic Abba of Jesus does not minimize the mystery of the Incarnation, but transposes it into an intercultural and interstellar symphony."[28] Other Christian theologians join in this effort to claim "the whole Jesus," whether by trying for a full affirmation of the goodness of creation in *Saving Paradise*[29] or in offering a theology of the cross in which we are *Saved from Sacrifice*.[30] In these developments, the systematic theologians are moving to reclaim the richness of the biblical texts. As for the cross itself, Jesus scholar Marcus Borg speaks for a broad consensus in noting that "at least five interpretations of the cross are found in the New Testament itself."[31] It is clear that increasingly we are coming to see that the biblical witness to Jesus speaks of one who taught, who healed, who lavishly revealed the vulnerable and triumphant love of God. The heirs of Whitehead have been specifically helpful in speaking of how God's creative transformation actually "works." John B. Cobb Jr., the most profound and prolific interpreter of Whitehead, writes movingly of a "field of force" generated by the Christ event: "The real past event of the crucifixion and resurrection of Jesus, involving his total being, has objectively established a sphere of effectiveness or a field of force into which people can enter. To enter the field is to have the efficacy of the salvation event become causally determinative of increasing aspects of one's total life."[32] Michael Welker, citing biblical testimony, has drawn on the same scientific language and has helpfully emphasized that people can be drawn into the force field quite without conscious engagement.[33]

Welker titles his book *God the Spirit,* and Trinitarian Christians may have been wondering whether in this account of God at work in the given there will be found any reference to the Third Trinitarian Person. We have earlier cited Whitehead's emphasis in *Adventures of Ideas* on the insight of the "theologians of Alexandria and Antioch" into "some sort of direct immanence of God in the world," which he links with the Third Person of the Trinity.[34] We should not perhaps expect a fuller development of this point in his writing of things cosmological.[35] But Kierkegaard can use the triune framework quite explicitly. An instance is his non-pseudonymous work *For Self Examination,* where the Spirit is particularly linked with the giving of life. Again, as with the permutations of the relationship between order and novelty, Kierkegaard stresses that this gift is *new* life. Here, the destabilizing is formulated strongly as death, a "dying to": "This life-giving in the Spirit is not a *direct* heightening of the natural life in a person in *immediate* continuation from and connection with it—what blasphemy! How horrible to take Christianity in vain this way!—it is a new life."[36] Nonetheless, the surprise of the new does open a new world of understanding. Michael Welker has made that point well, reaching back to the biblical first Pentecost: "The miracle of the baptism in the Spirit lies not in what is difficult to understand or incomprehensible, but in a totally unexpected comprehensibility and in an unbelievable, universal capacity to understand and act of understanding."[37] So Kierkegaard, while maintaining his deconstructive focus, speaks clearly of the gifts the Spirit brings: the faith and hope we reached for in the last chapter and the love which is our central focus in this one.[38]

So God is at work here, even (especially?) in the chaotic messiness of the middle in which we live. While God may not advertise that active presence, God is not simply "out there" as an anonymous third force, but rather is seeking an intimate relationship with the creature. Therefore, as we close this opening discussion of resources available in what is given, I underscore the place of prayer. After all, one of the works of the Spirit in biblical thought is to help us in praying, for "God . . . knows what is the mind of the Spirit" (Rom 8:26-27). Kierkegaard's writings are suffused with prayers of beauty and profundity. Recall the prayer to the "changeless God, moved by all things," cited in chapter 1.[39] The process-relational stream of reflection has very specific promise for understanding this form of relatedness. In her highly accessible book cited in the introduction, Marjorie Suchocki writes of how intercessory prayer works. She recalls praying for a Korean man who was in great need: "As God weaves together the circumstances of that man in order to fashion his best possibility for the next moment of his becoming, my praying offers new stuff for the weaving."[40] In interceding, we do not give God new information or seek to change God's fundamental will, but we trust God to use wisely and well the energy of our praying in the situation. We may be without access to that one for whom we pray; an omnipresent God is not.

The person of faith will find challenge aplenty in prayer. Praise and thanksgiving do not seem to come easily to our lips. There will be challenge coming *to* prayer and challenge coming *from* prayer. Even in intercessory prayer, Suchocki points out that "in a world of interdependence, we must recognize that God may use us in answer to our prayers."[41] In relation to this God-at-work in prayer, we will be changed. There is, after all, a "coming to oneself" in the experience of coming to God in prayer. Ann Belford Ulanov writes of this, "In prayer, we re-collect ourselves and feel touched by what or who we know ourselves to be. We recover a sense of ourselves, now disidentified somewhat from the different roles we take on during each day. For finally in prayer I am I for better or worse, before God, and not mother or teacher or wife or lover or some identity I share with my depressed or anxious or dulled feelings."[42] Ulanov echoes an almost Kierkegaardian sense of the true identity of the self before God. But she does not fail to recognize the need to re-enter those relationships in this new life. As that movement occurs, the person of faith will invariably discover the disturbing presence of another "other."

The Other Calls

In chapter 3, I drew on the writings of Emmanuel Levinas to emphasize that the strangeness of "the other" challenges us. This one eludes our knowing, tidily cataloging grasp. But our not-knowing does not eliminate the disturbing presence. As a number of authors have put it, the other is "always already there."[43] Edward Farley makes the point well: "The individual who wonders reflectively whether or how it experiences the other is already intersubjectively formed. . . . We can try to jump the gulf to the other only if the gulf is in some way already bridged by intersubjectivity."[44] The action on that bridge is not innocuous tourist traffic. This other, these others, interrupt my comfortable self-possession in a far more momentous way than the irritation of the camera-toting interloper who will soon go his way in peace.

This other is at once outside my control and comprehension and yet truly *my* other. Assuming that we are speaking of a "real" other, not some projection of our devising, the presence will disturb.[45] Levinas has spoken of this as the power of the "face": "The face resists possession, resists my powers. In its epiphany, in expression, the sensible, still graspable, turns into total resistance to the grasp."[46] He writes of the "nudity" of the face, of how the face serves the being and will of the other. This one contests my power, for she is not under my control. I do not take Levinas to be denying that one person can kill another person or that a human being can be manipulated and controlled. But then what we have—precisely *what we have*—is no longer a living human other. So there is a stubborn otherness in this one who enters my space and disturbs "my being at home with myself."[47] Yet there can be promise in this disturbance.[48] Levinas can write of how "the face speaks to me and thereby invites me to a relation incommensurate with a power exercised, be it enjoyment or knowledge."[49] He seems to be speaking of something more intimate and internal than what happens when we employ the other for momentary pleasure or add him to our securely self-possessed body of knowledge. How does that "something more" work? Levinas emphasizes how experiencing the vulnerability of the other draws the self into a suffering self-transcendence.

Our principal guides, Kierkegaard and Whitehead, come together to help us probe this process further. Kierkegaard has been misrepresented as the apostle of isolated subjectivity, brooding in his garret. Yes, he will put forward the self as a reality that "relates itself to itself, which is freedom."[50] But this is not a solipsistic self. Thus, the very next pair of sentences in *The Sickness unto Death* read, "The self is freedom. *But* freedom is the dialectical aspect of the categories of possibility and necessity."[51] Translating to our present discussion, one can speak of the other as both possibility and necessity. In the popular distortion of existentialism, one misses the necessity. That distorted reading fails to recognize that Kierkegaard vigorously exposes the despair of failing to face necessity in fashioning a life in freedom: "What is missing is essentially the power to obey, to submit to the necessity in one's life, to what may be called one's limitations."[52] Thus, the ethicist in *Either/Or* will speak of genuine repentance in truly relational ways, historically: "While in one way it isolates me, in another way it binds me indissolubly to the whole human race, because my life does not begin now and with nothing, and if I cannot repent of the past, then freedom is a dream."[53] Perhaps Kierkegaard saw the opposite extreme, "necessity's despair lacking possibility," as the dominant distortion to be exposed in his Denmark. But this spokesman for the individual was clear that the other meets me as possibility *and* necessity.

In his formulation of "internal relations," Whitehead adds further clarity as to how the other so functions, emphasizing how the other is objectively given *in* the descriptive becoming of the self. Other students of the human condition have pondered how the other seems essential *for* the moral reality of the self. Hannah Arendt looks to the sustaining power of promises for the one who makes the promise. The promise is not made only to oneself:

"Without being bound to the fulfillment of promises, we would never be able to keep our identities; we would be condemned to wander helplessly and without direction in the darkness of each man's lonely heart, caught in its contradictions and equivocalities—a darkness which only the light shed over the public realm through the presence of others, who confirm the identity between the one who promises and the one who fulfils, can dispel."[54] But it was Whitehead who went beneath and within the human self to detect the indwelling presence of the other, microscopically. Thus, he turns to "modern physics," which "has abandoned the doctrine of Simple Location": of course, "there is a focal region, which in common speech is where the thing is. But its influence streams away from it. . . . For physics, the thing itself is what it does, and what it does is this divergent stream of influence."[55] That stream carries the other(s) to us, *into* us. Our guides come together to say that relationships are constitutive but not exhaustive of the self.

Arendt rightly stresses that the other makes a claim on me. Levinas makes this point with unparalleled force. Jonathan Strandjord well summarizes Levinas here: "The Other as needy infinity summons me, placing me under the weight of exigency before I have done or said anything. I have not volunteered for this duty nor brought it on myself as recompense of guilty action; it comes to me unbidden, pure experience."[56] For Levinas, this is not a matter of balancing self and other. He writes of the "strange authority" and the "height" of the other in the "curvature of the intersubjective space."[57] Here an issue surely arises, as masochism offers its ugly face. The radical claim of the other invites theological assessment. Can a dispute between the claims of self and other somehow be arbitrated by appeal to their common Creator?[58] Levinas can actually say, "This 'curvature of space' is, perhaps, the very presence of God."[59] So, what would God have us do? Scripture is not silent at that point: "Love is the fulfilling of the law" (Rom 13:10). How are we to understand the divine call in which all the commandments are "summed up" (13:10)? How are we to understand and *live* the call to "love your neighbor as yourself" (cf. Matt 19:19)?

Loving Self and Other

Kierkegaard and Whitehead can help us with that question as well. Kierkegaard offers a nearly 400-page reflection in *Works of Love*. He gives major emphasis to the element of self-denial, "which is Christianity's essential form."[60] He is critical of "preferential love," "which selfishly can unite the two in a new selfish self. The spirit's self, in contrast, takes away from myself . . . all self-love."[61] A century later, Reinhold Niebuhr took up this critique in a very comprehensive analysis of the subtle diversity in which the sin of pride can manifest itself.[62] The classic statement of this critique of self-love is surely Anders Nygren's 741-page *Agape and Eros.* He points out how acquisitive Eros, on the one hand, can infect even "neighbourly love" and love for God. "Agape, on the other hand, excludes all self-love. Christianity does not recognize self-love as a legitimate form of love. Christian love moves in two directions, towards God and towards its neighbor; and in self-love it finds its chief adversary, which must be fought and conquered."[63] This critique is rooted in his concept of God, which leads him to identify the first two "main features" of Agape as "spontaneous and unmotivated" and "indifferent to value."[64]

Surely self-elevation can harmfully isolate the self from fully realizing the gift of creational relatedness. But one wonders also if a tendency to self-denigration can clothe itself in the righteous garment of sacrifice. Gene Outka has appropriately asked whether the consequences would not be self-frustrating if everyone acted self-sacrificially.[65] He argues for "equal regard" as a norm that includes self and other. Thus, he writes, "The recipient's willingness to respond to the agent's concern is one gauge of the other's personal well-being, and in this sense reciprocation may be the object of unselfish regard."[66] Moreover, he makes the point that "in any love-relation some self-love is *unavoidable* as a matter of psychological fact."[67] Of course, the unstinting theological critic of self-love might grant that point but read it as a mark of the universality of human fallenness. Yet Outka's recognition of the self is not grounded nontheologically. He writes, "The agent's basic self-regard, then, ought not to be simply dependent on the number of his achievements or the extent to which he is found likable, but on his being as well a man of flesh and blood and a creature of God, a person who is more than a means to some other end."[68]

More basically still, feminist authors have stressed the importance of self-development and self-affirmation, especially for women in Western culture. That cannot be a totally dominant concern. Thus, Whiteheadian authors certainly seek to recognize the call of the genuinely other. Marjorie Suchocki writes of "the transcendence of empathy" by which "one gains the ability to separate self from other and to see the other as fully other, even in relation to the self."[69] But she would likely not challenge the point made by her sister in feminist Whiteheadian thought, Catherine Keller: "The traditional notions of sin as pride and self-assertion serve to reinforce the subordination of women, whose temptations *as* women lie in the realm of underdevelopment or negation of the self."[70] Kierkegaard would not be made distraught by such feminist cautions. Commenting explicitly on the "second great commandment" (Matt 22:39), he emphasizes with italics that "'*as yourself'* does not leave self-love the slightest little excuse, the least little way of escape." But he knows that "this phrase . . . does not want to teach a person that he is not to love himself but rather wants to teach him proper self-love."[71] Could that be what Outka was describing as the agent's self-regard?

Whiteheadian authors agree with Kierkegaard that if we are to understand love, we must look first of all to God's love. At that point, Daniel Day Williams in *The Spirit and the Forms of Love* makes a major response to Nygren. Citing John's Gospel's language of Jesus in love "laying down his life for his friends" (John 15:13), he grants that the love of God is to be seen "as forgiveness poured out for the sinner, the grace of God toward the unworthy." But we must not forget this: God's love "is God the Father's love for the Son. It is the fulfilled communion of spirit." Williams rejects any sense of "a mere calculation of results," yet "love seeks out the other. That is surely a kind of motivation." So "the action of love is not a pointless fancy. It has an aim, the Kingdom of God."[72] Concerning those who "denounce self-love entirely," Edward Vacek pointedly asks, "Do they really think that God does not have self-love? And if Jesus and his Father can love themselves and accept being loved, the question arises, 'Why can't believers do the same?' "[73] Don Browning broadens that sense of God as the recipient of love: "Even divine love entails elements of investment, attachment, need, gratification and joy."[74] This surely reminds me of Kierkegaard's prayer to a God who is unchangeable but moved by all things.[75] People of faith may rest well in the assurance that God has got this dialectic figured out. But meanwhile, we remain emphatically human. We savor concreteness and so stubbornly persist in asking, "How on earth is one to love oneself Christianly?"[76]

Perhaps we can at least approach an answer to this question if we try to work back and out from the actual experience of love. Something happens to the self in the experience of loving. We should not assume an unchanging substantial self for which change is only accidental or incidental. Something radical happens to/in the self. Eberhard Jüngel has written insightfully of this experience. His characterization of love is "the event of a still greater selflessness within a great, and justifiably very great self-relatedness."[77] What happens in such an event or, one may want to say, process? Jüngel's description merits a long citation:

> The loving ego experiences both an extreme distancing of himself from himself and an entirely new kind of nearness to himself. For in love the I gives himself to the loving Thou in such a way that it no longer wants to be that I without this Thou. . . . The relationship he has had to himself until now is profoundly disturbed, and the relationships

he has had to the world are alienated in a remarkable way. The I is suddenly a stranger in the world. But it also becomes alien to itself. Yet that is only one side. For when love is fulfilled, then that peculiar alienation is transformed into an intensity of self-relation and world-relationship which was never there before. Lovers are aliens in the world and yet are more at home in it than others. Lovers are always alien to themselves and yet, in coming close to each other, they come close to themselves in a new way.[78]

Jüngel has caught something very important in this description. There is truly radical change, genuine transformation in love. How wide is the swath of this description?[79] Is he describing specifically Christian love? Such specification seems to be the terrain Kierkegaard traverses in *Works of Love*. Or does Jüngel illumine for us the nature of human loving more broadly? Unlike Kierkegaard, Jüngel affirms a preferential dimension in love. While acknowledging a distinction between "need-love" and "gift-love," he wisely warns against understanding agape and eros as opposing alternatives. Perhaps the ground for that inclusiveness is prepared in the Creator's very will for life. Some connection between self and other seems a creational given. Michael Welker expresses this well: "We are persons inasmuch as we are children of our parents, relatives of our relatives, friends of our friends, colleagues of our colleagues, contemporaries of our contemporaries."[80] So how widely may transformative love work its wonders? Both Whitehead and Kierkegaard refuse to juxtapose the actuality of the Christ figure to the work of the Creator God. Must self-love and neighbor love be opposed in the love to which Christ calls? In any case, such an opposition would seem to ignore something these loves share: the fact that both self and other are changed as they come together in love. In that transformation, a third word is added to love's lexicon. With need and gift, there is task as well.

The task is given. Self and other will be there in the doing of the task. In that doing, the self does not rule. Welker exegetes Paul's "gifts of the spirit" and finds them "defined by *free self-withdrawal and self-giving for the benefit of other creatures.*"[81] Clearly, the call is to something beyond "kin" or "reciprocal" altruism. But to put the matter in Lutheran language, the point is to serve the true needs of the neighbor, not to become preoccupied with sacrificing one's self.[82] There will be a self in this service. Family systems therapists wisely warn us against "fusion" in family relationships where "the togetherness force is so powerful that there is a loss of the separate 'I's' within the 'we.'"[83] Self and other remain distinct within the relationship(s). But this self is not a fortress. Thus, Sarah Coakley has responded strongly to feminist charges of masochism by appropriating the notion of kenosis (self-emptying) to speak of how in contemplative prayer self-emptying "is not a negation of self, but the place of the self's transformation and expansion into God."[84] Such discriminating self-negation will target specific dimensions of selfhood, preparing the way for new creation.

The creational self is a self created not only by and in relationships but also *for* relationships. As such, it is no crime to "need" the other(s). Levinas even speaks of this in terms of "desire."[85] This desire is a "luxurious need." He writes of "a will that is not egotist, a will that flows into the essence of desire, whose center of gravitation does not coincide with the I of need, the desire that is for the Other."[86] In this vision, we leave behind the self secure within— or stuck with—itself, the self free simply to fashion such relationships as it can and will. Such comfort and ease are no longer available, but in the call of the other, there is indeed the hopeful promise of the future. Once more from Emmanuel Levinas: "In need I can sink my teeth into the real and satisfy myself in assimilating the other, in Desire there is no sinking one's teeth into being, no satiety, but an uncharted future before me."

Called to Conversation

An uncharted future sounds pretty scary. The challenge of the truly new looms. How am I to live with the other(s)? For what strategies, tactics even, does love call? While the calling carries a vast range of implications and applications, Thomas Ogletree has well gathered this multiplicity in writing of what the other calls us to: "wonder and awe in the presence of the holy, receptivity to unconscious impulses arising from our being as bodied selves, openness to the unfamiliar and unexpected in our most intimate relation-ships, regard to characteristic differences in the experiences of males and females, recognition of the role social location plays in molding perceptions and value orientations, and efforts to transcend barriers generated by racial oppression."[87] The role of language in living with the other merits specific attention. Dorothee Soelle has spoken in this connection of the role of speech in empowerment: "If people are not to remain unchanged in suffering, if they are not to be blind and deaf to the pain of others, if they are to move from purely passive endurance to suffering that can humanize them in a produc-tive way, then one of the things they need is language."[88] We are called to conversation.

While Soelle has been especially articulate in her recognition of the role of lament in helping the one suffering move beyond "muteness," Wolfhart Pannenberg has been particularly helpful in illumining more broadly the nature of genuine conversation. He understands the human person as "exo-centric," as "open to the world."[89] Human instincts "operate in an uncertain way as compared with those of our animal relatives," for the human person has the ability to "turn to things without being limited by instinctual inter-ests."[90] "Yet precisely for this reason, human beings also have the ability to be present in a new way to what is other than themselves, that is, in such a man-ner that they are not absorbed into that other through being wholly at the mercy of the content of their perceptions. Human beings are present to what is other *as* other."[91] He then draws on Erving Goffman's understanding of "shared spontaneous involvement," which yields a coming together in which "a conversation has a life of its own."[92] There is a certain being together in a conversation that works for real change. Pannenberg cites Hans-Georg Gadamer to make the point that a successful conversation leads to "a trans-formation into a communion, in which we do not remain what we were."[93] In this, we are on the cusp of the transition from the modern world to the postmodern. Jürgen Habermas may well have pointed the way forward to us decades ago in seeking to distinguish in modernity an intersubjective, community-based "communicative rationality" from an instrumental subject/object rationality."[94]

In such conversation, "success" should not be defined in terms of bliss-ful unanimity. Thus, ethicist James Burtness writes of how the point of moral deliberation may well be to "come to *dis*agreement": "So it is necessary, however difficult it may be, to structure our reflection about morality in such a way that it is possible to recognize genuine disagreement when it does appear and to deal with it in a civil and productive manner."[95] A greater danger than disagreement lies in considering communication satisfactorily in place in the exchange of trivial tidbits invited by social media technology. In truly understanding the genuine difference of the other, I come to a new place in our speaking together.[96] But we will not reach that place without, in Whitehead's words, "venturing along the borders of chaos."[97] Getting there will often entail new language, as Mark Jordan has noted particularly with the churches' struggles over issues of sexual orientation: "Language wears down. . . . Finding new languages for Gospel truths might mean any number of things. It might mean making new vocabularies, contriving new images, experimenting with new shapes."[98]

There is a calling here. One is to practice the art of making free. Ted Peters speaks of how the Christian is to "educe" "authentic personhood in others" and of how, as that happens, "the fulfillment of our own human-ity is coming to expression."[99] There are no limits on who the other(s) may be. Once again, universalizing scope can be drawn from the reality that we are creatures drawn together as created together. Or it can be drawn from the universalizing and intensifying Christian imperative. My Luther Seminary colleague David Fredrickson has lifted up how Paul finds "those who are not wise, powerful, or well born, to be empowered for full participation in the church and to claim confidently their authority to do so."[100] Kierkegaard focuses on that Christian particularity. He revels in the freedom the Christian finds in not having to puzzle over the identity of the neighbor, since "'the neighbor' means 'all people.'"[101] This appeal to conversation may still seem simply too sweet. This talk about talk needs to face a further question: What if the effort to talk together fails? What then? Then there is a renewed calling.

Loving the Enemy: The Goodness of Being/Becoming

We have stressed the connectedness that comes with being creatures together in this universe. We have found some hope in that connectedness. Can the radical words of Jesus somehow be built on the mutuality of that connectedness? Making that link between the creational call of the other and knife-edge clarity of the mission of the Christ raises a question, or perhaps two questions: (1) Is the creational connectedness itself necessarily good news for the creaturely self if it truly finds expression in the call of Jesus? (2) Does that call of this strange itinerant preacher from Nazareth have any reasonable chance to prevail in the welter of competing claims in life? We surely know evil is very powerful around us and in us. So one asks if this Jesus calls to either masochism or, specifying the masochism in practical terms, suicide?

Jesus does not deny the real power of evil. He seems to walk into the very teeth of it in his imperatives: "You have heard that it was said, 'You shall love your neighbor and hate your enemy.' But I say to you, Love your enemies and pray for those who persecute you" (Matt 5:43-44). Some of his followers seem to have been caught up in the same strange rhetoric. Take that fiery convert Paul of Tarsus: "If your enemies are hungry, feed them; if they are thirsty, give them something to drink" (Rom 12:20). Or, leaping ahead to the twentieth century, Dietrich Bonhoeffer did not read the Nazi strangulation of the churches as a reason for Christians living safely among other Christians, writing instead that Christians belong "in the midst of enemies. There they find their mission, their work."[102] What kind of sense can such talk carry? Evil is real; there *are* enemies out there. Our guides in treading this troubling path know about the questions we are considering. Whitehead wrote that, among "the multifariousness of the world," that "philosophy may not neglect" is this: "Christ is nailed to the cross."[103] Kierkegaard did not back away from the imperative:

People think that it is impossible for a human being to love his enemy because, alas, enemies are hardly able to endure the sight of one another. Well, then, shut your eyes—then the enemy looks just like the neighbor. Shut your eyes and remember the commandment that *you* shall love; then you love—your enemy—no, then you love the neighbor, because you do not see that he is your enemy. In other words, when you shut your eyes, you do not see the dissimilarities of earthly life, but enmity is also one of the dissimilarities of earthly life.[104]

But how on earth (which is where we do reside) does this work? Doesn't such Jesus love-talk masochistically leave behind the self serving and *being served by* the reciprocity given in creation?

Walter Wink has suggested that the answer might have something to do with God: "What guilt was for Luther, the enemy has become for us: the goad that can drive us to God. What has often been a purely private affair— justification by faith through grace—has now, in our age, grown to embrace the world. . . . We can no more save ourselves from our enemies than we can save ourselves from sin, but God's amazing grace offers to save us from both."[105] That seems about right. This venture is going to sink or swim with God; it will go as God goes. After all, Jesus follows his troubling imperative with this: "so that you may be children of your Father in heaven; for he makes his sun rise on the evil and on the good, and sends rain on the righteous and on the unrighteous" (Matt 5:45). Paul, too, makes a God connection, emphasizing that if vengeance is called for, that call belongs uniquely to God (Rom 12:19).

Well, what have we come to say in these pages about God and God's power? In chapter 1 we have lifted up Kierkegaard's lesson from Socrates that somehow the "art of power is to make free," that God does not give up a real kind of power when God creates a real other for God.[106] If our meeting the enemy drives us to that kind of God, how will we emerge from thus meeting the enemy in God? Is there a sense that somehow one will newly have one's self even (only?—Matt 16:24) in denying oneself? Well, there will be change. The key to connecting with the given in creation is precisely to recognize that God is the *continuing* Creator. In that sense, Lutheran ethicist Gustaf Wingren points to the concrete connection between the natural law and the love imperative: "To care for one's children and to sacrifice oneself for one's enemies may appear to be two different things from the point of view of a barren ethical system. From the point of view of murder, however, they merge into one another in the commandment, 'Thou shalt not kill,' which Jesus interpreted: 'Everyone who is angry with his brother shall be liable to judgment.'"[107]

That seems a stretch.[108] But in love, our hearts *will* undergo change. Kierkegaard, ringing the changes on the theme that the outer is not the inner, found the essence of human action to lie within the self. In the *Postscript*, he wrote, "The actuality is not the external action but an interiority in which the individual annuls possibility and identifies himself with what is thought in order to exist in it. This is action."[109] He knew that "there is a place in a human being's most inward depths; from this place proceeds the life of love, for 'from the heart proceeds life.' "[110] Of course, he knew that "there is need in love to be recognizable by its fruits."[111] But he knew, more deeply, about love that "if it is really to bear fruit and consequently be recognizable by its fruit, it must *form a heart*."[112] But still we ask, How can one love the enemy and yet truly live *against* evil? Again, we stress that God the continuing Creator is at work for change. If we understand that love for the other does not will to leave them unchanged, then we might say that our own lovingly "working for their well-being" seeks the fruits of radical transformation.[113]

And then the second question: How can one be hopeful in this venture? Is following this way tantamount to suicide? We began this chapter on the Trail of Tears. Along that path, certain names came to mind: Auschwitz, Darfur, Wounded Knee. They cry out for this chapter's title, to live *against* evil. But do not the holocausts of history trade on the same creational connectedness of which we have been speaking? In introducing his five-hundred-page study of altruism, Stephen Post painfully asks "how empathy, which by its very nature is ethically neutral, can be used as a tool for nurture rather than for exploitative control."[114] Can an ethic be built on a foundation that seems so much up for grabs?

Well, matters are not frozen in the status quo. The genius of Whitehead's revolutionary prose was that change became the norm. So we can consider the enemy other differently. We can begin to resist the always-attractive temptation to demonize the other. Yes, evil is real, and the experience of being victimized is very real. But the story of that one who acts against me is not finished. Catherine Keller writes of loving the *potential* in the enemy: "A certain initiation of forgiveness acknowledges the potentiality for change: it loves the other in their potentiality for love. I love that potentiality in any terrorist, in any warrior, in any human."[115] She goes on to say, "I love it as a potentiality for peace, even as I love my own potentiality to outgrow fear and respond in love."[116] One does not demonize the target, even the target deep within oneself. Walter Wink has made the point strongly: "As we begin to acknowledge our own inner shadow, we become more tolerant of the shadow in others. As we begin to love the enemy within, we develop the compassion we need to love the enemy without."[117] So how can one hope?

In chapter 2 we pondered Whitehead's proposal that the poles of existence are "reversed" in God so that God acts with a unity of purpose that calls each entity toward a form that represents God's singular purpose. Faith finds hope in such words, hope amidst the uncertainties of the present. Hope fits the territory of freedom, but it is not without grounds.[118] It is a reasoning hope (1 Pet 3:15).

In Keller's hopeful loving, I hear something almost Augustinian about the nature of being itself. Augustine, (in)famously critiquing Pelagius's optimism, is seldom accused of minimizing the reality of moral evil. But he understood evil as parasitic, dependent on the fundamental goodness of being.[119] Keller echoes this outlook when she writes: "As early Christianity declared 'world' itself, or 'being' itself, intrinsically good—despite its profound implication in 'sin'—so we may declare relationship ontologically but not yet ethically good."[120] Keller places that Augustinian-like hope in Whitehead's more fully dynamic order of becoming. She connects this hopefulness with Paul's "My grace is sufficient for you, for my power is made perfect in weakness" (2 Cor. 12:9), writing of how "an honest embrace of our vulnerabilities may turn them into sources of empowerment. For those weaknesses seem to lie close to our strengths: our disorganization lies close to our creativity, for example, or our insensitivity close to our decisiveness."[121] So, too, have we not found that even the energy involved in the experience of suffering retains the potential to be drawn upon as a resource for healing? Perhaps grieving may not be merely a preparation for healing but can become part of that transformation for good. Perhaps even the energy in the enemy's action toward us can at times be reversed and contribute to a positive advance toward mutual transformation.

Keller and Augustine, despite dramatic differences, surprisingly come together to articulate a creational faith. As Langdon Gilkey in his classic statement of the Christian doctrine of creation makes clear, creational faith provides "basis for trust in the source of all being," and thus "we can have confidence in the fundamental goodness of life as promising fulfillment."[122] In such trust and confidence, both Keller and Augustine believe, differently, that God is the Creator. So perhaps we return to where we began: God is at work here. In this *inclusio* ("inclusion" or "inclusiveness"), we find a new image of power because we recognize a new image of God. Keller and Augustine together? There's something funny going on here. Bringing these two together does seem laughable. There may be a point to that response of laughter. Wink, stressing loving the enemy as "the criterion of true Christian faith" in our time, writes, "At no point is the inrush of divine grace so immediately and concretely perceptible as in those moments when we let go our hatred and relax into God's love."[123] Kierkegaard was fond of writing of humor as the border of the religious, for effective humor has a sense of the incommensurable realities in life: the philosopher constructing a theoretical castle, while living in life's uninvolved basement; the eternal in time; the despairing individual finding hope for the future.[124] Given the struggle to have faith (chapter 3) and the enormity of evil, it does seem funny to relax into God's love. But it is an empowering hilarity to which we are called. We may even be strong enough to face the questions that bedevil us. Lest we miss the punch line to this deadly serious joke, let us pause one more time to consider the conditions confronting a creative creaturely life.

Chapter 5

TO RESPECT OUR LIMITATIONS AND RECOGNIZE ACTUAL EVIL, WHILE LIVING CREATIVELY

We have been building some momentum, especially in the previous two chapters, writing of what is possible for people of faith. Believing, trusting, living with love even for the enemy—these are ambitious words of genuine transformation. We even ended chapter 4 on the note of hilarity. But things don't always go that smoothly. Have we forgotten that we live on earth and that life on earth contains many challenges to this call to transformation? Are we infected with the virus of a mindless enthusiasm, a destructive "ecstasy," where we stand insanely outside our true selves? We certainly do know of inhuman violence committed in religious fervor. Does religious faith call us to abandon the appropriate humility of shared life in an actual world? In a way, this question was recognized even in these chapters of affirmation, for we spoke of *facing* finitude and living *against* evil. There is a tone of challenge in such phrasing. But before drawing these reflections to a close, it seems wise to pause to note specifically the realities to be faced. Our guides, Kierkegaard and Whitehead, are not exempted from this task, as we shall see. They join us in the facing. They can help us identify the challenges and will provide some perspective as we proceed.

At the very least, we need to respect our limitations and recognize the actual evil around us. Let's start with respect. "Respect" has roots in the Latin *respicere*, "to look at." At the very least, we can do that—look at the challenging limitations seriously. But other meanings my dictionary provides for respect are "to show honor" and "hold in high regard."[1] I believe we can do that about our limitations, for the challenges need not shut us down and can provide a kind of cautionary service. But to do that, they need to be respected. And what about evil? In my dictionary, the ninth and final meaning of recognize is "to acknowledge as having the right to speak, as in a meeting." In the Robert's Rules for the meeting that this manuscript proposes, we do need thus to "recognize" actual evil, letting it speak to us—not least of our complicity.[2] That surely makes sense, for only if we are truly aware of and acknowledge the obstacles can we effectively seek to combat them.

Fair Finitude and Actual Evil

Most of the subsections of this chapter are phrased as questions. But we can begin with an affirmation. Looking at our finitude, Whitehead and Kierkegaard would have us begin "respectfully" with words of honor and regard, for these guides come together to value highly our finite existence. From Kierkegaard, we can receive his underlining of the power of the self. Every individual self has some power; this one can will to be herself, can shape the mix of necessity and possibility coming together in freedom. With Whitehead, we catch the pulse of potentiality; things are happening. Good things can happen, for the universe is aimed at beauty. There are "propositions" (proposals of possibility) that invite our interest.

These affirmations do not cancel the limitations we must face. Kierkegaard, of course, devoted an entire book to pondering the permutations of the created condition of anxiety. As one ponders one's own potential, one sees unsavory possibilities out ahead. More basically still, the self experiences "the anxious possibility of *being able*." Characteristically dialectical, regarding the self's relationship to this anxiety, Kierkegaard says, "He both loves it and flees from it."[3] One is called to move ahead, but one feels pretty unsteady at the moment. We reach out to steady ourselves, but/and we fall. For Whitehead, the experience of the passing of every precious moment of life stands out in any listing of limitations. Up to this point, I have not cited the striking statement of this passing in the final part of *Process and Reality*: "The ultimate evil in the temporal world is deeper than any specific evil. It lies in the fact that the past fades, that time is a 'perpetual perishing.' Objectification involves elimination. The present fact has not the past fact with it in any full immediacy."[4] Even as I experience a moment of sheer joy, I do so knowing that it will pass. It *is* passing. I may remember it, but the experience of remembering does not annul the passing.

These limitations are not the fruit of our fallenness. They go with the territory of finitude. Douglas John Hall has offered a very helpful account of the elements of this "suffering of becoming." He identifies four elements: loneliness, limitation, temptation, and anxiety.[5] I have made limitation the overarching category, but in its narrower reading, the theme of limitation does speak powerfully to us: we are not strong enough, smart enough, handsome enough. The list goes on. And there is something in us that says we don't live long enough. Somewhere in the rhetoric of finitude stands the line from the prayer book, "In the midst of life we are in death."[6] I certainly read the Genesis account as telling us that we *return* to the ground, for out of it we were taken (Gen. 3:19). Thus, in principle, death is part of fair finitude. But it surely has acquired a "sting" (1 Cor. 15:56).

There's where the other phrase from our section title comes into play: we need to recognize that evil is actual. As we set about to plan, to act, we need to let this grim reality speak to us. Whatever unclarity we may have about the absolute origin of evil, we have ample reason to recognize that evil is through and through part of the actuality of our existence. To be a candidate for temptation is part of finitude created with the gift of freedom, as Hall says. Perhaps anxiety is given with that gift and the sense of consequence attached to it. But we know something more, something distorting and damaging fair finitude. In Kierkegaard's terminology, we know "despair." Whether that despair is fashioned in the form of defiance or weakness, we are not so relating to the God who created us that we are "resting transparently" in that God.[7] We do not need to travel far to recognize this actual evil. The cartoon character Pogo has it right often enough: "We have met the enemy and he is us." I have drawn first on Kierkegaard in speaking of evil, but the Whiteheadian corpus would also illumine for us the efficacy of evil. Part of the "multifariousness of the world" that "philosophy may not neglect" is this: "Christ is nailed to the cross."[8] Moreover, such evil deeds do not lack efficacy. You tell one lie, and then ten more to cover up the first. Abused children so very often grow up to be abusers of children. The creativity that characterizes how the universe works does not fail to carry the power of evil along into the future. That evil can even be "clear-eyed," as we will knowingly against the will of God. There again, Kierkegaard's emphasis on defiance rings true.

Indeed, evil is so emphatically actual that we find ourselves drawn toward some concept of bondage, as Paul the apostle recognizes in writing that "I do not do the good I want, but the evil I do not want is what I do" (Rom. 7:19). We might try to find some absolution in what follows, where Paul writes, "Now if I do what I do not want, it is no longer I that do it, but sin that dwells within me" (Rom. 7:20). Kierkegaard is in many ways a Pauline theologian, but he will not let this sense of bondage eliminate a sense of responsibility. Thus, strikingly, he criticizes his beloved Socrates for failing to realize that sin lies not in the lack of understanding but in the will, and then adds that Christianity "fastens the end" by adding "the doctrine of hereditary sin," lest the sin and the sinner slip through without recognizing responsibility.[9] The doctrine of original sin is understood to underscore the individual sinner's responsibility!

Finitude is indeed fair, something to be shown honor and held in high regard. People of faith can make that affirmation because of their trust in the gracious work of the Creator. Still, it seems at times hardly fair to be faced with limitations at every hand and the created independence yielding natural and moral evil. At least we can "respect"—look at—those limitations and "recognize" that evil's actuality. As we do that, we become aware of questions.

What Is Real?

Do we adequately understand what is real? This very basic question troubles us. After all, if we are significantly in error in how we picture the shape of reality, how can we proceed confidently with the making of ethical or religious claims or the taking of any action in these spheres of existence? As I write these words, I am reflecting on one looming impression: there is so much we don't know. This is not a bare, speculative assertion. Things happen that leave us clueless as to causes, and even consequences. We are blown off our feet by sudden surprises we sense to be momentous, though we cannot fully calculate what these happenings hold for the future. In what we do think we know, there are elements that suggest to us that we are missing something important or simply mistaken in how we formulate what we receive/perceive as reality. In asking this question, I do not wish to abandon Kierkegaard and Whitehead, our guides through these pages of inquiry. I am convinced that they have a great deal to teach us along the lines the previous chapters have suggested. But they do not remove our question about the shape of reality. Indeed, the questions that arise as we receive their wisdom will illustrate our quandary. Attending once again to each of these giants can serve to specify that question.

We can begin by asking Kierkegaard some questions. The question put at the end of chapter 1 has not vanished. After struggling somewhat to recognize the self's relatedness to other selves, we asked, "May it be that whatever insufficiency one senses regarding relations between humans is tied into Kierkegaard's radical severing of human nature from the environing nature we inhabit with all the other creatures?" In my reading of Kierkegaard with students, I have formulated this question as a matter of "tipping" the human synthesis. If we formulate the synthesis in the terms of body and mind coming together in the "positive third" of spirit, the body seems to occupy a position inferior to that of the mind. In *The Sickness unto Death*, he elevates the mental pretty plainly: "Thus, consciousness is decisive. Generally speaking, consciousness—that is, self-consciousness—is decisive with regard to the self. The more consciousness, the more self; the more consciousness, the more will; the more will, the more self."[10]

But it is in *The Concept of Anxiety* that the most egregious tipping occurs, and this comes about in the association of the female with the body. Woman's ideal aesthetic aspect is said to be beauty; her ideal ethical aspect, procreation. Thus, "Venus is essentially just as beautiful when she is represented as sleeping, possibly more so, yet the sleeping state is the expression for the absence of spirit."[11] Of course, this "simple psychologically orienting deliberation" does say that woman also "is essentially qualified as spirit."[12] But what are we to make of the claim that "silence is not only woman's greatest wisdom, but also her highest beauty?"[13] Feminist scholars have agonized over these texts with differing evaluations, but a "tipping" of the synthesis does seem to be indicated.[14] The point here becomes a wider one when we hear that "nature's security has its source in the fact that time has no significance at all for nature."[15] In this time when we speak rather regularly of "the history of nature," can we trust a guide who seems to have a self in which body and world have an inferior status?[16] Would his writing of the spirit escape injury-free from his neglect of a crucial component? How can we better recognize the embodied character of our life on this earth? We have noted a stronger emphasis on body in Whitehead, of course. But can we simply glue Whitehead on body and Kierkegaard on consciousness together and call that creation "spirit"? Can spirit serve two masters so distinct from each other?

Other questions continue to trouble. Both Kierkegaard and Whitehead stress creaturely freedom. But we may ask today, "Just how free are we?" Rita Nakashima Brock and Rebecca Ann Parker put this question well for us in questioning the ancient emphasis on demons: "Today, most people speak of socialization instead of demons, and they seek therapy to improve their lives. They wonder about the limits of conscious choice and individual responsibility. The law allows an insanity plea, and psychologists offer the disease theory of addiction. Therapists struggle to alleviate the compulsions of sexual offenders, the entrenched cycles of domestic violence, and the suffering of post-traumatic stress. Scientists search for genetic causes of such behaviors, and social scientists study the sexism, racism and homophobia that spread harm through every society."[17] Such questioning of freedom strikes most directly at the Dane. My understanding is that most geneticists do not speak of genes as determinative, and I believe Kierkegaard has a vital word for us in his emphasis on the self as freedom.[18] The associated notion of individual responsibility is crucial in how we function as a society. But at the very least, in "locating" that freedom in its relational context, we need somehow to respect how limited we may be.

Whitehead, of course, places a major emphasis on that relationality. Again, can we cobble together Kierkegaard and Whitehead and proceed with confidence? That question needs to be engaged, but first we do need to recognize the questions Whitehead must face. There is the familiar problem discussed in the final pages of chapter 2 as to whether Whitehead offers a sufficient account of the unity and continuity of the human self. As we think of our own selves, can we settle for saying that "there is a becoming of continuity, but no continuity of becoming?"[19] What of the unity of the self in any single moment of becoming? Whitehead writes, "It is obvious that we must not demand another mentality presiding over these other actualities (a kind of Uncle Sam, over and above all the U.S. citizens)."[20] Is it obvious? What is more obvious, perhaps, is how limited our grasp of the self in relationship may be. At the end of chapter 2, I have summarized efforts to bolster the unity and continuity of the self within a Whiteheadian framework. Whitehead himself wrote, "The subject is responsible for being what it is . . . [and] also derivatively responsible for the consequences of its existence."[21] Yet one senses a lingering uneasiness as one tries to "get there" within the atomism so fundamental in his conceptual scheme.

Even in the central emphasis on relationship, there are questions to be considered. Is Whitehead's emphasis on "the causal independence of contemporaries" credible? Do I simply connect with the immediate past of that other person who stands before me, face-to-face? There have been discussions in physics around Bell's theorem suggesting some kind of direct relatedness of contemporaries.[22] J. Gerald Janzen has mined the theme of causal independence as having significant existential meaning: "What arises to intensely vivid consciousness is the fact of the other, not as one's benefactor, not as one's beneficiary (as important as these efficacious aspects undoubtedly are), but as a person charged with intrinsic worth in the absoluteness of that person's own self-enjoyment, actually present-to-himself-there-now."[23] Whitehead manifested an admirable openness to recognizing other contributions to the complexity of our relatedness in perception. He was, for example, interested in "the evidence for peculiar instances of telepathy."[24] Such interest fits his proposals' strong empirical character that resists dogmatic finality in formulation. It is quite like him to write that a question such as "the existence of purely spiritual beings other than God" could be decided "on more special evidence, religious or otherwise, provided that it is trustworthy."[25] This empirical philosopher awaited further work. That work is not complete. There is so much we do not understand.

As we ponder the limitations of our knowing, we may be tempted to give up on any venture that bids to offer a coherent account of "what is real." But surely the choices we face, the ventures we feel called to undertake, require some sense of the scheme of things. I am bold to say that, whatever else we may come to know, Kierkegaard's sense of the self's freedom and responsibility and Whitehead's emphasis on the pervasive reality of relationship call for our attention. These pieces will need to be there in the work of any theological bricoleur, an odd-jobs laborer making do constructively with whatever is at hand. But as we turn to our undertakings, another question arises.

What about God?

In speaking of God, people of faith may well ask themselves, "Who do we think we are, anyway?" Faith makes claims about *God*, whose being is "categorically supreme." I take the phrase from Charles Hartshorne, who offers this exposition for the notion:

> God is a name for the uniquely good, admirable, great, worship-eliciting being. Worship, moreover, is not just an unusually high degree of respect or admiration; and the excellence of deity is not just an unusually high degree of merit. There is a difference in kind. God is "perfect," and between the perfect and anything as little imperfect as you please is no merely finite, but an infinite step. The superiority of deity to all others cannot (in accordance with established word usage) be expressed by indefinite descriptions, such as "immensely good," "very powerful," or even "best" or "most powerful," but must be a superiority of principle, a definite conceptual divergence from every other being, actual or so much as possible. We may call this divergence "categorical supremacy."[26]

I like to try to convey this categorical supremacy to my students by saying, "God is not a smart Einstein or a tall Yao Ming." Hartshorne found a cleverly turned phrase, "the self-surpassing surpasser of all," to describe the combination of "perfection" and "livingness" in God's supremacy.[27]

But why do I presume to *speak* of such a categorically supreme being? That humbling question is asked from within the faith. Kierkegaard writes of

how with respect to God we are "separated by an infinite qualitative difference." His next sentence in *The Sickness unto Death* is "Humanly speaking,
any teaching that disregards this difference is demented—divinely understood, it is blasphemy."[28] Such difference and supremacy may make existential sense to anyone contemplating the vastness of the universe. Do I really
suppose that my sentences, launched from a tiny spot on a particular planet,
can speak truly of the Maker of a million universes? The Scripture has instruc-
tions for us. Through the psalmist, we are told, "Be still, and know that I am
God" (Ps. 46:10). Or consider this challenging word from the prophet:

> For my thoughts are not your thoughts,
>   nor are your ways my ways, says the LORD.
> For as the heavens are higher than the earth,
>   so are my ways higher than your ways
>   and my thoughts than your thoughts. (Isa 55:8-9)

So, why do we not fall silent in wordless adoration?

Certainly less dramatic but equally challenging questions of adequacy
arise with our guides, as well. They raise for us the suspicion that in our very
praise of God we somehow diminish God. With Whitehead, we have found
ourselves regularly engaged by the question "Is there enough God here to
warrant worship?" Kierkegaard does have that emphatic theme of "creation
out of nothing," but recall that he explicitly puts God at risk. God cannot do
otherwise than risk the response of offense.[29] Why? His response goes to the
heart of the matter in the relational character of this God: "What an unfathomable conflict in love! Yet in love he does not have the heart to desist from com-
pleting this act of love."[30] Whatever one will say about the absolute origin of
all, here in the middle where we do live, we are not *now* nothing. So Kierkegaard and Whitehead do come together in this. Whitehead, after all, has God
exemplifying Socrates's wisdom, calling the creatures toward greater freedom.
Thus, they—and surely *we*—face that second question: Is it (freedom!) worth
it? Believers know the line "God is great, and God is good." In the face of evil,
can one muster both adjectives?[31] Or must a conscientious believer put forward
one's faith as an outcry of protest against a God who so dangerously calls to
freedom?[32] If apologists for the faith were to respond to such whence questions about the origin of evil by appealing to the whither of God's response to
evil, they still would not be done with questions. There's that infamous "problem of particularity." Christians face the inevitably confessional character of
the highly particular Jesus of Nazareth. Why this one exclusively offering such
limited access to therapy for humankind's alleged universal problem?

But, of course, that is precisely the point: this God of whom faith speaks so particularly is a loving God—more than that, on message, *is* love (1 John 4). Accordingly, this God wills to be known, even if not always by name (Matt 25). Indeed, that highly particularly Jesus does not leave love an abstraction, for from him come the surprising words "I have called you friends" (John 15:15). The point of that? "I do not call you servants any longer, because the servant does not know what the master is doing. . . . I have made known to you everything that I have heard from my Father" (John 15:15). And there's more. Later in John's Gospel, this Jesus is speaking of sending the Spirit of truth who "will guide you into all the truth" (John 16:13). That Spirit, "blows where it wills" (John 3:8, RSV), and is notoriously hard to control. But this God wills to be known, by name or otherwise. This Jesus knew that he was sent so that the beloved "may have life and have it abundantly" (John 10:10). Life's abundance entails knowing, *mutual* knowing, whereby the Christian knows that he is known by God. We are called to such knowing. At some deep level we seek that: "As a deer longs for flowing streams, so my soul longs for you, O God" (Ps 42:1, RSV). But this deepest knowing does call for trust in the face of risk.

So people of faith will bid to speak of God. But it is truly essential that the limitations be recognized, be respected. Christians hear a call to "go tell it on the mountain," but the good tidings they bear are a kind of "learned ignorance."[33] Elizabeth Johnson catches the accent well: "The triune God is not simply unknown, but positively known to be unknown and unknowable—which is a dear and profound kind of knowledge."[34] Christians do not always act as if they realize that their learning is ignorant. Morris Cohen's classic charge against religions of the absolute needs to be heard:

> The fierce spirit of war and hatred is not of course entirely due to religion. But religion *has* made a *duty* of hatred. It preached crusades against Mohammedans and forgave atrocious sins to encourage indiscriminate slaughter of Greek Orthodox as well as of Mohammedan populations. It also preached crusades against Albigenses, Waldenses, and Hussite Bohemians. . . . Cruel persecution and intolerance are not accidents, but grow out of the very essence of religion, namely its absolute claims. So long as each religion claims to have absolute, supernaturally revealed truth, all other religions are sinful errors.[35]

Cohen's details drive his critique home for Christians. At their best, they will not head for escape routes such as the facile response that Christianity is not a religion, but revealed truth. So we face the questions anew. Indeed, have I not exacerbated matters in this very section by stressing the categorical supremacy of God? Must human trafficking with the absolute turn creatures against each other? We need the questions. To know how little one knows will be something Christians need constantly to recall, the more the learning-in-relationship develops. That will manifest itself in some falling silent precisely *in* one's speaking.[36] One will not cease praising the Christ, but one will do so the more by claiming that whatever this Jesus accomplished was done for *all* creatures. That will mean listening—to people of other faiths and to those who claim no faith and have questions aplenty for believers. It may mean a persistent mood of lament and protest as the believer puts her own challenges to God. Realizing how little one really knows will surely mean continuing to "live the questions" we ourselves have. Rainer Maria Rilke's word to "a young poet" fits people of faith well: "Have patience with everything unresolved in your heart and try to love the questions themselves. . . . Don't search for answers now, because you would not be able to live them. And the point is to live everything. Live the questions now. Perhaps, then, someday far in the future, you will gradually, without even noticing it, live your way into the answer."[37]

We will speak of God, as did Kierkegaard and Whitehead. We will cling to the reality of relationship with One who is truly absolute, qualitatively different from the creatures. But in that relationship, we will remember that this Christian story speaks surprisingly of what we have clumsily called transcendence in relationship, revealed in the Creator's unqualified love for all creatures. We will make our claims, trusting that coming to know of God what we do not now know would not undercut what we believe we do know. But we will respect, "hold in high regard," the questions. In that living of the questions, we find ourselves rather painfully pondering what comes to be in human response to God's will and work.

What about Our Troubled Response to God?

What God seems to be up to in this world involves freedom. God seems to know and exemplify what, on Kierkegaard's reading, Socrates knew: "that the art of power is to make free."[38] Perhaps freedom may not be the ultimate end in view in this relationship-making affair, but it surely seems a chosen means. Kierkegaard and Whitehead, despite their dramatically different styles, together reject the notion that creatures are simply expressions of divine determination. There is a calling. But if we are to respond honestly with the means we seem to have, we certainly need to look hard at the human track record in responding to God's call. In thus "respecting" our limitations, we find developments that disturb us. "Troubling" might be an understatement.

Well, what does God seek? Again, Kierkegaard and Whitehead offer illuminating illustrations. I have stressed that both our guides place a strong emphasis on relationship, and that entails something coming from the human side toward God. Thus, we speak of being called into a loving faith toward God and a loving justice toward the world. What is faith? Here the brew begins to boil, for the ingredients of faith do not come together easily. Conventionally, those ingredients are said to be *notitia* ("knowledge"), *assensus* ("assent"), and *fiducia* ("trust").[39] Perhaps these three go into two, distinguishing belief in propositions about God (classically, the *fides quae creditor*—the "faith which is believed") and trust in God (the *fides qua creditor*—the "faith by which we believe"). We thus distinguish between what is happening when we confess the Apostles' Creed in worship and what is happening when in praise or lament we turn passionately to the One who ultimately matters. These two, the propositions and the passions, surely keep close company in our lives. But this marriage between the more objective and the more subjective has not been a very stable one. In some ways, Kierkegaard and Whitehead, again exemplifying the challenges we face, can be read as representing the tendency to elevate one pole or the other.

The *fides quae creditor*, the objective dimension, may be seen in Whitehead's understanding of the nature of religion in *Religion in the Making*. His description certainly includes the subjective, for he writes, "You *use* arithmetic, but you *are* religious."[40] But he continues, "Religion is the force of *belief* cleansing the inward parts" (my emphasis). Thus, "in the long run your character and your conduct of life depend upon your intimate convictions."[41] His study of the emergence of religion in human history identifies four "factors": ritual, emotion, belief, and rationalization. But "the order of the emergence of these factors was in the inverse order of the depth of their religious importance."[42] The sentences of the *fides quae* will find their place in the third and fourth stages, leaving behind the passion of emotion and the routine of ritual. So his appeal is to "rational religion," which "appeals to the direct intuition of special occasions, and to the elucidatory power of its concepts for all occasions."[43] The point here is "that a rational religion must not confine itself to moments of emotional excitement. It must find its verification at all temperatures."[44] So it is that "generality is the salt of religion."[45]

The champions of the various orthodoxies in the story of religion, while perhaps variously uneasy with the particular "rational religion" to which Whitehead's emphasis leads him, surely agree in principle with this elevation of the claims of faith, the *fides quae creditor*. But that story also records

vigorous pietisms with their insistence that what really matters is a personal
relationship with God. In some way, Kierkegaard can be aligned with that
suspicion of objectifying propositions and with a favoring instead of the passionate commitment of the individual. The contrast is not absolute, for he can
be very specific in identifying the dialectical structure of the Christian paradox. But the recognition of the objective does not diminish the emphasis on
the subjective, the passion of faith. Thus, in *Works of Love*, he wrote, "It is true
that the pronouncement of the forgiveness of sin is pronounced also to you,
but the pastor does not have the right to say to you that you have faith, and
yet it is pronounced to you only if you believe. . . . See, this is the struggle of
faith in which you can have an occasion to be tried and tested every day."[46]

The dialectical structure of the Christ paradox, clearly offered as an
"objective" element, is most fully outlined in the *Concluding Unscientific
Postscript*. But even there, Kierkegaard's lean toward the *fides qua* is clear.
In the introduction, Johannes Climacus, writing from outside the faith, says,
"The objective issue, then, would be about the truth of Christianity. The
subjective issue is about the individual's relation to Christianity."[47] It is the latter that interests Johannes, asking already in *Philosophical Fragments* about
Christian talk of an "eternal happiness." That emphasis on the crucial role
of faith's venturing in any "advance on Socrates" in the subjectivity of the
individual prevails throughout the six hundred pages of the *Postscript*. Thus,
he writes infamously of the person praying "with all the passion of infinity"
but with his eyes "resting upon the image of an idol": this person "prays in
truth to God although he is worshipping an idol."[48] Consistently then, this
pseudonym has this to say in the *Postscript*'s conclusion: "Being a Christian is
defined not by the 'what' of Christianity but by the 'how' of the Christian."[49]
It is true that the very next sentence reaches for the objective in saying, "This
'how' can fit only one thing, the absolute paradox." This reaching out for the
other side reminds me of Whitehead, who with all his concern for generality
of formulation could still speak of the seminal religious intuition as "not the
discernment of a form of words, but of a type of character." Whitehead adds,
"It is characteristic of the learned mind to exalt words. Yet mothers can ponder many things in their hearts which their lips cannot express. These many
things, which are thus known, constitute the ultimate religious evidence,
beyond which there is no appeal."[50]

Thus do Kierkegaard and Whitehead come together to ponder the *quae*
and the *qua* of response to God. In respecting our limitations, we are called
to honor our own struggle with incorporating both dimensions, as they did
with differing emphases. We cannot do without the "objective" propositions,
for we do seek some identity within the cacophonous reality of religious

pluralism. We confess our creeds precisely together, for they do give us a kind of identity, even in our divisive struggles to "get it right." But we well know that there are times when even the most elegantly turned sentences seem brittle and threaten to turn to dust. Yet we seek to relate to a divine power or person even or especially when words fail us. We also know that there are people of winsome faith who do not muster or master the logistics of our theological propositions. Perhaps that is never clearer than in the quiet peace one senses when a sainted elder, not massaging the propositions, closes her eyes a final time and does so calmly, even eagerly. So how can people of faith hold together these dimensions of the faith? Perhaps the best we can do, for now at least, is to seek that identity of and in faith within a community where differentiation of roles and responsibilities may keep the creative tension between *quae* and *qua* alive.

That move to community may also be what we find ourselves doing when we look at the work of justice to be rendered in response to God. Perhaps this may be the more inclusive of the faith and justice pairing, if Matthew 25 is right in suggesting that those blessed ones providing deeds of mercy were serving Jesus, though they knew it not. In any case, if our topic is how things sort themselves out regarding the crying need for justice, we surely need not only to respect limitations. But we also sense a call to recognize, verily to repent of, actual evil. Of course, the two, respecting and repenting, are inextricably mixed together in our actual existence. The two verbs go together for us because their objects so often are mixed up with each other. Thus, the faith we decisively finite believers confess can sadly become a way we gain our communal identity by evilly excluding others who do not speak these sentences. Cohen and company stand ready to remind us how such exclusiveness can foster violence all too easily. When the *fides quae* functions in such exclusive claims to truth, we need to repair to the *fides qua*, which in a basic way links us with other mortals who, quite like us, reach out to their Creator.[51] There our life with "the others," as developed in chapters 3 and 4, comes into play. One hopes for mutual learning in that life, but of course, that learning draws on the creative differences conveyed by the conceptual identities expressed by the confessed propositions. The dialectic does not disappear.[52]

So how does faith function for this world? Must we not say that because of faith, things are better—and worse? Actual evil does not fail to visit our churches, synagogues, and mosques, often departing from those sacred spaces newly empowered for the doing of harm. That record is painfully clear. Would it not be better to eschew the high-temperature risk of religious passion altogether? Yet it is also clear that people of faith have worked for justice, dramatically and quietly. It is often difficult to sort out the mix of good and evil in humankind's long religious story. Perhaps it is not always so, for we have known seeming saints and may speak of clear-eyed actual evil, where we intend the harm we do to the other, or indeed even to ourselves. But part of the evil we face may be illustrated precisely by our tendency to classify behavior too readily as clear-eyed. Given the complexity of human life—in motivation and in consequence—it is well to heed Whitehead's frequently quoted maxim "Seek simplicity and distrust it."[53] Kierkegaard would remind us that there is a mystery about human freedom such that we need to be cautious in claiming certainty in judging the why of any act. But the efficacy of evil is evident to us. Moreover, evil does seem to have a leg up in the entropic character of much of our life together.[54] In any case, if we are aspiring to join God's work in the world, we seem fated to settle for a meliorism, muddling through with very mixed results. As we now have our lives, here in the middle of things, that mix of things seems the very stuff of our existence. We find ourselves crying out, "I believe, help my unbelief!" (Mark 9:24). Or, for that matter, with the psalmist, we may sing the song of lament, edging toward the attractiveness of a principled atheism. It is wise at the very least to "respect" such limitation in response and resist the self-deluding security of certainty too easily won. But perhaps there is a danger that lurks even in this recognition of the mix. We could fail to make the judgments that are needed to make our way creatively through this landscape. In our puzzlement, we may be driven to ask another question.

What More May Come?

Can we hope for something better—radically better? People of faith surely ask that question. Physicist-theologian John Polkinghorne understands that: "We shall all die with our lives incomplete, with possibilities unfulfilled and with hurts unhealed. This will be true even of those fortunate enough to die peacefully in honoured old age. How much more must it be true of those who die prematurely and painfully, through disease, famine, war or neglect."[55] Jürgen Moltmann expands on the latter point:

> Think of the life of those who were not permitted to live, and were unable to live: the beloved child, dying at birth; the little boy run over by a car when he was four; the disabled brother who never lived consciously and never knew his parents; the friend torn to pieces by a bomb at your side when he was sixteen; the throngs of children who die prematurely of hunger in Africa; the countless numbers of

the raped and murdered and killed. Of course their lives can take on a considerable meaning for others. But where will their own lives be completed, and how?[56]

Can Kierekgaard and Whitehead come together to help us with this urgent query?

In chapter 3, in writing of "a timely faith," I indicated the strong emphasis both Whitehead and Kierkegaard give to the temporal character of our lives. Characteristically, Kierkegaard calls for faith to attend to highly particular events, highlighting conversion, atonement, redemption, resurrection, and judgment.[57] Truly decisive things are happening *in time*. There is recognition that this can mean change for the better quite concretely. Thus, in his *Journals*, Kierkegaard writes of the Christian that "the possibility of faith presents itself to him in this form: whether he will believe by virtue of the absurd that God will help him temporally."[58] Whitehead, in contrast, develops cosmologically the theme that "all things flow." He very much rejects any Newtonian notion of "absolute time" and gives priority to the particular relations between actual occasions. I suggested that one could see Whitehead's emphasis systematically as a cosmological preparation for Kierkegaard's comparable critique of a flat linearity. Thus, both our guides believe that something new can occur with genuine significance. But I am standing on tiptoe here to ask whether we would be encouraged to expect "something more coming" in the sense of a change that radically speaks to the limitations and evil we experience so fully.

In asking this, we of course engage Christian hope about the ultimate future. We have biblical language speaking of death being swallowed up in victory (1 Cor 15:54), seeing God face-to-face (1 Cor 13:12), and God wiping away every tear (Rev 7:17). We don't see such things happening in our lives. We don't see the leopard lying down with the lamb (Isa 11:6), peacefully at least. Do Kierkegaard and Whitehead speak to such as yet unfulfilled promises? Much of the theological energy in Kierkegaard's corpus fits here, notably in the *Fragments* and *Postscript*, pondering the possibility of acquiring an "eternal happiness in time through a relation to something else in time."[59] This incarnational framing of the eternal stands as a kind of Archimedean point for Kierkegaard, though he does not devote many of his pages to a systematic development of the theme.[60] There are related references to God's action in the coming about of faith and the decisiveness of God's forgiveness, but no systematic development of eschatological themes.[61] I suspect that absence not only reflects Kierkegaard's aversion to the lecturing of "assistant professors" but also his unwavering focus on the need to bring Christianity into the Danish Christendom he found so troubling as he experienced it in his Copenhagen. Eschatological loci could be a distraction, but the Archimedean point stands.

Whitehead, in contrast, provides somewhat frequent references to what could be a cosmological connection point for theological eschatology. That lies in his notion of "cosmic epochs." In chapter 2, I mentioned his conviction that "the arbitrary, as it were 'given,' elements in the laws of nature warn us that we are in a special cosmic epoch."[62] In this notion of anticipating another cosmic epoch, we are certainly looking at radical change, for among the special elements in this epoch are "the electromagnetic laws, the four dimensions of the spatio-temporal continuum, the geometrical axioms, even the mere dimensional character of the continuum . . . and the fact of measurability."[63] Process theorists have pondered a series of worlds without beginning, attaching themselves to Whitehead's apparent disregard for the notion of absolute beginning.[64] But one can claim the notion of cosmic epoch as a launching pad for looking forward as well. Thus Jonathan Strandjord seems warranted in saying that this notion suggests that "fundamental change is not only possible but probable."[65] Could that be the basis for the rather remarkable optimism evident in the final part of *Process and Reality*, where Whitehead appeals to God's "tender care that nothing be lost"?[66] He writes, "The revolts of destructive evil, purely self-regarding, are dismissed into their triviality of merely individual facts; and yet the good they did achieve in individual joy, in individual sorrow, in the introduction of needed contrast, is yet saved by its relation to the completed whole."[67] Indeed, Whitehead states that we can actually "discern the defining characteristic of a vast nexus extending far beyond our immediate cosmic epoch. It contains in itself other epochs, with more particular characteristics incompatible with each other." He hopes for his successors "keener powers of discernment" with "the growth of theory."[68] This distinction between cosmic epochs is the basis for *Process and Reality* being subtitled "An Essay in Cosmology," rather than a "metaphysics," which would encompass more than the present epoch.

His successors have not failed to offer proposals for the construction of a Whiteheadian eschatology.[69] Perhaps most notable among them is the work of Marjorie Suchocki, who has been bold to write of the end of evil.[70] She formulates a notion of what one might call "triple transcendence": "One could envisage then a multiple transcendence of personality in God: first a transcendence of seriality into the fullness of the self; second a transcendence of selfhood through the mutuality of feeling with all other selves and occasions, and third and most deeply, a transcendence of selves into the Selfhood of God."[71] This is intoxicating stuff, but it is well prepared for in Whitehead's own work. Thus, in *Process and Reality*, he no sooner has told us that "in the temporal world, it is the empirical fact that process entails loss" than he adds, "But there is no reason, of any ultimate metaphysical generality, why this should be the whole story."[72] And on the book's penultimate page, he writes of the "peculiar completeness" involved in personal identity over time and adds, "The correlate fact in God's nature is an even more complete unity of life in a chain of elements for which succession does not mean loss of immediate unison."[73]

This is surely the territory of Christian hope. It is particularly helpful when such "end-time" proposals are launched from, or at least related to, the experience of God's presence and action in the chaotic middle, where we do live. Do we have here any basis for anticipating such a future? In the middle, we do experience the "emergence" of qualitatively new formulations of life.[74] Those new forms of life take up and integrate earlier forms. The truly new emerges from the old, but it also carries the old beyond itself. Polkinghorne has said that the first of many "metaphysical insights" emerging from science is that "*the world is full of surprises.*"[75] He proceeds to use the language of a "new regime" arriving in the figure of Jesus.[76] It is conventional for many Christians to say of the coming of the kingdom of God "already, but not yet." The crucial questions are whether and how faith's hope for the ultimate future connects with what we know of our life in the present. If the Christian looks to a time "beyond Eden," does that mean the precious and perilous gift of freedom will itself be no more? Jesus did respond to someone asking about that ultimate future by saying his message was of a God "of the living" (Matt 22:32). Christians do not aspire to a return to Eden and the prospect of something resembling Nietzsche's "eternal recurrence," as some interpreters view that notion. But can being "beyond freedom" be a fulfillment of freedom?[77]

So how does believing in an ultimate future of life with God function to inform life now, in the middle? As a distraction, a sedative for human striving, or as an inspiration and motivation for the work of justice and mercy? Sharon Betcher wisely warns us against the tendency to "theologize our frustration with dependence on the earth as a transcendent longing for elsewhere."[78] Jürgen Moltmann points us in the right direction when he writes of Jewish and Christian apocalypses: "They awaken the *resistance of faith* and the *patience of hope.* They spread hope in danger, because in the human and cosmic end they proclaim God's new beginning."[79] One hopes Moltmann is right about this and that Marx's judgment about the opiate-like function of faith is mistaken.[80] Certainly the misuse of biblical visions of the end time is widespread. Perhaps we do well to keep the focus on the middle, while recognizing that our experience in the middle includes experience of a God who shows a penchant for doing "new things" (Isa 43:9; Rev 21:5). Whatever more we say will have to emphasize the continuing creativity of that God, and not our troubled human response. In that emphasis, there must still be recognition of creaturely freedom. But we do well not to underestimate the dexterity and decisiveness of this God.

In the meantime, is not this life in the middle with God and all the "other others" quite enough to occupy us rather fully? We don't have to have a guaranteed reservation in a 100-percent certain future in order to join God's work in this precarious and yet promising world. Perhaps that was what Whitehead in *Adventures of Ideas* was driving at when he wrote of "the union of Zest with Peace: —That the suffering attains its end in a Harmony of harmonies."[81] He made clear there that peace was not "anesthesia," the "bastard substitute" into which peace "very easily passes."[82] Fully awake then, respecting our limitations and recognizing actual evil, we find ourselves in this time called to live creatively on and *for* the earth.

Living Creatively with an Earthbound Faith

We are bound to the earth—that is clear. We have lots of questions and gaps even in trying to understand what is real, how things work in the world we occupy. We are aware that we live in the chaotic middle, and we certainly don't own any empirical knowledge about any ultimate beginning or final end. We will speak of God, but we acknowledge that it is a learned ignorance upon which we draw. What God-talk we manage to muster is made in faith, but we struggle to hold both the propositions and the passion of faith with confidence, and to hold them together well seems to escape us. The deeds of our days are not less conflicted than our words. There is no question that by the Creator's will, we dwell on this earth, not in some blissful other world.

This overwhelming sense of being earthbound can be put theologically in a single sentence: "We belong with the creatures."[83] People of faith have not been particularly good at remembering this. Theologians have encouraged this forgetfulness by how they have spoken of humans being created in God's image. If we construct an order of being running from, say, specks of cosmic dust in outer space to God, it is easy to begin to think that we belong with the Creator.[84] Thus, we proceed to speak of humankind as the "crown" of the whole creative process. In such praise of human eminence, we ignore the biblical teaching that recognizes the creative role assigned to the (other) creatures: "let the waters bring forth" (Gen 1:20); "let the earth bring forth" (Gen 1:24). Moreover, we ignore the empirical reality that on the evolutionary clock, *Homo sapiens* appears only "at the last stroke" of midnight's bell.[85] Then there is the untidy little fact that we share 98 percent of our DNA with the chimpanzees.

Nonetheless, there has been a persistent tendency to claim such a special relationship with God that we are isolated from the other creatures. Whitehead and Kierkegaard can together help us set this right. Especially together. Kierkegaard repeatedly drives home the point of God's "infinite qualitative difference" from all other beings, surely including human beings. But we have seen that he is vulnerable, nonetheless, to a dualistic elevation of the human species. Whitehead clearly avoids such a dualism, notably by lowering the standing of consciousness in the human synthesis.[86] He might seem less clear about God's qualitative distinctness, as when he writes famously, "It is as true to say that God creates the World, as that the World creates God."[87] I have argued that such notions as "the reversal of the poles" of becoming entail what Charles Hartshorne has called a "categorical supremacy."[88] But certainly that God joins us here in this creaturely world should serve to make the more forcefully the positive point that we belong with the creatures. If we leave this world to ascend to the stars, we leave God behind with the creatures.

Very well, we belong with the creatures, and our faith is bound to the earth decisively. The question that remains for us in this chapter is whether, respecting our limitations and recognizing actual evil, we can still live creatively. Can the emphatic earthiness of our lives be recognized as a positive thing? Or must the finitude and even more the fallenness rehearsed in this chapter's preceding pages simply leave us without grounds or energy for significant human life? I believe the answer to that second question is no. The most important reason for that answer for people of faith is what was just suggested: that it turns out that God is right here in this earthly struggle. I use the adverb *creatively* to characterize a significant human life, for that term does resonate with the theological point that we are created in the image of the Creator. Of course, there are no guarantees of success, but Whitehead and Kierkegaard have made clear for us that God too seems to have adopted the "ethic of risk" that fits freedom.[89] Confessing faith in this adventurous God, we need to set aside such familiar self-defeating notions as the idea that individual initiative always represents prideful self-assertion and that social amelioration is forever pointless because nobody can fix it all. How shall we think positively of our situation? What will it take to "live creatively"?

Our guides can help us with this fundamental question. Whitehead can call us to imagine the possibilities, the "propositions," that present themselves in the processes of our lives. Something new beckons, and we can find it "interesting."[90] He refuses to settle for a reductionist understanding of experience in which a barren "world" seems pretty uninteresting. Kierkegaard can call us to will to bring such possibility into "actuality." Thus, he cites Luther at the Diet of Worms willing "with all the decision of subjectivity" and hence regarding mere possibility "as temptation."[91] A longer passage from the *Postscript* can serve us here: "In asking ethically with regard to my own actuality, I am asking about its possibility, except that this possibility is not esthetically and intellectually disinterested but is a thought-actuality that is related to my own personal actuality—namely, that I am able to carry it out."[92] Whitehead's understanding of God's empowering and shaping presence at the beginning of each moment of the self's becoming can make the "I am able to carry it out" something other than bravado. Thus, the American electorate in the remarkable campaign of 2008 seemed to believe, "Yes, we can." Racism, deeply embedded in American life and potent still, need not prevail.

Living creatively will not be dominated by focusing on "results." Kierkegaard was particularly critical of efforts to bolster Christianity by heralding the "results" of faith. In *Practice in Christianity*, he asks, "Is the Result of Christ's Life More Important Than His Life?"[93] His answer: No! He continues, "That God has lived here on earth as an individual human being is infinitely extraordinary. Even if it had had no results whatever, it makes no difference; it remains just as extraordinary, infinitely extraordinary, infinitely more extraordinary than all the results."[94] Kierkegaard's point here is to underscore the sheer incarnational reality of God's presence in Jesus of Nazareth. Whitehead affirms that presence and connects it with the broader creational work of God. He will remind us that even in the "purely self-regarding" "revolts of destructive evil," there is something that can be saved by a "tender patience" leading with a "vision of truth, beauty, and goodness."[95] There *will* be results.

I have been writing here of faith living creatively *on* the earth. As people of faith do that, they may come to learn *from* the earth. For example, Sallie McFague has challenged Christians to learn from the dominating reality of climate change: "Climate change, quite simply, is the issue of the twenty-first century. It is not one issue among many, but, like the canary in the mine, it is warning us that the way we are living on our planet is causing us to head for disaster. . . . All of the other issues we care about—social justice, peace, prosperity, freedom—cannot occur unless our planet is healthy. It is the unifying issue of our time."[96] Karen Baker-Fletcher comes forward as one who gets it, finding not only challenge but resource in turning to the earth: "Without the life-sustaining warmth of the sun, the quenching power of rain, the oxygen the air provides, there would be no hope for the physical sustenance of the bodies that enflesh our spirits. The entire cosmos, then, is engaged in God's activity of providing resources for survival and wholeness."[97] Such talk of learning from the earth may be a stretch for literalistic readers of Kierkegaard, but it connects with and extends the keen sense of context he reveals in his discerning critique of Danish Christendom's appropriation of Luther.[98]

On this matter of learning from the earth, ecofeminists are currently making an important contribution.[99] Closely related is the lively conversation between religion and science, which holds great promise. Scholars following Whitehead's vision have been prominent in this conversation, reaching back to John Cobb's early book *Is It Too Late?*[100] It is crucial in this connection to examine with care the images we use to speak of the relationship human beings have with other creatures. We have perhaps seen the last of a "spaceship earth" mentality, but even such a traditional notion as "steward" may be questioned as permitting too managerial an authority for humankind. Whiteheadian thought would seem receptive to such a suggestion as Paul Santmire's proposal that we speak of the relationship with entities in wild or fabricated nature not as "I-Thou" or "I-it," but as "I-Ens," from the Latin participle for "being."[101] We share created being. For Whiteheadians, that might suggest well the partnership reflecting the commonality and primacy of feeling in all living beings.

In partnerships, there are distinctions to be recognized, such as "senior" and "junior." Perhaps we might manage to speak in some such way of humankind's life with the other creatures. Such distinctiveness would support responsibility as the calling of human privilege. A Kierkegaardian trying to learn from the evolutionary emergence of humankind will be sure to emphasize the distinctiveness of the human. But perhaps that intuitively strong point can be converted into a creative living *for* the earth. That is the kind of move Holmes Rolston III makes in writing of the presence of kenosis at many points in the evolutionary process: "a great deal of one kind of thing being sacrificed for the good of another. The lives of individuals are discharged into, flow into, 'emptied into' these larger currents of life."[102] At the emergent level of the human, he recognizes "the possibility of kenosis in a still richer sense, where self-interested humans impose limits on human welfare on behalf of the other species."[103] Perhaps a Kierkegaardian Christian, heeding the universality of the call to love, could move creatively in our context to claim this "Christian calling for the next millennium."[104]

CONCLUSION: AVAILING POWER

To what have we, guided by Søren Aabye Kierkegaard and Alfred North Whitehead, come in our attempt to understand the power of love? What emerges is a view of power as "availing." My dictionary says this of the Middle English and Old French roots of the word *avail*: "to be of use, help, worth or advantage (to) in accomplishing an end."[1] It does not list *compel* or even *control* as synonyms. This understanding is importantly different from a familiar understanding of power suggested by verbs deriving from a view of unlimited power. In these final pages, I will seek to clarify the difference in explicating the nature of power, human or divine.

The difficulties with a notion of unlimited power are familiar by now:

(a) Starting with divine power, what are we to make of the stubborn sense of some genuine creaturely agency, a sense essential to meaningful concepts of purpose and responsibility? Even in the familiar "vertical" piety I am criticizing, human beings get credit at least for their sins. William Placher conveys such an approach in writing of "irrational events that are somehow not caused by God."[2] How does such agency not qualify, indeed limit, God's power?

(b) Speaking of sins, the visceral human sense that God is good and loving can easily become a producer of guilt consciousness when combined with a barely qualified divine power (a). In a world no better than this, an almighty and all-good God must have decreed that my sufferings are proper punishment for my sins. So the believer, called to repentance, is invited to seek out her secret sins. That search may waste precious creaturely time and uncover nothing. Or worse yet, perhaps, it may lead to the reclassifying of simple creaturely characteristics and imperfections as candidates for repentance and suppression.

(c) If we claim that saying God does all things is compatible with non-divine agency, can the causal link be identified?[3] Does appeal to "the paradox of two agents" involving different language strata simply restate the problem?[4] While theologians regularly emphasize differences in the level of God's involvement in the range of creaturely acts, clarity in specifying that difference is often hard to come by.[5] Placher writes, "Theologians get in trouble when they think they can clearly and distinctly understand the language they use about God."[6] Perhaps, yet surely Anselm was right that faith does seek understanding.

(d) Finally, regarding power divine or human, if control is the nature of the connection, what does the one who controls actually secure by such control? It would not seem that a genuine relationship can exist without some element of shared freedom. Of course, an all-powerful God could easily deceive us, creating in us the mistaken sense of freedom. But what would God gain in that? Not a genuine relationship with the creatures.[7] So, too, human life rooted in the image of a controlling God of unlimited power will not favor the fruit of such genuine relationships. Pastors, for example, can be tempted, perhaps unconsciously, to model the all-determining God they suppose themselves somehow to serve.[8]

In any case, the view I seek now to summarize, a view to which Kierkegaard and Whitehead both would guide us, does make a major point in speaking of power in the terms of both freedom and relationship. To think those two realities together, to hold them together in living—that is the crucial matter, even as one may agree with Michael Peterson that over against all-determining power, "there may be a range of modes of divine power, such as 'productive power' or 'sustaining power' or 'enabling power.'"[9]

Freedom in Relationship

In summing up, we can begin with the human self and Kierkegaard's evocation of the ineluctable reality of that self. He has driven home the fact that the human self has efficacious power, power to produce an effect in the decisive resolution of the anxious possibilities that present themselves. He speaks thus of the self in protest against all efforts to swallow the individual, whether in the omnivorous dialectic of Hegel's philosophy or the popularizing pull of the "press." He challenged a Christendom where he saw the individual's responsibility evaporating in a culture where to be a Christian was reduced to being a Danish citizen. The first sentence in his first major work, *Either/Or*, voices his concern: "It may at times have occurred to you, dear reader, to doubt somewhat the accuracy of the familiar philosophical thesis that the outer is the inner and the inner is the outer."[10] Within the self, there is genuine power that makes a difference for the self as "the relation relating itself to itself," and potentially—in power—for the world outside the self.[11] In *The Concept of Anxiety* and elsewhere, he steadfastly resists all attempts, philosophical or practical, to eviscerate the self's freedom. There is in the self the power to will to be itself. I can "choose" myself, choose how the mix of possibility and necessity comes together exactly in me. I can choose the values that will orient my life. I can know who I am, uniquely. This is availing power, for in this self-relating, there is worth.[12] Against all pious self-denigration, I can claim that worth. That claiming draws on faith in the goodness of the Creator: it is good that I come to be. Kierkegaard's steadfast insistence at this point serves to correct a dangerously disjunctive tendency in popular piety to believe one can praise the Creator by cursing the creature.

It is good as well that I continue to be, continue to come to be. This worth must be affirmed even in the face of the horror that my misuse of freedom regularly brings to be. Kierkegaard cannot credibly be regarded as "soft on sin," but he knew what the Lutheran confessors of the sixteenth century knew when they produced *The Formula of Concord*. In the very first article, tellingly devoted to the topic of "original sin," they say this: "We believe, teach, and confess that there is a difference between original sin and human nature—not only as God originally created it pure, holy and without sin, but also as we now have it after the fall. Even after the fall this nature still is and remains a creature of God."[13] Terence Fretheim has made the same point biblically about the Creator's evaluation "good" remaining in place despite sin. Indeed, he writes, "In the wake of sin many texts actually will reinforce that evaluation, sometimes in even stronger terms."[14] Sin wreaks havoc on God's precious creatures but cannot invalidate the reality that the Creator has brought into being. Accordingly, Kierkegaard wisely calls us to resist all efforts to demean, neglect, or more aggressively, to swallow up the individual's unique identity.

But the self is never simply by itself. The world surrounds, supporting or suppressing; the "others" are "always already there."[15] I have not organized my discussion in historical terms. But, in the introduction, I mentioned Stephen Toulmin's analysis of the "modern" world in terms of the self–world relationship. One could trace historically the pull of polarization in this polarity.[16] There have been powerful cultural currents that have in effect taken Kierkegaard's emphasis on the self and run with it to a place where the world seems effectively to have collapsed into the self. Taste rules in the self's choices, and philosophy becomes a call to "edification," rather than any attempt to "mirror" nature.[17] Lawrence Cahoone has summarized this development trenchantly: "This gradual loss of the transcendental, the breakdown of the subjectivist-transcendental synthesis that had made subjectivism workable since the seventeenth century, initiated a profound alteration of the subjectivist categories themselves. The subject and object categories were thereby freed to be universally and radically applied, unencumbered by God or reason or any other trans-subjective factor. . . . It becomes impossible to conceive of subjectivity and objectivity as being independent existences *and yet* as being interrelated, mutually involved."[18]

In the polarization of self and world, both self and world are changed. That changed self can seem threatened by the disturbing "other," even when the wound holds the potential to be a healing one. Eberhard Jüngel has put well this prospect of healing: "[A human being] . . . is that creature, whose being is not in immediate correspondence with itself, but is capable of being interrupted at any moment by other things that exist, and in fact is always being so interrupted. . . . Human life occurs, then, when the continuity of earthly life and existence is interrupted, in that something intervenes and is apprehended (and thus comes to be known). Human life, therefore, *is* the interruption of the continuity of created life by the occurrence of truth."[19] How could interruption be healing in our current sense of things? Perhaps modernity's polarizing of the elements that together constitute life will be interrupted by a call to connection. Enter the postmodern critics as well summarized by Ted Peters: "We moderns, say the postmodern critics, have separated human consciousness from the world of extended objects, separated value from truth. We have separated humans from nature, from God, and from one another; and should we finally detonate our nuclear weapons— weapons that represent the height of the modern achievements in technological thinking—then we may even separate ourselves from our own future. Our world continues to break into more and more pieces. Voices from many quarters can be heard crying out, 'Enough of this! Let's put the world back together again.'"[20]

The Dane who died trying to call the state church to repentance would disown the pervasive individualism present in, for example, American culture. That is clear in Kierkegaard's understanding of "the ethical." He emphasizes the ethical as the decisive first "stage on life's way" beyond the immediacy of the "aesthetic." Moreover, he will not leave the individual alone on that path, for "the ethical and the religious, insofar as they seek their expression in something particular, find this best in the marriage ceremony." This does not become an isolating rhapsodizing of any single couple, for the ceremony "binds the new marriage in the great body of the human race. It thereby provides the universal, the purely human."[21] Thus, "the ethical view of marriage . . . does not show how a pair of very specific people can become happy because of their extraordinariness but how every married couple can become happy. It sees the relationship as the absolute."[22] Marriage serves to concretize a broader point about human existence. Writing about "a social, a civic self," Kierkegaard makes the point about the individual: "If he thinks that the art is to begin like a Robinson Crusoe, he remains an adventurer all his life."[23] That is not the human calling.

This deep recognition of the other has been neglected in the theological appropriation of Kierkegaard, perhaps particularly in viewing the decisively Christian as wholly separated from the ethical.[24] I believe the emphasis on such a separation is a misreading of Kierkegaard. Early and late, he lifted up the "ethico-religious." At the midpoint of the authorship in the *Postscript*, in commenting on "a contemporary effort [his] in Danish literature," he wrote, "There are three stages, an esthetic, an ethical, a religious. . . . But despite this tripartition, the book is nevertheless an either/or. That is, the ethical and the religious stages have an essential relation to each other."[25] But even more telling is Kierkegaard's emphasis in "the intermediate clause" between the generally religious ("Religiousness A") and the decisively Christian ("Religiousness B"): "Religiousness A is not the specifically Christian religiousness. On the other hand, the dialectical is decisive only insofar as it is joined together with the pathos-filled and gives rise to a new pathos."[26] The ethical call of the other is never abandoned in Kierkegaard's understanding of things Christian. In the intense particularity of religious passion, the ethical may be "teleologically suspended" in fear and trembling, but it is never abandoned.[27] Thus, "the ethical is reduced to the relative. From this it does not follow that the ethical should be invalidated; rather the ethical receives a completely different expression, a paradoxical expression."[28] That narrower reading of Christian particularity is mistaken, but its development and relative dominance can be understood, given Kierkegaard's powerful emphasis on the individual. It is evident that in understanding power, something more is needed along with his recognition of the inward freedom of the human self.

Whitehead can make that contribution to our effort to understand power. His notion of "internal relations" is decisive here. He is relentless in criticizing the notion of "simple location," stressing instead the "agitation" by which any "thing" cannot be separated from its "divergent stream of influence."[29] This is not less true of "higher" orders of being, as Charles Hartshorne showed in his incisive criticism of "the assumption *that relativity as such is a deficiency.*"[30] To use Kierkegaard's opening sentence from *Either/Or* again, we can speak of how the "outer" enters, becomes "objectified" in, the "inner."[31] It is characteristic that the entering "outer" does not refer simply or even primarily to other minds entering our minds, but to the world, the earth, fleshly bodies bearing in on us as embodied beings.

This Whiteheadian affirmation of the central role of body in our being and knowing has become one of several contact points with contemporary feminist thought. Sallie McFague, for example, is particularly insistent in challenging the spiritualizing or rationalist denigration of the body, which is so commonly paired with the denigration of women: "We ought to love and honor the body, our own bodies, and the bodies of all other life-forms on the planet. The body is not a discardable garment cloaking the real self or essence of a person . . . ; rather it is the shape or form of who we are. It is how each of us is recognized, responded to, loved, touched, and cared for—as well as oppressed, beaten, raped, mutilated, discarded, and killed."[32] Whitehead does not write with McFague's passion, but he stresses so persistently the "withness" of the body—we receive the world "with" our bodies. Our bodies do link us decisively with the raw materiality of the world. Philip Schultz expresses that well in "The Music":

> There is music in the spheres of the body.
> I mean the pull of the sea in the blood
> of the man alone on his porch watching
> the stars wind bands of light around his body.
> I mean the roll of the planet that is the rhythm
> of his breath & the wilderness of his perception
> that is the immensity of light flowering like stars
> in the lights of his eyes. I mean the singing
> in his body that is the world of the moment of his life,
> Lord![33]

David Griffin, one of the directors for the Center for Process Studies in Claremont, California, has issued a series of books detailing the differences between "constructive" postmodernism and "deconstructive" postmodernism, where effective reference to the world is threatened. The key difference is constructive postmodernism's refusal to relinquish a claim on a shared and knowable actual world.[34]

If we put these two insights together, what do we have? We have a recognition of freedom in relationship. Relationship becomes the empowering source and the destined telos of the self's freedom in every moment of human life. In between that alpha and omega, relationship serves as the measure of the self, as Kierkegaard recognizes: "The criterion for the self is always: that directly before which it is a self, but this in turn is the definition of 'criterion.'"[35] His language merits close attention: "but this in turn." He recognizes that these two—the self and the relationship—go together, each needing the other. He adds of the self, "That which is its qualitative criterion [Maalestok] is ethically its goal [Maal]."[36] He clearly recognizes the element of risk entailed in relationship, and we surely need to avoid romanticizing abusive "relationships." But the solution is not to seek to withdraw from relationships altogether, for to do so would be to deny the Creator's will for humankind. Dietrich Bonhoeffer, revered for his fateful decision to resist Hitler violently, echoes this risky recognition of the self in relationship: "In truth, freedom is a relation between two persons. Being free means 'being free for the other' because I am bound to the other. Only by being in relation with the other am I free."[37]

Making Claims without Certainty

Kierkegaard and Whitehead share a strong recognition of the temporal, the movement marking this self in relationship. That movement is a metaphysical given in process thought. But it is crucial to remember as well that for Kierkegaard, the self is a "relation relating itself to itself."[38] Something is happening, not merely "to," but also "within" the self. That we are speaking of a self "on the move" means something when we inquire as to what that self can claim to know with certainty. Kierkegaard was fond of making the point against Hegel and all comers that "a system of existence cannot be given." In his aptly titled Concluding Unscientific Postscript, one of the six hundred pages includes this sentence: "System and conclusiveness correspond to each other, but existence is the very opposite."[39] Whitehead would not quarrel with that restriction. Indeed, even his ambitious cosmological sketch is rendered with the realization that "the proper test is not that of finality, but of progress."[40] Both men kept writing.[41] Why? While accepting and indeed insisting upon limitation, both would plead for the qualified legitimation Paul Ricoeur expresses: "The Word is my kingdom and I am not ashamed of it. . . . As a University professor, I believe in the efficacy of instructive speech; in teaching the history of philosophy I believe in the enlightening power, even for a system of politics, of speaking devoted to elaborating our philosophical memory. As a listener

to the Christian message I believe that words may change the 'heart,' that is
the refulgent core of our preferences and the position we embrace."[42]

Both men wrote more than a few words. At the same time, both would
welcome the postmodern emphasis on the service of suspicion, of doubt.[43]
Kierkegaard expressed that the more vividly in praising Lessing, who "has
said that, if God held all truth in His right hand and in His left the lifelong
pursuit of it, he would choose the left hand."[44] Heeding their counsel, suspicion will be warranted when encountering formulations that compromise
that earnest pursuit. Apologists for faith can err in this matter. In *The Sickness
unto Death*, Kierkegaard offers a scathing critique of anyone who would seek
to rescue Christianity by defending it. That person is "*de facto* a Judas No. 2;
he, too, betrays with a kiss, except that his treason is the treason of stupid-
ity."[45] Nonetheless, I read his employment of "stages on the way of life" as an
apologetic of sorts, for he will engage the passionate seeker of truth and lead
that person toward a decision about the passion-intensifying, paradoxical
proposal that he exists "before" God. The argument goes like this: "Faith is a
marvel, and yet no human being is excluded from it; for that which unites all
human life is passion, and faith is a passion."[46] Reading Kierkegaard on the
suffering (literally, the "passion") of human life, one is reminded of Dorothee
Soelle's affirmation: "To be able to believe means to say yes to this life, to
this finitude, to work on it and hold it open for the promised future."[47] His
apologetic, then, in Jonathan Strandjord's words, is "a defense neither of the
believer nor of God but of the public availability of hope. It is fully ecstatic,
abandoning the safety of every form of private right and refuge and stepping
outside the confines of every social boundary."[48] The offered word avails for
passionate hope.

This self in relationship, on the move, is called to trust. The creational
basis for that act of trust is given in the gift of imagination, which finds a
decisive expression in trust. Both the cosmologist speaking of God's aim for
the coming-to-be occasion and the theologian speaking of the self existing
"before" God see that. Surprisingly, perhaps, it may have been seen also by
William Young, the author of the popular religious best seller *The Shack*. God
is portrayed as Elousia, a sassy African American woman. She urges Mack,
the human protagonist of the piece, to realize that freedom is "an incremental
process," that "freedom is a process that happens inside a relationship."[49] Just
a little later, Mack gets another lesson, this time from Sarayu, the personifica-
tion of the Third Person of the Trinity: "Trust is the fruit of a relationship in
which you know you are loved."[50] Perhaps Sarayu had read the first epistle of
John, for she understands that "perfect love casts out fear" (4:18). For Young,
all this talk of freedom and trust is most fundamentally God-talk. That has

been our theme as well—how in our imagining the future, we can image the God who acts in power to create freedom. Young also gets us to our material focus in these pages, the power of love, when the divine "Papa" tells Mack, "The God who is—the I am who I am—cannot act apart from love."[51] But we need to be very clear about what is to be said about this God and, derivatively, of power.

The Power of the Creator and of the Creature

We have highlighted Kierkegaard's profound insistence that God's "omnipotence is in the power of love."[52] So what does that power, which we are to image, look like? Kierkegaard and Whitehead come together to specify two fundamental ingredients: (1) the decisiveness of the commitment; and (2) the intimacy of the connection.

On the first of these, I recall Paul Tillich stressing in class that a decision is like an incision: it involves painful cutting. Kierkegaard finds that, in decisive love, God "cannot" do certain things. This will seem sacrilegious to theologians whose notion of divine power will not permit them to imagine placing the words *God* and *cannot* in the same sentence. However, Kierkegaard sees this reality not as a limitation but as a *manifestation* of God's power. God has the power to make a commitment and fulfill it. The contrast, you recall, is to a king who can pretend to be a servant but who can always throw off his disguise and exercise his royal power. But this "is no perfection in the king (to have this possibility) but merely manifests his impotence and the impotence of his resolution, that he actually is incapable of becoming what he wanted to become."[53] This beautiful parable is an explicitly christological framing of God's decisiveness. But recall from chapter 1 the God who wills "*one* thing" in creation and redemption. God may be terribly distressed by our sin, but God does not change.[54]

Concerning the second ingredient, the intimacy of the connection, Whitehead will particularly help us. In decisiveness, the Creator will be there for the creature. And God will always be there *first*, at the beginning of every creaturely moment. You will recall the language of aim: "The immediacy of the concrescent subject is constituted by its living aim at its own self-constitution. Thus the initial stage of the aim is rooted in the nature of God."[55] These two sentences merit dissection. It would be understating the matter simply to say we start "from" God. We start "in" God, as do all things. To be sure, a distinction arises between God and the emerging reality, for panentheism is not pantheism. If Kierkegaard is right that the art of power is to create freedom, then this God is artful. Whitehead writes of the subject's "*self*-constitution."

(And Kierkegaard knows a God who, in creating, risks "the possibility of offense.") But that self's immediacy "is constituted by its living aim," and "the initial stage of the aim" is rooted in the nature of God. In Whitehead, the intimacy of God's powerful purposing draws on the decisiveness, for as a thread of becoming continues, God is always there with the initial aim. In this, there is the promise of availing power.

In any case, what kind of power will "avail"—will actually help in a relationship of freedom? We know the power that compels: we pay our taxes, we plan our funerals. But in the messy middle of genuine relationships entailing freedom, such coercive power is not possible. If we hanker after such power, we may despairingly suppose that God's power is simply frustrated. Douglas John Hall has written of this as he ponders the place of God in relation to human suffering: "There are situations where power is of no avail. *They are most of the situations in which as human beings we find ourselves!* May we not also dare to say that, from the standpoint of a faith tradition which posits love, not power, as God's primary perfection, they are most of the situations in which God finds God's Self too?"[56] I appreciate Hall's critique of the power of coercion, his steadfast emphasis on love as the "category proper" in Christian God-talk, and his sensitive recognition of divine suffering. He will not posit in God a power that denies divine love in genuine relationship with real creaturely freedom. But I am claiming his own word to say that in this relationship, there *is* a power that can "avail"—the power of love.[57]

According to the dictionary, to avail is to have "worth." Martha Nussbaum captures something of this worth, writing of "a kind of human worth that is inseparable from vulnerability, an excellence that is in its nature other-related and social, a rationality whose nature it is not to attempt to seize, hold, trap, and control, in whose values openness, receptivity, and wonder play an important part."[58] Does it not seem likely that a God "worth" having in a world no better than this is such a God? Moreover, given the reality of selves in relationship (most intimately with God), would not such a God be a powerfully availing God? In Bonhoeffer's memorable phrase from the prison letters, "Only the suffering God can help."[59]

Bonhoeffer knew that we are tempted toward another God. In that letter of July 16, he wrote, "Man's religiosity makes him look in his distress to the power of God in the world: God is the *deus ex machina*. The Bible directs man to God's powerlessness and suffering."[60] A half dozen sentences earlier in this remarkable letter, he made his point about the difference between the "Gods" in nine words: "Before God and with God we live without God." That is not easy living. We lust after that other God, for we fatally believe with one of Walker Percy's characters that "in the end the world yields only to violence, that only the violent bear it away, that short of violence all is in the end impotence."[61] But we are called to the discovery "that violence leads to annihilation and not redemption or transformation."[62]

Kierkegaard ("before God") and Whitehead ("with God") come together in that discovery. Bonhoeffer is pointing the way to a theology of the cross, citing the cry of forsakenness from the cross in a quite Kierkegaardian manner. But both these Lutherans knew that this availing God is none other than the Creator. That God is well described by their Anglican brother in the faith as one who is to be found in "the tender elements in the world, which slowly and in quietness operate by love."[63] At their best, Christians together know that "love neither rules, nor is it unmoved."[64] The point about not being unmoved is essential for Whitehead. It is precisely the continuing Creator's work to suffer the world and to claim a power for transformation even in and through that suffering.[65] Thus, in this remarkable final part to his magnum opus, he writes, "The revolts of destructive evil, purely self-regarding, are dismissed into their triviality of merely individual facts; and yet the good they did achieve in individual joy, in individual sorrow, in the introduction of needed contrast, is yet saved by its relation to the completed whole."[66] So it is that "the creative action completes itself" as the transformed suffering "passes back into the temporal world."[67]

That temporal world is surely where we find ourselves, as we scramble and struggle for power. That is where God is to be found as well. God is unfailingly here, "avail-able." It matters mightily what we imagine power to be. Perhaps this is indeed the "more hopeful world" Marjorie Suchocki envisioned.[68] Relational power connects with the integrity and freedom of the other and so images the Creator's love for all and the resultant capacity for change. We should have learned from Gandhi in India and Martin Luther King Jr. in the United States that there is transforming power in love.[69] If a third continent is wanted, we could travel to Africa to learn of the transforming power of love from Nelson Mandela in South Africa, and from nameless citizens in Cairo in February 2011. The lesson can be learned from many sources, in many places, and indeed preeminently from Jesus of Nazareth on Golgotha, despite distorting voices outside of and within the churches.

In this world, one at least doesn't need to waste one's time seeking to discover and repent of some secret sin responsible for the suffering a distant God delivers. That was a chief strategy of Job's "comforters," a strategy rejected by book's end, where God praises the loudly lamenting Job for having "spoken of me what is right" (Job 42:7).[70] God is here, able to avail. Carol Newsome, pondering the book of Job with its surprises for Job and for us, writes, "This new image is one of God as a power for life, balancing the needs of all creatures, not just humans, cherishing freedom, full of fierce love and delight for each thing without regard for its utility, acknowledging the deep interconnectedness of death and life, restraining and nurturing each element in the ecology of all creation."[71] Job undergoes a stunning reversal in his understanding of God. In his trip out into the wild beauty of creation, he has been faced with "things too wonderful" (Job 42:3), and he sees God speaking out of the whirlwind. As William Brown has made clear, "God does not rule with an iron fist, grinding the wicked into the dust and coercing obedience from earthly subjects. Rather, Yahweh governs with an open hand, sustaining creation in all of its variegated forms, leaving both good and bad characters to weave their existence into the complex network of life."[72]

In this time, when the suffering of Jobian innocents seems to abound, Christians may face no less a challenge to their attempt to hold and live the faith. The tasks at hand as the century's second decade begins are considerable: caring for this imperiled creation, welcoming "the other" as in churchly issues of the ordination of noncelibate gay and lesbian candidates, finding a peaceable way to live together with people of other faiths or no faith.[73] The list continues and is daunting enough. But people of faith can live now with hope as befits residents in a world where studies of emergence and complexity could tell them to expect constant surprises.[74] Living before and with a creating God, they experience an availing power.

That is an empowering experience, for this God is an indwelling God. Thus, the creature is called to image that God, living availably in the routine and the revolutions of this unpredictable life. That is enough—to be available to those in need. The creature is not called to a greater power than that of the Creator. We are tempted to seek such power. Fear is not hard to come by, and fundamentalism thrives on fear. Fear finds force attractive.[75] But the creature is called to remember how paltry is the victory won by coercion. Remembering that, the creature can come to live the truth that being available is being present. Perhaps the Creator's perfect love can cast out creaturely fears (1 John 4:18). The one who is present is one who enters. To enter is not to invade, to occupy. Entering, one empowers. One empowers with some effort at discernment, seeking that the entered one will in turn empower others.[76] Here the Christian joins other humans in hearing the Creator's call to a ministry of presence. At the end of his life, Kierkegaard, battling what he saw as a decadent Christendom, expressed the desire to spend some time with Socrates, if even "for only a half hour."[77] He had learned from the gadfly of Athens that "the art of power is to make free." That is the Creator's teaching, actually.

And if one cannot be present, what then? If the limitations of finitude seem to separate, if the other's freedom seems bound in resisting one's presence, what then? It is wise first of all to recognize that in our despairing, we may have underestimated how pervasively presence works.[78] There the Whiteheadian insight informs us: even in the darkest moment, it is indeed the *many* who become one. God is at work within each one of that becoming one many.[79] A God who orders all possibility, "primordially," is a God for whom there is always possibility in any anxious moment.[80] We err if we let David Hume's exclusive emphasis on sense impressions define presence for us. On that definition, our common parlance makes no sense. Why say, "I'll be thinking of you" to a person headed into surgery? Why promise, "I'll send you my best energy" to the student facing an onerous final examination? What's the point of saying such things? Perhaps our practice is wiser than our propositions about perception. People of faith sometimes say something more: "I'll pray for you." It is well said. It is well *lived*, as we remember that the Creator will draw on every resource, spoken or unspoken, in the artful venture of making truly free. To that end, the creature, imaging God in believing in the face of finitude and living against evil, can claim power that avails in a truly creative life.

NOTES

Preface

1. Thomas Jay Oord appropriates this Johannine foundation in writing that "my own proposal of an adequate doctrine of God begins with the claim that love is an essential divine attribute." See his *Defining Love: A Philosophical, Scientific, and Theological Engagement* (Grand Rapids: Brazos, 2010), 189. While insisting that "loving others is not an arbitrary divine decision," Oord does recognize divine freedom in *how* God loves. I, too, will seek to retain a genuine sense of divine freedom, but the "category proper" of love modifies the meaning of freedom so that as love God knows not "freedom *from* relationship but freedom *in* relationship." In "Putting the Cross in Context: Atonement through Covenant," in *Transformative Lutheran Theologies: Feminist, Womanist, and Mujerista Perspectives,* ed. Mary J. Streufert (Minneapolis: Fortress Press, 2010), 107–22, Marit Trelstad develops this understanding of relational freedom emphatically, drawing on the work of Jürgen Moltmann.

2. Eberhard Jüngel, *God as the Mystery of the World* (Grand Rapids: Eerdmans, 1983), 315. Jüngel does not underestimate the difficulty facing theology thus understood: "And in doing so, it must accomplish two things. It must, on the one hand, do justice to the essence of love, which as a predicate of God may not contradict what people experience as love. And on the other hand, it must do justice to the being of God which remains so distinctive from the event of *human* love that 'God' does not become a superfluous word."

3. Jonathan Standjord, "What Contributions Should Teaching Theologians Make to the Life and Mission of the Church? How Is This Best Done?," 124–33 in *Lutherans and Theological Method: Perennial Questions and Contemporary Challenges,* ed. David C. Ratke (Minneapolis: Lutheran University Press, 2010), 128. Standjord makes the point (125) that in this time of "enormous technological innovation and social shifts" the need for theological activity is increased.

4. In chapter 1 I will discuss Kierkegaard's view of "the impossibility of direct communication" as conveyed in *Practice in Christianity*, ed. and trans. Howard V. Hong and Edna H. Hong (Princeton: Princeton University Press, 1991), 124–43.

5. See Alfred North Whitehead, *The Aims of Education* (London: Williams & Norgate, 1955).

6. Sallie McFague, *A New Climate for Theology: God, the World, and Global Warming* (Minneapolis: Fortress Press, 2008).

7. In this book I occasionally cite prominent feminist theologians, such as Elizabeth Johnson and Sharon Welch, who have so much to teach us about God's love. But my learning here has been too limited to make a major statement in print. Indeed, I am aware that feminist thought could have been a major part of the context for the contemporary coming together of Kierkegaard and Whitehead. There has been a remarkable confluence between feminist/womanist and Whiteheadian vitalities (for example, Marjorie Suchocki, Catherine Keller, Monica Coleman). Furthermore, feminist theologians have argued with and over the Kierkegaard corpus (for example, Sylvia Walsh, Wanda Warren Berry, Jamie Ferreira). Were I to stress that aspect of the context, I would find myself attempting with Kierkegaard what sixteen women have done in engaging Martin Luther in the *Transformative Lutheran Theologies* work already cited. I regret that this rich collection of essays was not available to me during most of the time I was writing these chapters. That volume advances the pathbreaking relational work of such women as Mary Solberg (*Compelling Knowledge: A Feminist Proposal for an Epistemology of the Cross* [Albany: State University of New York Press, 2004]), and Deanna Thompson (*Crossing the Divide: Luther, Feminism, and the Cross* [Minneapolis: Fortress Press, 2004]).

8. Søren Kierkegaard, *Christian Discourses*, ed. and trans. Howard V. Hong and Edna H. Hong (Princeton: Princeton University Press, 1997), 127.

Introduction

1. An alternative framing might be "subject/object."

2. Stephen Toulmin, *Cosmopolis: The Hidden Agenda of Modernity* (New York: Free Press, 1990), 108. He offers this summary: "Human actions and experiences were *mental* or spontaneous outcomes of reasoning; they were performed willingly and creatively; and they were active and productive. Physical phenomena and natural processes by contrast involved brute matter and were *material;* they were mechanical, repetitive, predictable effects of causes; they merely happened; and matter in itself was passive and inert."

3. See especially the second and sixth of the Meditations on First Philosophy in René Descartes, *The Philosophical Writings of René Descartes*, trans. John Cottingham, Robert Stoothoff, and Dugald Murdoch, 2 vols. (Cambridge: Cambridge University Press, 1984).

4. I have discussed this development somewhat more fully in two previous works: *God: The Question and the Quest* (Philadelphia: Fortress Press, 1985), 7–13; and *Faith and the Other* (Minneapolis: Fortress Press, 1993), 6–12.

5. An early statement of this direction is Philip Rieff, *The Triumph of the Therapeutic: The Uses of Faith after Freud* (New York: Harper & Row, 1966).

6. Robert Soloman, *Continental Philosophy since 1750: The Rise and Fall of the Self* (New York: Oxford University Press, 1988), 6, speaks of this mentality as the "transcendental pretense."

7. David Hume, *Dialogues Concerning Natural Religion*, ed. Henry D. Aiken (New York: Macmillan/Hafner, 1948, 1975), 17, 43. For Hume's fuller statement of this reductive empiricism, see his *An Enquiry Concerning Human Understanding*, 2nd ed., ed. L. A. Selby-Bigge (Oxford: Oxford University Press, 1902); and his *A Treatise of Human Nature*, ed. L. A. Selby-Bigge (Oxford: Oxford University Press, 1888).

8. Richard Dawkins, *The God Delusion* (Boston: Houghton Mifflin, 2006), 56–59. I will address this more fully in chapter 3.

9. Richard Rorty, "The Priority of Democracy to Philosophy," in *The Virginia Statute for Religious Freedom*, ed. Merill D. Peterson and Robert C. Vaughan (New York: Cambridge University Press, 1988), 269.

10. Readers curious to check my take on each of these figures can still consult my earlier lengthy studies: *Kierkegaard on Christ and Christian Coherence* (New York: Harper, 1968); and *Faith and Process: The Significance of Process Thought for Christian Faith* (Minneapolis: Augsburg, 1979). This present project takes off from the analyses of Kierkegaard and Whitehead in those works.

11. An exception would be the work of Helene Russell. Particularly helpful is her seminar paper "Solitude: A Theological Dialogue: Søren Kierkegaard and Process Theology," Summer 2001, available through the Center for Process Studies Web site: www .ctr4process.org. With Kierkegaard, Russell has given sustained attention to *Purity of Heart Is to Will One Thing* (See Kierkegaard's *Upbuilding Discourses in Various Spirits*, ed. and trans. Howard V. Hong and Edna H. Hong [Princeton: Princeton University Press, 1988]). David Tracy has given considerable attention to both traditions—see, for example, *The Analogical Imagination: Christian Theology and the Culture of Pluralism* (New York: Crossroad, 1981)—but has not to my knowledge discussed them together.

12. Thus, after stressing that "as soon as the spirit is posited, the moment [in which time and eternity touch each other] is present," Kierkegaard says, "Nature's security has its source in the fact that time has no significance at all for nature. Only with the moment does history begin." *The Concept of Anxiety*, trans. Reidar Thomte (Princeton: Princeton University Press, 1980), 88–89. In chapter 2, I will cite the widely shared opposing recognition of "the history of nature." Cf. Larry Rasmussen, *Earth Community; Earth Ethics* (Maryknoll, N.Y.: Orbis, 1996), 256: "Nature and history are one." The classic formulation of this point is Carl Friedrich von Weizsäcker, *The History of Nature* (Chicago: University of Chicago Press, 1949).

13. Alfred North Whitehead, *Process and Reality*, ed. David Ray Griffin and Donald W. Sherburne (New York: Free Press, 1978), 35: "There is a becoming of continuity, but no continuity of becoming."

14. For a fuller statement, see my theological autobiographical statement, "A Living Conversation," *dialog* 42, no. 3 (Winter 2003): 368–75.

15. See Bernard E. Meland, *The Realities of Faith: The Revolution in Cultural Forms* (New York: Oxford University Press, 1962).

16. I will not offer an elaborate soteriological statement either, but I will argue that anything to be well said there depends on the fundamental concept of a living God in actual relationship with the creatures. That is my theme.

17. Don Cupitt, *Taking Leave of God* (London: SCM, 1980), 106.

18. Ibid.

19. H. P. Owen, *Concepts of Deity* (New York: Herder & Herder, 1971), 24–25. Cf. Karl Rahner's critique of Jürgen Moltmann, that a suffering God "does not help me" and his appeal that "God is in a true and authentic and consoling sense the God who cannot suffer" in Jürgen Moltmann, "The Crucified God: Yesterday and Today: 1972–2002," in *Cross Examinations: Readings on the Meaning of the Cross Today,* ed. Marit Trelstad (Minneapolis: Fortress Press, 2006), 134–35. In a posthumously published letter, Moltmann stresses "that God does not suffer as finite creatures do does not mean that he is incapable of suffering in any way. God is capable of suffering because he is capable of love" (ibid.). For a comparable Roman Catholic response to Rahner, see Elizabeth A. Johnson, *She Who Is: The Mystery of God in Feminist Theological Discourse* (New York: Crossroad, 1992), 254. She notes, "The pathological tendency in the present culture of First World countries to deny suffering and death in human experience, which leads to banality in thought and superficiality in values. In this context speech about redemptive

suffering and the power of the suffering God is genuinely countercultural." In this book, I have tried to follow Johnson's counsel that "what is needed is to step decisively out of the androcentric system of power over versus victimization and think in other categories about power, pain, and their deep interweaving in human experience."

20. Eberhard Jüngel, *God as the Mystery of the World,* trans. D. L. Guder (Grand Rapids: Eerdmans, 1983), 315.

21. Søren Kierkegaard, *Christian Discourses,* ed. and trans. Howard V. Hong and Edna H. Hong (Princeton: Princeton University Press, 1997), 128. Thus, Geddes MacGregor, *He Who Lets Us Be: A Theology of Love* (New York: Seabury, 1975), 15, writes of divine power as an "unlimited capacity for creative love."

22. Marjorie Suchocki, *In God's Presence: Theological Reflections on Prayer* (St. Louis: Chalice, 1996), 24.

23. Bernard of Clairvaux, Sermon 64.10, in *Bernard of Clairvaux: On the Song of Songs III,* trans. Kilian Walsh and Irene M. Edmonds (Kalamazoo, Mich.: Cistercian, 1979), 177–78. I am indebted to my Luther Seminary colleague David Fredrickson for this reference.

24. Suchocki, *In God's Presence,* 24.

25. Tom Beaudoin has drawn on the writings of Michel Foucault to clarify the uses of power in supporting structures of oppression. See his *Witness to Dispossession* (Maryknoll, N.Y.: Orbis, 2008).

26. Anders Nygren, *Agape and Eros,* trans. Philip S. Watson (London: SPCK, 1953). A helpful summary statement is Carter Lindberg, *Love: A Brief History through Western Christianity* (Malden, Mass.: Blackwell, 2008). Werner G. Jeanrond's *A Theology of Love* (London: T & T Clark, 2010) takes as its focus the *praxis* of love with noteworthy attention to the "institutions" and "politics" of love. The literature on love is vast. See Jeanrond's list, ibid., 7–9. An excellent ethical statement is Margaret A. Farley's *Just Love: A Framework for Christian Sexual Ethics* (New York: Continuum, 2007).

27. Thomas Jay Oord, *Defining Love: A Philosophical, Scientific, and Theological Engagement* (Grand Rapids: Brazos, 2010), 15. In chapter 2, Oord specifically engages Nygren and suggests how *agape, eros,* and *philia* all find a place in his own definition.

28. Michael E. Lodahl, "Creation out of Nothing? Or Is *Next* to Nothing Enough?" in *Thy Nature and Thy Name Is Love: Wesleyan and Process Theologies in Dialogue,* ed. Bryan P. Stone and Thomas Jay Oord, 217–38 (Nashville: Abingdon, 2001), 236. In my focusing on "life in the middle," I need not explicitly engage Lodahl's questioning appreciation of *creatio ex nihilo* in order to resonate with his emphatic recognition that the God we know is always creating in love. He cites the familiar, more dualistic process emphasis in which God does not bear total responsibility for every event, but wants with John Wesley to "nudge the Whiteheadian tradition at least a little toward *creatio ex nihilo.*" I am attracted to a more emphatic move in this direction in imagining that divine love irreversibly limits itself in the commitment that creation represents. One can trust a power that freely works faithfully in love. In class I have often heard my colleague Terry Fretheim make this point biblically about God's commitment. For a recent statement see his *Creation Untamed: The Bible, God, and Natural Disasters* (Grand Rapids, Mich.: Baker Academic, 2010), 32.

29. In *Adventures of Ideas* (New York: Free Press, 1967), 169, he pointedly laments that these theologians "made no effort to conceive the World in terms of the metaphysical categories by means of which they interpreted God, and they made no effort to conceive God in terms of the metaphysical categories which they applied to the World."

Chapter 1

1. I am indebted to the staff at the Domestic Abuse Project on Franklin Avenue in Minneapolis for their forceful statement of this point of personal responsibility. In *The*

Concept of Anxiety, Kierkegaard is particularly concerned to avoid collapsing the individual into the race, as he sees happening in certain understandings of original sin.

2. Søren Kierkegaard, *Either/Or*, ed. and trans. Howard V. Hong and Edna H. Hong (Princeton: Princeton University Press, 1987), 2:214. I have found Bruce Kirmmse's *Kierkegaard in Golden Age Denmark* (Bloomington: Indiana University Press, 1990) particularly helpful for biographical material.

3. See George Connell, *To Be One Thing: Personal Unity in Kierkegaard's Thought* (Macon, Ga.: Mercer University Press, 1985). Cf. James Giles, ed., *Kierkegaard on Freedom* (New York: Palgrave, 2000).

4. Søren Kierkegaard, *Concluding Unscientific Postscript*, ed. and trans. Howard V. Hong and Edna H. Hong (Princeton: Princeton University Press, 1992), 1:312.

5. Ibid.

6. Ibid., 348.

7. Kierkegaard, *Either/Or*, 2:214. One can find this theme richly developed in Kierkegaard's *Purity of Heart Is to Will One Thing: Stages on Life's Way*, ed. and trans. Howard V. Hong and Edna H. Hong (Princeton: Princeton University Press, 1988) and the second volume of *Either/Or*. The first of these works is more accurately titled in the Hongs' translation: "An Occasional Discourse," which is the first part of *Upbuilding Discourses in Various Spirits*, ed. and trans. Howard V. Hong and Edna H. Hong (Princeton: Princeton University Press, 1993). Douglas Steere's 1938 titling of his translation is well chosen as far as representing a prevailing theme in the discourse.

8. Kierkegaard, *Either/Or*, 2:248. In *The Human Embrace: The Love of Philosophy and the Philosophy of Love* (University Park: Pennsylvania State University Press, 2000), 2. Ronald L. Hall draws Kierkegaard together with Stanley Cavell and Martha Nussbaum in the thesis that "a unique feature of human being is that we humans must decide to be human, to embrace our humanness."

9. Kierkegaard, *Either/Or*, 2:252, 258.

10. Calvin Schragg, *The Self after Postmodernity* (New Haven: Yale University Press, 1997), 62.

11. Niebuhr is very explicit about his debt to Kierkegaard: "Kierkegaard's explanation of the dialectical relation of freedom and fate in sin is one of the profoundest in Christian thought." *The Nature and Destiny of Man* (London: Nisbet, 1941, 1943), 1:279. He proceeds to quote extensively from the German edition of *The Concept of Anxiety*.

12. See Jean-Paul Sartre, *Being and Nothingness: An Essay on Phenomenological Ontology*, trans. Hazel E. Barnes (New York: Philosophical Library, 1956), where Sartre explicitly adopts Kierkegaard's distinction between "anguish" (SK: "anxiety") and fear, and specifically ties that distinction to Heidegger's emphasis on anguish as the apprehension of nothingness.

13. Paul Tillich, *The Courage to Be* (New Haven: Yale University Press, 1952), 125.

14. *Søren Kierkegaard's Journals and Papers*, ed. Howard V. Hong and Edna G. Hong (Bloomington: Indiana University Press, 1970), 2:1251.

15. Kierkegaard, *Concluding Unscientific Postscript*, 201–2. Three years later, writing as the decisively Christian pseudonym Anti-Climacus, he makes the point even more explicitly. In pleading for "a little Socratic ignorance with respect to Christianity," he writes, "Let us never forget that it was out of veneration for God that he was ignorant, that as far as it was possible for a pagan he was on guard duty as a *judge* on the frontier between God and man, keeping watch so that the deep gulf of qualitative difference between them was maintained." Søren Kierkegaard, *The Sickness unto Death*, ed. and trans. Howard V. Hong and Edna H. Hong (Princeton: Princeton University Press, 1980), 99.

16. Søren Kierkegaard, *The Moment and Late Writings*, ed. and trans. Howard V. Hong and Edna H. Hong (Princeton: Princeton University Press, 1998), 343.

17. I am making final changes in mid-February 2011, after the astounding non-violent ousting of Hosni Mubarek in Egypt. I note that it was a secularist uprising that accomplished this strike for freedom.

18. Søren Kierkegaard, *Christian Discourses*, ed. and trans. Howard V. Hong and Edna H. Hong (Princeton: Princeton University Press, 1997), 127–28.

19. Ibid.

20. Joyce M. Cuff and Curtis L. Thompson, *Nature Alive: A Scientist and a Theologian Conversing on the Divine Promise of Possibility* (forthcoming).

21. Stephan G. Post, *Unlimited Love: Altruism, Compassion, and Service* (Philadelphia: Templeton Foundation Press, 2003), 20.

22. See the introduction to this book for a comment on Michael Lodahl's discussion of *ex nihilo* doctrines.

23. Kierkegaard, *The Sickness unto Death*, 126. This was a lesson Karl Barth learned from Kierkegaard. See Barth's *The Epistle to the Romans*, trans. Edwyn C. Hoskyns (London: Oxford University Press, 1933), 99.

24. Kierkegaard, *The Sickness unto Death,* 126. Of Christ, he writes with exceptional eloquence: "He can debase himself, take the form of a servant, suffer, die for men, invite all to come to him, offer up every day of his life, every hour of the day, and offer up his life," and then "but he cannot remove the possibility of offense."

25. The pseudonym Anti-Climacus is particularly rich in describing the range of offense. In *Practice in Christianity* (1850), he offers a christological framing of offense in relation to "loftiness" ("that an individual human being speaks or acts as if he were God," 94) and "lowliness" ("that the one who passes himself off as God proves to be the lowly, poor, suffering, and finally powerless human being," 102). (Søren Kierkegaard, *Practice in Christianity*, ed. and trans. Howard V. Hong and Edna H. Hong [Princeton: Princeton University Press, 1992].) This distinction follows his discussion of offense related to Christ "simply as an individual human being who comes into collision with an established order" (85). I will shortly refer to the anthropological framing of offense in *The Sickness unto Death* (1849), where among the many descriptions of despair, the distinction between "defiance" and "weakness" particularly stands out.

26. Kierkegaard, *Practice in Christianity*, 104.

27. Søren Kierkegaard, *Philosophical Fragments*, ed. and trans. Howard V. Hong and Edna H. Hong (Princeton: Princeton University Press, 1985), 55. It is noteworthy that this formulation of divine decisiveness is put forward by Johannes Climacus, a pseudonym who does not claim to be a Christian but asks about an advance beyond Socrates. The Christian claim about the "art of power" does not depend on faith for intelligibility. If one were to appeal to the language of faith to make this point, one would not be restricted to specifically Christian texts. From the Hebrew scriptures, for example, in Climacus's use of this parable, I hear an echo of Hosea 11, where God cries out over the prospect of judging Israel: "How can I give you up. . . . How can I hand you over. . . . My heart recoils within me; my compassion grows warm and tender. I will not execute my fierce anger, . . . I will not come in wrath" (Hos 11:6).

28. Ibid.

29. Kierkegaard, *Practice in Christianity*, 131.

30. Kierkegaard, *The Moment and Late Writings*, 268.

31. Ibid., 278.

32. Ibid., 281.

33. Robert W. Jenson, "Triune Grace," in *The Gift of Grace: The Future of Lutheran Theology*, ed. Niels Henrik Gregersen, Bo Holm, Ted Peters, and Peter Widmann, 17–30 (Minneapolis: Augsburg Fortress, 2005), 30.

34. Ted Peters, "Grace, Doubt and Evil," in Gregersen et al., *The Gift of Grace*, 307–325, quoting from 311.

35. Kierkegaard, *Journals and Papers*, 2:1348.

36. Gustaf Wingren, *Creation and Law*, trans. Ross Mackenzie (Philadelphia: Muhlenberg, 1961), 38.

37. Kierkegaard, *Journals and Papers*, 3:2554.

38. Jürgen Moltmann, *God in Creation*, trans. Margaret Kohl (Minneapolis: Fortress Press, 1993), 88. In "Putting the Cross in Context: Atonement through Covenant," 107–22, in *Transformative Lutheran Theologies: Feminist, Womanist, and Mujerista Perspectives*, ed. Mary J. Streufert (Minneapolis: Fortress Press, 2010), Marit Trelstad links herself with Moltmann and terms the continuity in God's action "ontological." She writes vividly: "Before the cross, there was the covenant. And after the cross, there is the covenant." In the same volume in "God's Heart Revealed in Eden," 57–67, Deanna Thompson reaches back behind Kierkegaard to find a comparable continuity in Luther's understanding of a *protevangelion* in Genesis 3. Geddes MacGregor, *He Who Lets Us Be* (New York: Seabury, 1975), 104, cites similarly the Russian theologian Sergei Bulgakov writing of "the creation of heaven and earth" as "a metaphysical 'kenosis,'" with respect to divinity itself." In *On the Moral Nature of the Universe: Theology, Cosmology, and Ethics* (Minneapolis: Fortress Press, 1996), Nancey Murphy and George Ellis offer a fulsome discussion of the universe as "created by kenosis." What is at stake in these converging references is the affirmation of the gracious character of the Creator's work.

39. Eberhard Jüngel, *God as the Mystery of the World*, trans. Darrell L. Guder (Grand Rapids: Eerdmans, 1983), 384.

40. Ibid., 328. MacGregor, *He Who Lets Us Be*, 75, cites Simone Weil's affirmation in *Waiting on God* of "self-emptying" as "belonging to the essential nature of God." Catherine LaCugna has offered a comparable reflection on the relationship of love and freedom in God's creating. See her *God for Us: The Trinity and Christian Life* (New York: HarperCollins, 1991), 355: "While the world is the gracious result of divine freedom, God's freedom means *necessarily* being who and what God is. From this standpoint the world is not created *ex nihilo* but *ex amore, ex condilectio*, that is, out of divine love." Cf. Paul Fiddes, *The Creative Suffering of God* (Oxford: Clarendon, 1988), 71.

41. Kierkegaard, *Journals and Papers*, 2:1251.

42. Terence E. Fretheim has particularly emphasized how, biblically, the promises of God do "limit the options available for action": "God cannot use power in such a way as to violate a promise God has made; that would mean unfaithfulness." See his *The Suffering of God: An Old Testament Perspective* (Philadelphia: Fortress Press, 1984), 72.

43. Cf. above, in the section "The Art of Power."

44. Kierkegaard, *The Sickness unto Death*, 126. It is striking that the recognition of divine risk is not compromised even in writing of God's foreknowledge. Thus, in *Practice in Christianity*, 222, he can write of "how this life here upon earth is a time of testing": "Governance certainly can know that it will happen, although human beings still are responsible for its happening."

45. Kierkegaard, *Practice in Christianity*, 238–39. I will later point out that there is strong recognition, ibid., that the prototype must also be "*unconditionally* behind . . . in order to be able to capture and include all . . . and [yet] in order to propel forward those who are to be formed according to it."

46. Kierkegaard, *Philosophical Fragments*, 15. In the language Paul Ricoeur has sketched (*The Symbolism of Evil*), Kierkegaard is clearly an "Adamic" theologian, locating sin's responsibility with the human.

47. Cf. Arnold Come's discussion in *Kierkegaard as Theologian: Recovering My Self* (Montreal: McGill-Queen's University Press, 1997), 349ff. See also Helene Tallon Russell, *Irigaray and Kierkegaard: Multiplicity, Relationality, and Difference* (Macon, Ga.: Mercer University Press, 2009), for her discussion of three pairs of polar elements, temporal and eternal, within three spheres of existence.

48. Cuff and Thompson, *Nature Alive*, offer a comprehensive discussion of emergence, weak and strong, within their presentation of "consilience."

49. Kierkegaard, *The Concept of Anxiety*, 41.

50. See Stuart Kauffman's discussion of that complexity in *At Home in the Universe: The Search for Laws of Self-Organization and Complexity* (New York: Oxford University Press, 1995); and *The Origins of Order: Self-Organization and Selection in Evolution* (New York: Oxford University Press, 1993). Arthur Peacocke notes, "Harold Morowitz has . . . identified some twenty-eight emergent levels in the natural world." *All That Is: A Naturalistic Faith for the Twenty-First Century*, ed. Philip Clayton (Minneapolis: Fortress Press, 2007), 15. The basic conception is well outlined in I. Prigogine and I. Stengers, *Order out of Chaos* (London: Heinemann, 1984). These complexity theorists make the case that self-organization needs recognition along with natural selection as a factor in the evolutionary story.

51. Ian Barbour, *Nature, Human Nature, and God* (Minneapolis: Fortress Press, 2002), 17–18. Adding such self-organizing complexity to random variation and natural selection in the story of evolution can bring Kauffman to say, "We should see ourselves not as a highly improbable historical accident but as an expected fulfillment of the natural order." Ibid. For a very rich theological discussion of such emergence, see Philip Clayton, *Adventures in the Spirit: God, World, Divine Action* (Minneapolis: Fortress Press, 2008), part 2, where the line of argument reaches all the way "From Emergent Nature to the Emerging Church." Barbour and Clayton differ somewhat on the question of whether "interiority" is to be found "all the way down." See the summary of the disagreement in Thomas Jay Oord, *Defining Love: A Philosophical, Scientific, and Theological Engagement* (Grand Rapids: Brazos, 2010), 134–35.

52. Kierkegaard, *The Sickness unto Death*, 13.

53. Ibid., 30.

54. Ibid., 25.

55. Cf. Arnold Come's argument for translating the Danish as "a relation, which relates to itself." The point he is making is that the reflexive movement in the self "is not transitively forward toward an object but reflexively backward in reference to some hidden action of the relation within itself." That hidden action is the reality of freedom by which "the relation chooses to become a self." See Come, *Kierkegaard as Humanist: Discovering My Self* (Montreal: McGill-Queen's University Press, 1995), 8–11.

56. Kierkegaard, *Either/Or*, 2:262.

57. Kierkegaard, *The Sickness unto Death*, 14.

58. Ibid., 16.

59. Kierkegaard, *The Concept of Anxiety*, 35.

60. Ibid., 42.

61. Ibid., 43.

62. Ibid., 44.

63. Ibid., 41.

64. Ibid., 45.

65. Ibid.

66. Ibid., 61. Cf. John M. Hoberman, "Kierkegaard on Vertigo," in *International Kierkegaard Commentary: Sickness unto Death*, ed. Robert L. Perkins, 19:185–208 (Macon, Ga.: Mercer University Press, 1987).

67. Ibid., 22.

68. Ibid., 23.

69. Ibid., 162.

70. Ibid., 16.

71. Kierkegaard, *Purity of Heart Is to Will One Thing*, in *Upbuilding Discourses in Various Spirits*.

72. Ibid., 154.

73. For a detailed discussion of two different meanings for repentance, see my chapter "God's Changelessness: The Triumph of Grace in Law and Gospel as 'Archimedean

Point,'" in the International Kierkegaard Commentary on *The Moment*, ed. Robert Perkins (Macon, Ga.: Mercer University Press, 2009), 101–28. Amy Laura Hall has relentlessly emphasized the need for repentance in *Kierkegaard and the Treachery of Love* (Cambridge: Cambridge University Press, 2002).

74. Kierkegaard, *The Concept of Anxiety*, 61.

75. Ibid., 49.

76. Ibid., 62.

77. Ibid.

78. Ibid., 61.

79. Ibid., 49.

80. Kierkegaard, *The Sickness unto Death*, 92–93.

81. Kierkegaard, *The Concept of Anxiety*, the subtitle for the work.

82. Kierkegaard, *The Sickness unto Death*, 93.

83. Ibid., 49.

84. Marjorie Suchocki, writing as a leading interpreter of the Whiteheadian legacy, has offered a sustained critical response to Reinhold Niebuhr's influential emphasis on sin as conscious and prideful rebellion against God. See her *The Fall to Violence: Original Sin in Relational Theology* (New York: Continuum, 1994), 16–29. See also Céline Léon and Sylvia Walsh, *Feminist Interpretations of Kierkegaard* (University Park: Pennsylvania State University Press, 1997). In that volume (19) and elsewhere, Wanda Warren Berry has offered a discerning appropriation of Kierkegaard, claiming "the liberatory potential of his religious existentialism."

85. In an extended footnote in *Sickness unto Death*, 50, Kierkegaard pleads, "I am far from denying that women may have forms of masculine despair and, conversely that men may have forms of feminine despair, but these are exceptions."

86. Ibid., 21.

87. Paul Tillich, *The Courage to Be* (New Haven: Yale University Press, 1952).

88. Ibid., 87–88.

89. Mary Louise Bringle, *Despair: Sickness or Sin?* (Nashville: Abingdon, 1990).

90. Ibid., 173.

91. Ibid., 174.

92. Kierkegaard, *The Sickness unto Death,* 15.

93. Ibid., 26, 44, 62, 67.

94. Ibid., 131.

95. I use here Robert L. Perkins's rendering of the "Anti." See his response to Howard Hong's formulation in *International Kierkegaard Commentary: Practice in Christianity*, ed. Robert L. Perkins (Macon, Ga.: Mercer University Press, 2004), 1–7. Perkins argues from the journals that the first idea Kierkegaard had about the "reckless" "anti" is to move against Climacus back toward the aesthetic. In *Sickness* and *Practice*, the move is against Climacus to a recklessly decisive Christianity.

96. Kierkegaard, *Practice in Christianity*, 160.

97. Kierkegaard, *The Moment and Late Writings*, 292.

98. Ibid., 341. "I, who am not even a Christian" expresses his concern to "keep the ideal free" and reflects his formulation in *Concluding Unscientific Postscript* (see "The Conclusion," 607–16) of the distinction between "being" and "becoming" a Christian.

99. Søren Kierkegaard, *Judge for Yourself*, ed. and trans. Howard V. Hong and Edna H. Hong (Princeton: Princeton University Press, 1990), 193.

100. Kierkegaard, *Journals and Papers*, 3:2503. For a comparably dialectical reading of Luther, see ibid., 3:2513.

101. Kierkegaard, *The Sickness unto Death*, 129.

102. Kierkegaard, *Either/Or*, 2:93–94.

103. See the sustained development of the theme in ch. 2 of the *Postscript*, 189–251.

104. Ibid., 578ff. with the "retroactive" effect entailing "the consciousness of sin" (583).

105. Søren Kierkegaard, *Works of Love*, ed. and trans. Howard V. Hong and Edna H. Hong (Princeton: Princeton University Press, 195), 383–84.

106. Ibid., 107.

107. Ibid., 142.

108. Ibid., 384.

109. Cf. Arnold Come's quest in *Kierkegaard as Theologian* to locate such a Kierkegaardian view of sociality and community.

110. Curtis Thompson has called my attention to a remarkable passage in *Works of Love*: "Let us for a moment look at nature. With what infinite love nature or God in nature encompasses all the diverse things that have life and existence!" (269). The potential present in such a passage seems largely unfulfilled in Kierkegaard, though there certainly is strong recognition of God's omnipresence and providence.

111. Kierkegaard, *The Concept of Anxiety*, 48.

112. Ibid., 49.

113. Donald Capps makes such a case for "relocating soul in the body and its processes." "Enrapt Spirits and the Melancholy Soul: The Locus of Division in the Christian Self and American Society," in *On Losing the Soul: Essays in the Social Psychology of Religion*, ed. Richard K. Fenn and Donald Capps (Albany: State University of New York Press, 1995), 146. He claims Martin Luther as an ally in this, and has sharp words for Melanchthon, who "spiritualized" Luther's understanding of God.

114. Dietrich Bonhoeffer, *Creation and Fall*, trans. Douglas Stephen Bax (Minneapolis: Fortress Press, 1997), 76–77.

115. Walker Percy, *Lost in the Cosmos: The Last Self-Help Book* (New York: Farrar, Straus & Giroux, 1983), 1. He continues severely: "Every advance in an objective understanding of the Cosmos and in its technological control further distances the self from the Cosmos precisely in the degree of the advance—so that in the end the self becomes a space-bound ghost which roams the very Cosmos it understands perfectly." Ibid., 12–13.

116. Ibid.

117. Bradley R. Dewey, "Walker Percy Talks about Kierkegaard: An Annotated Interview," 273–98, *Journal of Religion* (July 1974): 281–82.

118. I have discussed that influence in American literature and other fields in "America," 9–36; "Kierkegaard Research," *Bibliotheca Kierkegaardiana*, ed. Niels Thulstrup and Marie Thulstrup (Copenhagen: Reitzels, 1987).

119. See Alasdair MacIntyre, *After Virtue: A Study in Moral Theory* (Notre Dame: University of Notre Dame Press, 1981); and Robert Bellah, *Habits of the Heart: Individualism and Commitment in American Life* (Los Angeles: University of California Press, 1985).

120. Richard Rorty, *Philosophy and the Mirror of Nature* (Princeton: Princeton University Press, 1979), 367.

121. See, for example, Walter Kaufmann's concerns about fideism and irresponsible choice in *From Shakespeare to Existentialism* (Boston: Beacon, 1959). C. Stephan Evans has particularly taken up the task of defending Kierkegaard's christological formulations as something quite other than nonsense. See his *Passionate Reason, Making Sense of Kierkegaard's Philosophical Fragments* (Bloomington: Indiana University Press, 1992). Evans notes that Climacus says, "The paradox is the most improbable," and so is not a logical contradiction, which would be impossible, not improbable. Evans notes that a logical contradiction would not meet Kierkegaard's concern to speak of the paradox as unique, as *the absurd*. *Faith beyond Reason* (Edinburgh: Edinburgh University Press, 1998), 83. Evans is prominent among a line of authors employing analytic philosophy in reading Kierkegaard. Here the influence of Paul Holmer, at the University of Minnesota and at Yale, was powerful.

122. Kierkegaard, *The Sickness unto Death*, 100.

123. Kierkegaard, *Concluding Unscientific Postscript*, 1:568. This commitment to truth speaking is strikingly illustrated in his reaction to H. L. Martensen's funeral eulogy for Bishop J. P. Mynster. Martensen, who had been Kierkegaard's teacher at the university, praised Mynster as a "witness to the truth." The outraged student spends some eleven months writing biting attacks but waits to publish them. Bruce Kirmmse's explanation emphasizes the possibility of a lawsuit by either Martensen or the conservative government. Such a suit "would have obscured the broader and deeper intent of SK's assault, namely to alter the entire ordering of boundaries between the spiritual and the political realms." Kirmmse, *Kierkegaard in Golden Age Denmark*, 450.

124. Kierkegaard, *Concluding Unscientific Postscript*, 1:568.

125. See Stephen Dunning, *Kierkegaard's Dialectic of Inwardness: A Structural Analysis of the Theory of Stages* (Princeton: Princeton University Press, 1985), 8–9, for an attempt to distinguish paradox from the dialectics of contradiction, reciprocity, and Hegelian mediation

126. George Bernard Shaw, *Major Barbara* (New York: Brentano's, 1907), 152. Cf. Martin Luther, *Table Talk*, 5677, in *Luther's Works*, ed. and trans. Theodore C. Tappert (Philadelphia: Fortress Press, 1967), 54:476.

127. Kierkegaard, *Practice in Christianity*, 125.

128. The discussion of "indirect communication" could well involve consideration of Kierkegaard's complicated use of pseudonymity. I have offered a perspective on this in *Kierkegaard on Christ and Christian Coherence* (New York: Harper & Row, 1968), part 1. In the present chapter, I have followed the approach of James Giles, who draws on Kierkegaard's extensive use of irony to undercut the claim that the pseudonymous works are not to be seen as containing Kierkegaard's ideas. See *Kierkegaard on Freedom*, 2–13.

129. Kierkegaard, *The Concept of Anxiety*, 43. Cf. 23 on the distinction between psychology and dogmatics with regard to the leap into sin.

130. Ibid., 32.

131. Ibid., 42–43.

132. To make the transition to the next chapter, we may recall Whitehead's much-quoted statement: "Religion is what the individual does with his own solitariness." But he also speaks of "the internal life" depending not only on the individual but also on "what is permanent in the nature of things." *Religion in the Making* (1926; New York: Fordham University Press, 1996), 16.

Chapter 2

1. A comprehensive biographical account is Victor Lowe's *Alfred North Whitehead: The Man and His Work*, 2 vols. (Baltimore: Johns Hopkins University Press, 1985, 1990).

2. Alfred North Whitehead, *Religion in the Making* (1926; New York: Fordham University Press, 1996), 16.

3. Ibid., 16–17.

4. Ibid., 74.

5. *Process and Reality*, corrected ed., ed. David Ray Griffin and Donald W. Sherburne (1929; New York: Free Press, 1978), 348.

6. Philip Clayton and Arthur Peacocke, eds., *In Whom We Live and Move and Have Our Being: Panentheistic Reflections on God's Presence in a Scientific World* (Grand Rapids: Eerdmans, 2004).

7. Whitehead, *Religion in the Making*, 60. Cf. 137: "There is no such thing as absolute solitariness. Each entity requires its environment. Thus man cannot seclude himself from society."

8. Cf. Martin Heidegger, *Being and Time*, trans. John Macquarrie and Edward Robinson (New York: Harper & Row, 1962), "The Worldhood of the World," 91–148. I am indebted to Curtis Thompson for this reference.

9. Lowe, *Alfred North Whitehead*, 2:128–30. He also cites the notes Whitehead wrote for a second edition of the *Principles of Natural Knowledge* just before sailing for America.

10. It is true that Whitehead introduces his "God-talk" under the heading of "Some Derivative Notions" in the second chapter of *Process and Reality* (31). In this chapter, I will argue that this makes good sense in the empirical development of his system, but that the distinctive and essential role of God is already recognized in speaking of God as the basis for the "relevance" of "unrealized abstract form" (32) without which the ordered novelty of the system—as discussed in chapter 1—is impossible.

11. Whitehead, *Religion in the Making*, 84.

12. Alfred North Whitehead, *Adventures of Ideas* (1929; New York: Free Press, 1978), 25.

13. This concern should not be confused with views arguing that any metaphysical effort is in principle mistaken. A moderate criticism of this discriminating sort is the influential comment of Langdon Gilkey regarding process theology: "The Process school so far has emphasized far too strongly the significance, for good or for ill, of metaphysical concepts in theology and its history." See Langdon Gilkey, "Process Theology," 5–29 *Vox Populi* 43 (1973), 12. Yet he grants that "process theology, we must now recognize, has been correct in its insistence that ontological or metaphysical speculation is necessary for theology, and that the metaphysical vision they champion presents us with many creative possibilities in the present theological situation" (14).

14. In *Faith and Process: The Significance of Process Thought for Christian Faith* (Minneapolis: Augsburg Publishing House, 1979), I distinguish "tactical, ethical, conceptual, and constitutive" elements in the contribution that process thought may make to faith.

15. Whitehead, *Adventures of Ideas*, 163–68.

16. Whitehead, *Religion in the Making*, 79.

17. Whitehead, *Adventures of Ideas*, 168.

18. Ibid., 163.

19. Ibid., 166.

20. Ibid.

21. Ibid., 167.

22. In "The Passion of Christ: Grace Both Red and Green," in *Cross Examinations: Readings on the Meaning of the Cross Today*, ed. Marit Trelstad (Minneapolis: Fortress Press, 2006), 196–207, Jay B. McDaniel takes up the very specific challenge to think in such a way about the cross that one can "appreciate its wisdom in light of grace both red and green," 197.

23. Whitehead, *Adventures of Ideas*, 167.

24. Ibid.

25. Ibid., 168.

26. Ibid.

27. Ibid.

28. Ibid., 168–69.

29. Ibid., 169. A striking variety of process approaches to the doctrine of the Trinity is available in Joseph A. Bracken and Marjorie Suchocki, eds., *Trinity in Process: A Relational Theology of God* (New York: Continuum, 1999).

30. Whitehead, *Adventures of Ideas*, 169.

31. Ibid.

32. Whitehead, *Process and Reality*, 343.

33. Ibid., 9.

34. Ibid., 17.

35. See *Process Perspectives* 31, no. 3 (Winter 2009), for a report ("Beyond Metaphysics?") on a conference held in Claremont, December 4–8, 2008, to debate whether these later works represent a new turn in Whitehead's approach. For Whitehead's famous claim that "the true method of discovery is like the flight of an aeroplane," see *Process and Reality*, 5.

36. Robert W. Jenson, "The Triune God," in *Christian Dogmatics*, ed. Carl E. Braaten and Robert W. Jenson, 79–196 (Philadelphia: Fortress Press, 1984), 1:154.

37. Cf. above, ch. 1.

38. Whitehead, *Adventures of Ideas*, 169. Whitehead's analysis critiquing the notion of creation out of nothing is not specifically targeted by Philip Hefner in his vigorous defense of that doctrine. But Hefner offers a sharply different view on the theodicy question. See his "The Creation," in Braaten and Jenson, *Christian Dogmatics*, 1:265–357: "There is scarcely a more offensive idea for the Christian than one that holds God in some way responsible for evil. Perhaps the only idea more repugnant is the alternative we mentioned—that God is limited in power over anything, including evil" (1:312). Later in the chapter, I will suggest that Whitehead's explicit rejection of creation out of nothing needs to be understood in the light of the location of his experiential venture in the middle of things.

39. H. P. Owen, *Concepts of Deity* (New York: Herder & Herder, 1971), 36. In ch. 2, Owen offers his critique of process theology. A more recent example is Thomas Weinandy, *Does God Suffer?* (Notre Dame, Ind.: Notre Dame University Press, 2001).

40. Whitehead, *Adventures of Ideas*, 169.

41. Søren Kierkegaard, *Christian Discourses*, ed. and trans. Howard V. Hong and Edna H. Hong (Princeton: Princeton University Press, 1997), 127. Cf. my discussion of this point in chapter 1, including the claim that this Creator calls for a response from the (human) creatures.

42. Whitehead, *Process and Reality*, 342.

43. Ibid., 343.

44. Ibid., 346. For a discussion of the difficulties in the *ex nihilo* doctrine, see Thomas Jay Oord, *Defining Love: A Philosophical, Scientific, and Theological Engagement* (Grand Rapids: Brazos, 2010), 151–66. He notes the lack of biblical support (citing Jon Levenson and Claus Westermann), as well as the theological alternatives regarding absolute origin (citing Catherine Keller and David Ray Griffin). Cf. above, note 28 in the introduction for my comment on the relation of my project to Michael Lodahl's "Next to Nothing."

45. It is interesting that David Griffin speaks of God creating out of "relative nothing," chaos. *Two Great Truths: A New Synthesis of Scientific Naturalism and Christian Faith* (Louisville: Westminster John Knox, 2004), xxi.

46. Ted Peters, *God—The World's Future*, 2nd ed. (Minneapolis: Fortress Press, 2000), 98.

47. Whitehead, *Process and Reality*, 344.

48. Tyron L. Inbody, *The Transforming God: An Interpretation of Suffering and Evil* (Louisville: Westminster John Knox, 1997), 148.

49. Whitehead, *Process and Reality*, 345.

50. Ibid., 351.

51. Elizabeth A. Johnson, *She Who Is: The Mystery of God in Feminist Theological Discourse*, 2nd ed. (New York: Crossroad, 2002), 228, cf. 236. For Johnson's appreciative comment on "process theology's concepts of the reciprocal relation between God and the world, and the consequent nature of God," see 250–51.

52. To summarize: David Ray Griffin makes the point that if to be is to have power to produce an effect, in a relational world God simply could not have all the power. See Griffin's *Evil Revisited: Responses and Reconsiderations* (Albany: State University of

New York Press, 1991), chs. 6–7. In any case, the Whiteheadian God seems committed to calling creatures to a greater freedom. In this respect, Whitehead's God does bear responsibility for an increased risk of evil in human responses to God's initiative, even if one does not speak of an originating creating out of nothing.

53. Whitehead, *Process and Reality*, 58–59.
54. Ibid.
55. Ibid., 208.
56. Ibid.
57. Ibid., 21.
58. Alfred North Whitehead, *Modes of Thought* (New York: Free Press, 1938), 101–2.
59. Whitehead, *Adventures of Ideas*, 177.
60. Whitehead, *Process and Reality*, 27.
61. Ibid., 151.
62. Ibid., 17.
63. Whitehead, *Adventures of Ideas*, 226.
64. Whitehead, *Modes of Thought*, 73.
65. Ibid., 71.
66. Ibid., 72.
67. Ibid.
68. Ibid.
69. Ibid., 73.
70. Whitehead, *Symbolism: Its Meaning and Effect*, 52.
71. Whitehead, *Process and Reality*, 170.
72. Ibid.
73. Curtis Thompson has called my attention to a comparable passage in Kierkegaard's *Journals* where we hear that "a possibility is a beckoning by God" (3:337).
74. Ibid., 259. He immediately adds that "the importance of truth is, that it adds to interest."
75. Whitehead, *Adventures of Ideas*, 265.
76. See McDaniel, "The Passion of Christ," 206, on combining harmony and intensity "in openness to grace, both red and green."
77. Gilkey, "Process Theology," 20. Here Whitehead would find ethical significance in the dialectic pondered by contemporary students of "complexity." Thus, Ian Barbour writes, "Too much order makes change impossible; too much chaos makes continuity impossible." *Nature, Human Nature, and God* (Minneapolis: Fortress Press, 2002), 18. Cf. notes 50 and 51 in chapter 1. How closely the work of leading complexity theorist Stuart Kauffman coheres with Whitehead's understanding is debated within the process community. See *Process Perspectives* 31, no. 2 (Fall 2008), for the report of a seminar featuring Joseph Bracken and Philip Clayton on the theme of emergence. At issue is whether Kauffman's self-organizing systems have the subjectivity of Whitehead's actual occasions and whether the same laws of complexification work "all the way up."
78. Curtis Thompson has called my attention to a passage from a Harvard lecture in April 1925, when Whitehead was working out his atomic theory of time: "Wherever you get the aspect of continuity in space-time relation, you are dealing with possibilities." See Lewis S. Ford, *The Emergence of Whitehead's Metaphysics, 1925–1929* (Albany: State University of New York Press, 1984), app. 1, 285.
79. Whitehead, *Process and Reality*, 21.
80. Ibid., 351.
81. Whitehead, *Adventures of Ideas*, 207.
82. Marjorie Suchocki, *God, Christ, Church: A Practical Guide to Process Theology*, rev. ed. (New York: Crossroad, 1992), 55.
83. Whitehead, *Process and Reality*, 342.

84. Ibid.

85. Whitehead, *Religion in the Making*, 75.

86. Ibid., 153.

87. Above, "The Galilean Vision" section of this chapter, quoting Whitehead, *Process and Reality*, 344.

88. Whitehead, *Process and Reality*, 47.

89. Ibid., 87. A very helpful recent discussion of the reversal of the poles is available in Marjorie Hewitt Suchocki, "The Dynamic God," 39–58, *Process Studies*, 39:1 (Spring–Summer 2010).

90. Ibid., 164.

91. Whitehead, *Adventures of Ideas*, 113.

92. Ibid., 112.

93. Whitehead, *Process and Reality*, 88.

94. Whitehead, *Adventures of Ideas*, 172.

95. Whitehead, *Process and Reality*, 67; cf. 189, 344.

96. Thomas Jay Oord notes that "God exerts oscillating and diverse causal efficacy" and cites David Ray Griffin's recognition in Whitehead of "variable divine influence." *Defining Love*, 196.

97. Whitehead, *Process and Reality*, 188.

98. Whitehead, *Adventures of Ideas*, 296.

99. Ibid., 285.

100. Walter Brueggemann, *A Social Reading of the Old Testament: Prophetic Approaches to Israel's Communal Life*, ed. Patrick Miller (Minneapolis: Fortress Press, 1994), 224.

101. Walter Brueggemann, *The Prophetic Imagination*, 2nd ed. (Minneapolis: Fortress Press, 2001), 64.

102. Whitehead, *Process and Reality*, 65.

103. Terence E. Fretheim, *God and World in the Old Testament: A Relational Theology of Creation* (Nashville: Abingdon, 2005), 278–84.

104. Ibid., 278.

105. Cf. Whitehead, *Process and Reality*, 164, on God's decision in relation to "the *entire* multiplicity" of forms of relatedness ("eternal objects" in Whitehead's technical vocabulary). Cf. ibid., 257, on how "the general relationships of eternal objects to each other, relationships of diversity and of pattern, are their relationships in God's conceptual realization."

106. Ibid., 33–34. Whitehead also considers *appetition* and *intuition* as possible terms to characterize the primordial nature.

107. Ibid., 245. In her 2011 Claremont doctoral dissertation, "Living Poetry: The Community of Actual Imagination in the Image of God," Kirsten Mebust analyzes the twenty-some references to imagination in *Process and Reality*, emphasizing the role played in the becoming of an actual occasion.

108. Ibid., 32.

109. Ibid., 4–5.

110. Cf. Walker Percy, *Lost in the Cosmos: The Last Self-Help Book* (New York: Farrar, Straus & Giroux, 1983), 1.

111. Edith Wyschogrod, *Saints and Postmodernism: Revisioning Moral Philosophy* (Chicago: University of Chicago Press, 1990), 234.

112. Catherine Keller, "'To Illuminate Your Trace': Self in Late Modern Feminist Theology," *Listening* 5, no. 3 (1990): 221. A fuller statement is available in her *From a Broken Web: Separation, Sexism and the Self* (Boston: Beacon, 1986).

113. See, e.g., Whitehead, *Process and Reality*, 91: "The arbitrary, as it were 'given,' elements in the laws of nature warn us that we are in a special cosmic epoch." Among the special elements are the electromagnetic laws, "the four dimensions of the spatio-

temporal continuum, the geometrical axioms, even the mere dimensional character of the continuum . . . and the fact of measurability."

114. Cf. Arthur Peacocke, *Paths from Science to God* (Oxford: Oneworld, 2001), 72, on our arrival "at midnight's bell"; and Alan Weisman's remarkable *The World without Us* (New York: St. Martin's, 2007).

115. Robert C. Neville, *The Cosmology of Freedom* (New Haven: Yale University Press, 1974), 28.

116. Whitehead, *Process and Reality*, 108.

117. Whitehead, *Modes of Thought*, 27–28.

118. Ibid., 27.

119. Whitehead, *Process and Reality*, 47.

120. The most striking examples would be John B. Cobb Jr., writing extensively on ecological and economic issues, and David R. Griffin, energetically critiquing "American empire" politics.

121. Alfred North Whitehead, *Science and the Modern World* (New York: Macmillan, 1925, 1967), 89.

122. Ian Barbour, *Nature, Human Nature, and God* (Minneapolis: Fortress Press, 2002), 98. Barbour responds favorably to Joseph Bracken's efforts to speak of the self as "an ongoing structured field of activity for successive actual occasions as momentary subjects of experience."

123. Catherine Keller, *From a Broken Web*, 230. She is quoting Whitehead from *Adventures of Ideas*, 195, where he appeals to this notion of causal independence of contemporaries to be "the preservative of the elbow-room within the Universe."

124. For a spirited defense of Whitehead's understanding of selfhood as adequate to feminist concerns, see Marit Trelstad, "Relationality Plus Individuality: The Value of Creative Self-Agency," *dialog* (Summer 1999): 193–98. In "Lavish Love: A Covenantal Ontology," 109–24, in *Cross Examinations,* she argues that "the active love of God is directed to invigorate human action, not suppress it" (121).

125. Caryn D. Riswold appropriates the Lutheran language in *Coram Deo: Human Life in the Vision of God* (Eugene, Ore.: Wipf & Stock, 2006), an insightful dialogue between Luther's writings and process thought.

126. Søren Kierkegaard, *The Sickness unto Death*, ed. and trans. Howard V. Hong and Edna H. Hong (Princeton: Princeton University Press, 1980), 29: "Thus, consciousness is decisive. Generally speaking, consciousness—that is, self-consciousness—is decisive with regard to the self. The more consciousness, the more self; the more consciousness, the more will; the more will, the more self. A person who has no will at all is not a self; but the more will he has, the more self-consciousness he has also."

Chapter 3

1. See Dee Brown, *Bury My Heart at Wounded Knee: An Indian History of the American West* (New York: Holt, Rinehart & Winston, 1971). Brown notes that one in four Cherokees died during the winter march in 1838–39. He also notes that other native nations (the Choctaws, Chickasaws, Creeks, Seminoles, Shawnees, Miamis, Ottawas, Hurons, and Delawares) experienced such forced relocation.

2. Colum McCann, *Let the Great World Spin* (New York: Random House, 2009), 365–66.

3. It is *one* target, of course. See, for example, Isabelle Stenger's comment in "The Answer of a Happy Elephant," *Process Studies* 37, no. 2 (Fall–Winter 2008): 164–89, on how "thinking with Whitehead" (the title of her book forthcoming in translation from Harvard University Press) makes a decisive difference in how we regard tradition: "The efficacy of religious propositions demands their own adventure, reclaiming the

empowering environment of worship practices, without which those propositions risk remaining mute metaphors, vainly calling for the kind of leap they require" (187–88). More generally, she writes, "Whitehead's task was to reclaim rationality as an adventure" (187). David Brown has contributed two important volumes to this challenge of the "moving text." See *Tradition and Imagination* (New York: Oxford University Press, 1999); and *Discipleship and Imagination* (New York: Oxford University Press, 2000).

4. Søren Kierkegaard, *The Concept of Anxiety*, ed. and trans. Reidar Thomte (Princeton: Princeton University Press, 1980), 90.

5. From 1844 *Philosophical Fragments*, ed. and trans. Howard V. Hong and Edna H. Hong (Princeton: Princeton University Press, 1985), and from 1846 *Concluding Unscientific Postscript to Philosophical Fragments*, ed. and trans. Howard V. Hong and Edna H. Hong (Princeton: Princeton University Press, 1992).

6. See the discussion in chapter 2, citing *Process and Reality*, ed. David Ray Griffin and Donald W. Sherburne (New York: Free Press, 1984), 208–9.

7. Alfred North Whitehead, *Symbolism: Its Meaning and Effect* (New York: Fordham University Press, 1985), 36.

8. John B. Cobb, *A Christian Natural Theology* (Philadelphia: Westminster, 1965), 69.

9. Ted Peters, "The Terror of Time," 56–66, *dialog* 39, no. 1 (Spring 2000): 60. Peters is citing C. J. Isham's "Creation of the Universe as a Quantum Process," in *Physics, Philosophy and Theology*, ed. Robert John Russell, William R. Stoeger, and George V. Coyne (Vatican City-State: Vatican Observatory; Notre Dame: University of Notre Dame Press, 1988) on Einstein's understanding of general relativity and special relativity. Jonathan P. Strandjord makes a related point in "Varieties of Temporal Experience," *Process Studies* 17, no. 1 (Spring 1988), 19–25.

10. In a study of 1 Cor. 15:20-28, David E. Fredrickson offers a biblical rendition of this priority. He sees in Paul "a destruction of order as the separation and hierarchical arrangement of physical effects. In its place comes a narrative order, an order of time." David E. Fredrickson, "Paul Playfully on Time and Eternity," 21–26, *dialog* 39, no. 1 (Spring 2000): 25.

11. Ian G. Barbour, "Creation and Cosmology," in *Cosmos as Creation*, ed. Ted Peters (Nashville: Abingdon, 1989), 143. There is a debate over the matter as to how to read Einstein's theory of special relativity and the block universe which seems to favor rather a "spatialization of time." In "A Response to David Bohm's 'Time, the Implicate Order and Pre-Space,'" 209–18, in *Physics and the Ultimate Significance of Time*, ed. David Ray Griffin (Albany: State University of New York Press, 1986), 211, Robert John Russell puts the question succinctly: "From the standpoint of physics, are irreversible processes at the macrolevel reducible to reversible microprocesses, or is there an irreducible physical basis for time's arrow?" I find helpful Ian Barbour's summary elsewhere: "In relativity theory there are some events that are past for one observer and future for another observer, but for any two events that could be causally related there is an absolute distinction of past and future for all possible observers. There is no way in which a future event could influence the past or present, according to relativity theory." "Bohm and Process Philosophy: A Response to Griffin and Cobb," 161–71 in *Physics and the Ultimate Significance of Time*, 168. See also Chris J. Isham and John C. Polkinghorne, "The Debate over the Block Universe," in *Quantum Cosmology and the Laws of Nature: Scientific Perspectives on Divine Action*, ed. Robert J. Russell, Nancey C. Murphy, and Chris J. Isham (Vatican City-State: Vatican Observatory Publications; Berkeley: Center for Theology and the Natural Sciences, 1993).

12. See Joyce Cuff and Curtis Thompsons, *Nature Alive: A Scientist and a Theologian Conversing on the Divine Promise of Possibility* (forthcoming), ch. 3.

13. Ian Barbour, *Religion in an Age of Science* (San Francisco: HarperSanFrancisco, 1990), 158.

14. Rita Nakashima Brock and Susan Brooks Thistlethwaite have made this point well in an insightful study of prostitution. They write of how "the body stores our spiritual and material legacy." See their *Casting Stones: Prostitution and Liberation in Asia and the United States* (Minneapolis: Augsburg Fortress, 1995), 277.

15. Søren Kierkegaard, *The Sickness unto Death*, ed. and trans. Howard V. Hong and Edna H. Hong (Princeton: Princeton University Press, 1980), 38–39.

16. Barack Obama, *Dreams from My Father: A Story of Race and Inheritance* (New York: Three Rivers, 1995, 2004), 242.

17. Cf. Sydney Mead, *The Lively Experiment* (New York: Harper, 1963).

18. Ibid., 7.

19. Bill Gates, *The Road Ahead* (New York: Viking Penguin, 1995).

20. See the discussion of Augustine and Plotinus in Wolfhart Pannenberg, "Eternity, Time and the Trinitarian God," 9–14, *dialog* 39, no. 1 (Spring 2000): 10.

21. Claus Westermann, *Creation,* trans. John J. Scullion (Philadelphia: Fortress Press, 1974), 56.

22. Terence E. Fretheim, *Creation Untamed: The Bible, God, and Natural Disasters* (Grand Rapids: Baker Academic, 2010), 14. See the full first chapter, "God Created the World Good, Not Perfect."

23. Paul Ricoeur, *Time and Narrative* (Chicago: University of Chicago Press, 1984), 1:3.

24. Leslie Marmon Silko, *Ceremony* (New York: Viking, 1977), 2.

25. Patricia O'Hanlon Hudson and William Hudson O'Hanlon, *Rewriting Love Stories: Brief Marital Therapy* (New York: Norton, 1991).

26. Michael Walzer, *Interpretation and Social Criticism* (Cambridge: Harvard University Press, 1987). I have discussed this category in *The Pulse of Creation: God and the Transformation of the World* (Minneapolis: Fortress Press, 1999), 78–83.

27. I am thinking of the optimistic tone of Thomas Berry and Brian Swimme's *The Universe Story* (San Francisco: Harper San Francisco, 1992).

28. Obama, *Dreams from my Father,* 191.

29. Ibid., 195.

30. William Shakespeare, *Shakespeare's Sonnets,* ed. Edward Bliss Reed (New Haven: Yale University Press, 1925), 33.

31. Victor Lowe, *Alfred North Whitehead: The Man and His Work* (Baltimore: Johns Hopkins University Press, 1985, 1990), 2:34.

32. Neal Gabler puts this question to *TIME* magazine's "Man of the year" for 2009, Mark Zuckerberg, regarding his contention that e-mail, "the last link to traditional, epistolary, interpersonal communication," is "outmoded," soon to be replaced by a "social Inbox device." Gabler's charge is not trivial: "Zuckerberg is the anti-Gutenberg, creating a typography in which complexity is impossible and meaninglessness reigns supreme." See "A Modern-Day Gutenberg without the Helpful Impact," *Minneapolis StarTribune,* December 5, 2010. There is ambiguity also in these developments, for one surely appreciates the transformative power of social media as illustrated in the Arab world so dramatically in February 2011.

33. See Ray Kurzweil, *The Age of Spiritual Machines* (New York: Viking, 1999); and Hans Moravec, *Robot: Mere Machine to Transcendent Mind* (New York: Oxford University Press, 1999). I am indebted to Ned Hayes for these references. Joel Garreau, *Radical Evolution: The Promise and Peril of Enhancing Our Minds, Our Bodies—and What It Means to Be Human* (New York: Broadway, 2005), paints a revolutionary picture of what is ahead through the technologies of genetics, robotics, information technology, and nanotechnology. As I make final revisions in February 2011, the news chan-

nels are energized by the victory of the computer "Watson" over the top two *Jeopardy!* champions.

34. For an accessible discussion of these questions, see Cuff and Thompson, *Nature Alive*, chs. 3, 6. They draw on Steven Pinker, *The Blank State: The Modern Denial of Human Nature* (New York: Penguin, 2002), 78–87, where emphasis is placed on environmental inputs interacting with the biological neural networks of the genetic program.

35. Philip Clayton, *Transforming Christian Theology: For Church and Society* (Minneapolis: Fortress Press, 2009), 44.

36. Emmanuel Levinas, *Totality and Infinity: An Essay on Exteriority*, trans. A. Linguis (Pittsburgh: Duquesne University Press, 1969), 39.

37. Richard Kearney, "Others and Aliens: Between Good and Evil," in *Evil after Postmodernism: Histories Narratives, and Ethics*, ed. Jennifer L. Geddes, 101–13 (New York: Routledge, 2001), 106. Kearney calls for bringing together "an *aporetics of hospitality* represented by Derridean deconstruction" and "an *ethics of judgment* inspired by Ricoeurian hermeneutics."

38. Kierkegaard questions the necessity of the past in a dense "Interlude" in *Philosophical Fragments*.

39. See Alfred North Whitehead, *Modes of Thought* (New York: Free Press, 1938, 1966), 1–19, 103–4.

40. Søren Kierkegaard, *The Concept of Anxiety*, 44–45.

41. The record for our guides seems somewhat mixed as well. Kierkegaard's famous failure is to be found in breaking his engagement with Regina Olson. See his own account in *Søren Kierkegaard's Journals and Papers*, ed. and trans. Howard V. Hong and Edna H. Hong (Bloomington: Indiana University Press, 1970), 5:5521 for his remorseful "My sin was that I did not have faith, faith to believe that with God all things are possible." In *Kierkegaard and the Treachery of Love* (Cambridge: Cambridge University Press, 2002), Amy Laura Hall uses *Works of Love* to draw out the theme of how our lives with the other invariably flounder. Whitehead could be quite venturesome, as in leaving a secure professorship at Cambridge to go to London, leaving "the groove," experiencing unemployment in the academic year 1901–1902, and setting out for Harvard's Cambridge at the age of sixty-three. See Lowe, *Alfred North Whitehead*.

42. Douglas John Hall, "Theology of the Cross: Challenge and Opportunity for the Post-Christendom Church," 252–53, in *Cross Examination: Readings on the Meaning of the Cross Today*, ed. Marit Trelstad (Minneapolis: Fortress Press, 2006), 254.

43. Richard Dawkins, *The God Delusion* (Boston: Houghton Mifflin, 2006); Sam Harris, *The End of Faith* (New York: Norton, 2004); and Daniel Dennett, *Breaking the Spell: Religion as a Natural Phenomenon* (London: Viking, 2006), represent a wider group of "new atheists."

44. David Hume, *Dialogues Concerning Natural Religion*, ed. Henry D. Aiken (New York: Hafner, 1948), 66.

45. Ibid., 71.

46. See chapter 2 and the discussion of the difficulties of the *ex nihilo* doctrine as summarized by Thomas Jay Oord, *Defining Love: A Philosophical, Scientific, and Theological Engagement* (Grand Rapids: Brazos, 2010), 151–66.

47. Søren Kierkegaard, *Christian Discourses*, ed. and trans. Howard V. Hong and Edna H Hong (Princeton: Princeton University Press, 1997), 127. Cf. my discussion of "The Art of Power" in chapter 1.

48. John Polkinghorne, *Quarks, Chaos and Christianity: Questions to Science and Religion*, rev. ed. (New York: Crossroad, 1994, 2005), 59. Christopher Southgate's *The Groaning of Creation: God, Evolution and the Problem of Evil* (Louisville: Westminster John Knox, 2008), 42, helpfully locates Polkinghorne (with Nancey Murphy and George Ellis) in the "developmental" form of "Good-Harm Analyses" in his chapter "Strategies of

Evolutionary Theodicy." For the biblical grounding of Polkinghorne's point, see Terence Fretheim, *Creation Untamed,* 21, on the "mess of creativity."

49. Polkinghorne, *Quarks, Chaos and Christianity,* 61.

50. Ibid., 54–55.

51. Pierre Bayle asks this question powerfully in his famous *Historical and Critical Dictionary* (London: Harper, 1710). Bayle greatly influenced Herman Melville in his dark reading of conflict in *Moby Dick.*

52. Simone de Beauvoir, *The Ethics of Ambiguity,* trans. Bernard Frechtman (New York: Philosophical Library, 1948, 1976), 10.

53. The title is Greg Boyd's. Boyd is one of several evangelical writers (e.g., William Hasker, Clark Pinnock) who join process thought in this recognition that, in some measure, the future is open for God. For a treatment of this dialogue, see John B. Cobb and Clark H. Pinnock, eds., *Searching for an Adequate God* (Grand Rapids: Eerdmans, 2000). Terence E. Fretheim develops this theme in biblical literature in *The Suffering of God: An Old Testament Perspective* (Philadelphia: Fortress Press, 1984), ch. 4.

54. John Hick, *Evil and the God of Love* (New York: Harper, 1966), 317.

55. Barack Obama, *The Audacity of Hope: Thoughts on Reclaiming the American Dream* (New York: Three Rivers, 2006).

56. Simone de Beauvoir, *The Ethics of Ambiguity,* 129.

57. That wide-ranging secular hope is exhaustively portrayed by Ernst Bloch in *The Principle of Hope* (Cambridge, Mass.: MIT Press, 1986).

58. George Steiner, *Real Presences* (Chicago: University of Chicago Press, 1989), 3.

59. Whitehead apparently was attracted to agnosticism early in his life. See Lowe, *Alfred North Whitehead,* 1:140–41, for his attraction to Newman and his comment in his student days that one should either go to Rome or in the other direction. Lowe speaks of his agnostic period lasting "about a quarter of a century" (188). Atheism found a formidable representative in Bertrand Russell, with whom he had a ten-year collaboration, marked notably by the coauthorship of the three volumes of *Principia Mathematica* (1910–1913). Lowe reports (2:138) that Russell and daughter Jessie agree that Whitehead's turn to religion was at least occasioned by son Eric's death in World War I and adds the comment that the war "decisively ended an age of secular progress and hope" (2:188).

60. Sigmund Freud, *The Future of an Illusion,* trans. James Strachey (New York: Norton, 1961), 56.

61. Richard Dawkins, *The God Delusion,* 56–57, 59. Gould's work is *Rocks of Ages: Science and Religion on the Fullness of Life* (New York: Ballantine, 1999).

62. I have discussed the science and religion conversation in *Speaking of God* (St. Louis: Chalice, 2006), ch. 6.

63. Richard Dawkins, *The God Delusion,* 18–19; cf. his emphasis on the "supernatural" in his definition of religion (31). Fortunately, there are more considered challenges. See, for example, John Rawls, *A Brief Inquiry into the Meaning of Sin and Faith,* ed. Thomas Nagel (Cambridge, Mass.: Harvard University Press, 2009). Unfortunately, they do not receive the attention Dawkins's tirades do.

64. For a collection of panentheistic positions, see Philip Clayton and Arthur Peacocke, eds., *In Whom We Live and Move and Have Our Being: Panentheistic Reflections on God's Presence in a Scientific World* (Grand Rapids: Eerdmans, 2004). It is interesting that the editors pretty well represent the two magisteria.

65. I have written of this in "The Knowledge of God," in *Christian Dogmatics,* ed. Carl Braaten and Robert Jenson, 193–264 (Philadelphia: Fortress Press, 1984). See especially "The Legitimation and Limitation of the Knowledge of God," 207–10.

66. Aristotle, *Nichomachean Ethics,* trans. W. D. Ross, 8th ed. (London: Oxford University Press, 1915), 3:9.

67. Søren Kierkegaard, *Either/Or*, ed. and trans. Howard V. Hong and Edna H. Hong (Princeton: Princeton University Press, 1987), 1:3. Kierkegaard's dissertation, *On the Concept of Irony with Constant Reference to Socrates*, was actually published first, but he always regarded his authorship to have begun with *Either/Or.*

68. Søren Kierkegaard, *Concluding Unscientific Postscript to Philosophical Fragments*, ed. and trans. Howard V. Hong and Edna H. Hong (Princeton: Princeton University Press, 1992), 1:46–49.

69. See chapter 2, "A Deeper Experience," on Whitehead's reading of the "withness of the body" in our perception. I am indebted to Kirsten Mebust for her emphasis on the importance of embodiment.

70. Sponheim, *Speaking of God*, 8.

71. William James, "The Will to Believe," in *Religion from Tolstoy to Camus*, ed. Walter Kaufmann, 221–38, (New York: Harper, 1961), 235.

72. Ibid., 237.

73. See especially William James, *A Pluralistic Universe*, in *William James: Writings 1902–1910* (New York: Library of America, 1987).

74. Ibid., 815.

75. Ibid.

76. Kierkegaard, *The Sickness unto Death*, 31.

77. Kierkegaard, *Journals,* 1:1030. Cf. ibid., 1:1025.

78. Samuel Taylor Coleridge, *The Complete Works of Samuel Taylor Coleridge*, ed. W. G. T. Shedd (New York: Harper, 1884), 3:491. For a contemporary statement, see Arthur H. Modell, *Imagination and the Meaningful Brain* (Cambridge, Mass.: MIT Press, 2003), for a discussion of the role of the imagination in the "metaphoric process" involved in the brain's constructing and reconstructing a world.

79. John Dewey, *Reconstruction in Philosophy* (Boston: Beacon, 1920, 1948), 103. Mark Johnson has drawn heavily on Dewey in writing of how the imagination can be creative and transformative in constructing a world for the self. See his *The Meaning of the Body: Aesthetics of Human Understanding* (Chicago: University of Chicago Press, 2007).

80. Whitehead, *Process and Reality*, 5.

81. William Stafford, "Bi-Focal," as quoted in Donald Capps, *The Poet's Gift: Toward the Renewal of Pastoral Care* (Louisville: Westminster John Knox, 1993), 152.

82. S. T. Coleridge, quoting from the *Notebooks* (March, 1808), as cited in *Coleridge's Responses,* ed. Samantha Harvey (London: Continuum, 2008), 3:3290.

83. Whitehead, *Process and Reality*, 111.

84. Dewey, *Reconstruction in Philosophy*, 211.

85. Coleridge, *Complete Works* (Shedd), 3:363.

86. Walter Brueggemann, *The Prophetic Imagination* (Philadelphia: Fortress Press, 1978), 97. The crucial doubleness of the imagination's role is well stated by Michael Fishbane in *Sacred Attunement: A Jewish Theology* (Chicago: University of Chicago Press, 2008), 140–42, in speaking of "the double ellipse of religious speech."

87. Brueggemann, *The Prophetic Imagination*, 106. For a comparably dialectical statement from a feminist perspective, see Krista E. Hughes, "In the Flesh: A Feminist Vision of Hope," 212–23, in *Cross Examinations.*

88. Craig R. Dykstra, *Vision and Character: A Christian Educator's Alternative to Kohlberg* (Mahwah, N.J.: Paulist, 1981), 83.

89. Søren Kierkegaard, *Practice in Christianity*, ed. and trans. Howard V. Hong and Edna H. Hong (Princeton: Princeton University Press, 1991), 67.

90. Arnold Come, *Kierkegaard as Theologian: Recovering My Self* (Montreal: McGill-Queen's University Press, 1997), 335.

91. Iris Murdoch, "The Darkness of Practical Reason," *Encounter* 27 (July 1966), as cited by M. Jaimie Ferreira, "Faith and the Kierkegaardian Leap," in *Cambridge*

Companion to Kierkegaard, ed. Alastair Hannay and Gordon D. Marino, 207–34 (Cambridge: Cambridge University Press, 1998), 231.

92. Ferreira, "Faith and the Kierkegaardian Leap," 226.

93. Ekkehard Muhlenberg, "*Synergia* and Justification by Faith," in *Discord, Dialogue, and Concord: The Lutheran Reformation's Formula of Concord,* ed. L. W. Spitz and W. Lohff, 15–37 (Philadelphia: Fortress Press, 1977), 34. My emphasis.

94. Kierkegaard, *Practice in Christianity,* 160.

95. M. Jamie Ferreira, *Transforming Vision: Imagination and Will in Kierkegaardian Faith* (Oxford: Clarendon, 1991), 124.

96. See Arnold Come, *Kierkegaard as Humanist: Discovering My Self* (Montreal: McGill-Queen's University Press, 1995), ch. 8.

97. Kierkegaard, *The Sickness unto Death,* 35–37.

98. David J. Gouwens, *Kierkegaard's Dialectic of the Imagination* (New York: Peter Lang, 1988), 277. David Brown has written creatively of the role of imagination in claiming in fresh contexts the message of the "moving text" of the biblical witness. See his *Tradition and Imagination* and *Discipleship and Imagination.* See the discussion above in note 3 of this chapter.

99. Cf. above, ch. 2, "A Deeper Experience."

100. Brueggemann, *The Prophetic Imagination,* 66.

101. Whitehead, *Process and Reality,* 5.

102. In her pathbreaking "epistemology of the cross" Mary Solberg calls for criticism of "the neat partnership between epistemological hubris and the quasi-religious belief in progress." See *Compelling Knowledge: A Feminist Proposal for an Epistemology of the Cross* (Albany: State University of New York Press, 1997), 110.

103. For a discussion of a distinction between hope and optimism, see Thomas Jay Oord, *Defining Love: A Philosophical, Scientific, and Theological Engagement* (Grand Rapids: Brazos, 2010), 69–71. Citing the studies of Patricia L. Bruininks, he stresses the specificity of hope. A useful introduction to attempts to justify believing hope is Michael L. Peterson, *God and Evil* (Boulder, Colo.: Westview, 1998). Jeff Astley, David Brown, and Ann Loades, eds., *Evil: A Reader* (New York: T & T Clark, 2003) provides an excellent sample of sources. My own venture here is *God: The Question and the Quest* (Philadelphia: Fortress Press, 1985).

104. Kierkegaard, *The Sickness unto Death,* 79. The Danish for "directly before which" is *lige overfor hvilket. Søren Kierkegaards Samlede Vaerker* (København: Gyldendalske Boghandel, 1905), 11:191.

105. Kierkegaard, *The Sickness unto Death,* 79. A little later (85; cf. 123), he adds a christological intensification, writing of any individual human being, "For this person's sake, also for this very person's sake, God comes to the world, allows himself to be born to suffer, to die, and this suffering God—he almost implores and beseeches this person to accept the help that is offered to him."

106. Ibid., 113–14.

107. Kierkegaard, *The Concept of Anxiety,* 17. Cf. Amy Hall, *The Treachery of Love.*

108. Kierkegaard, *Practice in Christianity,* 67.

109. Cf. Nelson Pike, *God and Timelessness* (London: Routledege & Kegan Paul, 1990). Pike puzzles over how a timeless God could be said to know the future, or indeed anything at all.

110. The language used in the classic formulation of the Council of Chalcedon, 451.

111. Paul R. Sponheim, *God: The Question and the Quest,* ch. 3.

112. Søren Kierkegaard, *Søren Kierkegaard's Journals and Papers,* ed. and trans. Howard V. Hong and Edna H. Hong (Bloomington, Ind.: Indiana University Press, 1970), 3: 2554. Cf. ch. one, "God Willing One Thing in Creation and Redemption."

113. Kierkegaard, *Journals and Papers,* 5:5468.

114. Alfred North Whitehead, *Adventures of Ideas* (1929; New York: Free Press, 1978), 170.

115. I have also discussed these offerings in *God: The Question and the Quest*, chs. 5–7.

116. So Philip Clayton argues in the order of the Christian triad—"belonging, behaving, believing"—in *Transforming Christian Theology for Church and Society* (Minneapolis: Fortress Press, 1010), 39–42.

117. An eloquent Jewish theology of protest is David R. Blumenthal's "Theodicy: Dissonance in Theory and Praxis," in *The Fascination of Evil*, ed. David Tracy and Hermann Häring, 95–106 (Maryknoll, N.Y.: Orbis, 1998).

118. Dietrich Bonhoeffer, *Creation and Fall*, trans. Douglas Stephen Bax, ed. John W. de Gruchy (Minneapolis: Fortress Press, 1997), 63.

119. Ibid.

120. Ibid.

121. See especially *Life Together: Prayerbook of the Bible*, trans. Daniel W. Bloesch and James H. Burtness (Minneapolis: Fortress Press, 1996).

122. Bonhoeffer, *Creation and Fall*, 66–67.

123. Paul Ricoeur states the ironically connecting character of dying in *Living Up to Death*, trans. David Pellauer (Chicago: University of Chicago Press, 2009), 14: "It is perhaps only in the face of death that the religious gets equated with the Essential and that the barrier between religions, including the nonreligions (I am thinking, of course, of Buddhism) is transcended. But because dying is transcultural, it is transconfessional, transreligious." In *Let the Great World Spin*, 107, Colum McCann makes the point powerfully in the words of Claire, a Park Avenue lioness meeting with other women who have lost sons in Vietnam, women from very different socioeconomic settings: "Death, the greatest democracy of them all. The world's oldest complaint. Happens to us all. Rich and poor. Fat and thin. Fathers and daughters. Mothers and sons."

124. Jonathan Strandjord, "Suffering, Desire, Temptation, and Ecstatic Apologetics," in *God, Evil, and Suffering: Essays in Honor of Paul R. Sponheim*, ed., Terence Fretheim and Curtis Thompson, 136–42 (St. Paul: Word & World, 2000), 142.

Chapter 4

1. This is the appeal of Harold Kushner's best-selling *When Bad Things Happen to Good People* (New York: Shocken, 1981). I am not thinking of care that reduces the efficacy of the suffering for the victim, but of action that "lives against" the *causes* of the suffering. I do recognize the importance of the former, as well represented by such a theologically informed "practical" response as Jerry K. Robbins's *Carevision: The Why and How of Christian Care-Giving* (Valley Forge, Pa.: Judson, 1993). Similarly, Jürgen Moltmann identifies two questions as "the so-called theodicy question" and "the existential question about community with God in suffering." See his "The Crucified God: Yesterday, and Today: 1972–2002," in *Cross Examinations: Readings on the Meaning of the Cross Today*, ed. Marit Trelstad, 127–38 (Minneapolis: Fortress Press, 2006), 128–29. Citing Whitehead, he takes the second question as his focus. I want to hold these two questions together, but in this chapter the second question presses.

2. Emmanuel Levinas, *Ethics and Infinity: Conversations with Phillipe Nemo*, trans. Richard Cohen (Pittsburgh: Duquesne University Press, 1985), 77.

3. Alfred North Whitehead, *Process and Reality: An Essay in Cosmology*, corrected ed., ed. David Ray Griffin and Donald W. Sherburne (1933; New York: Free Press, 1978), 88.

4. Ibid., 247.

5. Ibid., 88.

6. Ibid., 339. For a one-hundred-page treatment of this larger point, see part 1 of *Adventures of Ideas* (New York: Macmillan, 1933, 1961).

7. Whitehead, *Process and Reality*, 339. Terence Fretheim connects the biblical expression of "created good not perfect" with the command to "subdue" the earth (Gen. 1:28) thusly: "the best sense for the verb is 'to bring order out of continuing disorder.'" See his *Creation Untamed: The Bible, God, and Natural Disasters* (Grand Rapids: Baker Academic, 2010), 13–14.

8. I have found reason to cite particularly the work of Stuart Kauffman in chapters 1 (nn50–51) and 2 (n77).

9. For a brief summary of this conversation, see Paul R. Sponheim, *Speaking of God: Relational Theology* (St. Louis: Chalice, 2006), 65–66. An outstanding example of the conversation is Joyce M. Cuff and Curtis L. Thompson, *Nature Alive: A Scientist and a Theologian Conversing on the Divine Promise of Possibility* (forthcoming). More-detailed discussions are available in Keith Ward, *Divine Action* (London: Collins, 1990) (stressing "bottom-up"); and John Polkinghorne, *Quarks, Chaos and Christianity* (New York: Crossroad, 2001) (stressing "top-down"). The most comprehensive sorting of the options is Herb Gruning, *How in the World Does God Act?* (Lanham, Md.: University Press of America, 2000).

10. See my discussion in *Speaking of God,* 60–66.

11. Dietrich Bonhoeffer, *Ethics*, ed. Clifford J. Green, trans. Reinhard Krauss, Charles C. West, and Douglas W. Stott (Minneapolis: Fortress Press, 2005), 178.

12. Ibid., 4, 389.

13. Ibid., 70. Cf. 428.

14. Ibid., 394. In "A Theology of the Cross for the 'Uncreators,'" 181–95 in *Cross Examinations,* Cynthia Moe-Lobeda stresses Bonhoeffer's call for action "recognizing social evil, naming it and 'putting a spoke in the wheel' of earthly powers that demand disobedience to God," 192.

15. Søren Kierkegaard, *The Moment and Late Writings*, trans. Howard V. Hong and Edna H. Hong (Princeton: Princeton University Press, 1998). See, for example, issue no. 3 (141–53). Such criticism is not rare in Kierkegaard's journals either, where he writes of the "barbaric behavior" in this mixing of church and state.

16. Kierkegaard, *The Moment*, 271. A fascinating secondary study here is Patrick Sheil's *Kierkegaard and Levinas: The Subjunctive Mood* (Surrey, U.K.: Ashgate, 2010).

17. Vitor Westhelle, "The Word and the Mask: Revisiting the Two-Kingdoms Doctrine," in *The Gift of Grace: The Future of Lutheran Theology,* ed. Niels Henrik Gregersen, Bo Holm, Ted Peters, and Peter Widmann, 167–78 (Minneapolis: Fortress Press, 2005), 177.

18. Deanna A. Thompson, *Crossing the Divide: Luther, Feminism, and the Cross* (Minneapolis: Augsburg Fortress, 2004), 102. In "Experiencing the Spirit: The Magnificat, Luther and Feminists," in *Transformative Lutheran Theologies: Feminist, Womanist, and Mujerista Perspectives,* ed. Mary J. Streufert, 165–76 (Minneapolis: Fortress Press, 2010), 173, Lois Malcolm makes the point that Mary's "story of God 'seeing' her undid not her pride, but the 'cultural unraveling' she knew only too well." In *Holy Spirit: Creative Power in our Lives* (Minneapolis: Fortress Press, 2009), 57, Malcolm writes of how the Spirit can bring freedom from "our compulsive obsessive ways of being that keep us trapped in destructive patterns of behavior."

19. Søren Kierkegaard, *Concluding Unscientific Postscript to the Philosophical Fragments*, ed. and trans. Howard V. Hong and Edna H. Hong (Princeton: Princeton University Press, 1992), 1:245; cf. 243.

20. Whitehead, *Process and Reality*, 338.

21. Whitehead, *Adventures of Ideas*, 167.

22. Ibid.

23. Søren Kierkegaard, *Practice in Christianity*, ed. and trans. Howard V. Hong and Edna H. Hong (Princeton: Princeton University Press, 1991), supp.: 279.

24. Søren Kierkegaard, *The Sickness unto Death*, ed. and trans. Howard V. Hong and Edna H. Hong (Princeton: Princeton University Press, 1980), 100.

25. Kierkegaard, *Practice in Christianity*, 182–83. Similarly, "to forgive sinners is in the most decisive sense a qualification in terms of God." Ibid., 101; cf. 61. So, too, in *The Sickness unto Death*, Anti-Climacus writes, "There is one way in which man could never in all eternity come to be like God: in forgiving sins" (122).

26. Kierkegaard, *Practice in Christianity*, 239. Cf. 238: "He who is truly to be the prototype and be related only to imitators must in one sense be *behind* people, propelling forward, while in another sense he stands *ahead,* beckoning."

27. Martin Luther, "Two Kinds of Righteousness," in *Martin Luther's Basic Theological Writings*, ed. Timothy Lull, 155–64 (Minneapolis: Fortress Press, 1989), 156–57.

28. Mark Thomsen, *Christ Crucified: A 21st Century Missiology of the Cross* (Minneapolis: Lutheran University Press, 2004), 33.

29. Rita Nakashima Brock and Rebecca Ann Parker, *Saving Paradise: How Christianity Traded Love of This World for Crucifixion and Empire* (Boston: Beacon, 1989).

30. Mark Heim, *Saved from Sacrifice: A Theology of the Cross* (Grand Rapids: Eerdmans, 2006). Drawing on René Girard's understanding of scapegoating, Heim writes of Christ going to the cross in order to *end* sacrifice. He is clear that "the God who paid the cost of the cross was not the one who changed it" (329).

31. Marcus J. Borg, *The Heart of Christianity: Rediscovering a Life of Faith* (San Francisco: HarperSanFrancisco, 2004), 92. He distinguishes "rejection and vindication," "the defeat of the powers," "the revelation of 'the way,'" the revelation of the depth of God's love, and the sacrificial, "Jesus died for our sins." He notes that the fifth is not fuly developed in the New Testament, "yet it is the one most emphasized in popular Christianity" (94). He argues that "Jesus died for our sins" "was originally a subversive metaphor," for "it was a metaphorical proclamation of radical grace" (95).

32. John B. Cobb Jr., *Christ in a Pluralistic Age* (Philadelphia: Westminster, 1975), 117. Cobb draws on the biblical studies of Walter Grundmann here.

33. Michael Welker, *God the Spirit*, trans. John F. Hoffmeyer (Minneapolis: Fortress Press, 1994), 238: "People are also drawn into this community and this force field independently of their knowledge of the Spirit (cf. Acts 19:2), independently of their works (see Titus 3:5), but also in and with their readiness to let themselves be filled by the Spirit (cf. e.g., Eph. 5:18)." On the conscious level, the cross and resurrection of Jesus may take priority in our knowing, but in God's doing the base is set in the Creator's work. If that is not clear in a given theology, distortions will arise in the understanding of Christ's work itself, as Gustaf Wingren was fond of pointing out to fervent Barthians.

34. Whitehead, *Adventures of Ideas,* 168–69.

35. For a strikingly diverse range of process-relational interpretations of the doctrine of the Trinity, see Joseph A. Bracken and Marjorie Suchocki, eds., *Trinity in Process: A Relational Theology of God* (New York: Continuum, 1999).

36. Søren Kierkegaard, *For Self-Examination* and *Judge for Yourself,* ed. and trans. Howard V. Hong and Edna H. Hong (Princeton: Princeton University Press, 1990), 76.

37. Welker, *God the Spirit,* 230–31.

38. Kierkegaard, *For Self-Examination,* 81–84.

39. Above, ch. 1, "God's Omnipotent Resolution." Perry Lefevre has usefully gathered many of these prayers in *The Prayers of Kierkegaard* (Chicago: University of Chicago Press, 1956).

40. Marjorie Hewitt Suchocki, *In God's Presence: Theological Reflections on Prayer* (St. Louis: Chalice, 1996), 46.

41. Suchocki, *In God's Presence*, 50. Similarly, Michael Fishbane writes, "Thus the praying self may thus reflect on its own responsibilities as a conduit of these divine forces, and the effect of its actions on God's presence." *Sacred Atunement: A Jewish Theology* (Chicago: University of Chicago Press, 1996), 139.

42. Ann Belford Ulanov, "What Do We Think People Are Doing When They Pray?" *Anglican Theological Review* 60, no. 4 (1978): 387–98, quoting from 388.

43. Edward Farley gathers these references (e.g., to Maurice Bondel, Martin Heidegger, Alfred Schutz, and Maurice Merleau-Ponty) in *Good and Evil: Interpreting a Human Condition* (Minneapolis: Fortress Press, 1990), 36–37.

44. Ibid.

45. David Tracy points out how "both the 'pagan' and the 'Jew' have too often served as the projected other of 'Christian' self-understanding." *Dialogue with the Other: The Inter-Religious Dialogue* (Grand Rapids: Eerdmans, 1990), 5. Sarah Pinnock, *Beyond Theodicy: Jewish and Christian Continental Thinkers Respond to the Holocaust* (Albany: State University of New York Press, 2002), is a particularly eloquent warning against "taking over" the other.

46. Emmanuel Levinas, *Totality and Infinity: An Essay on Exteriority*, trans. Alphonso Lingis (Pittsburgh: Duquesne University Press, 1969), 198.

47. Ibid., 39.

48. See Cuff and Thompson, *Nature Alive*, ch. 5, on how the other can function both as confrontation and invitation.

49. Levinas, *Totality and Infinity*,, 198.

50. Kierkegaard, *The Sickness unto Death*, 29.

51. Ibid., (my emphasis).

52. Ibid., 36. Kierkegaard does not fail to see the sinister side of that connectedness. Note the discussion of repentance in chapter one. That the self simply by itself is a distortion is recognized by other existentialist authors following in Kierkegaard's train. Jean-Paul Sartre, for example, writes of what he sees to be the "facticity of freedom": "the given which it has to be and which it illuminates by its project. . . . It is my place, my body, my past, my position in so far as it is already determined by the indications of Others, finally my fundamental relation to the Other." *Being and Nothingness*, trans. Hazel E. Barnes (New York: Philosophical Library, 1948), 494–96. Thus, Sartre can close the lyrical prose of his autobiography by speaking of "a whole man, composed of all men and as good as all of them and no better than any." Jean-Paul Sartre, *The Words*, trans. Bernard Frechtman (New York: George Braziller, 1964), 255.

53. Søren Kierkegaard, *Either/Or*, ed. and trans. Howard V. Hong and Edna H. Hong (Princeton: Princeton University Press, 1987), 2:239.

54. Hannah Arendt, *The Human Condition* (Chicago: University of Chicago Press, 1958, 1969), 237. In my discussion of this point in *Faith and the Other* (Minneapolis: Fortress Press, 1993), ch. 3, I cite the work of Lawrence Kohlberg concerning moral development where an increase in self-determination *and* increase in the reciprocity of relationship are linked in the movement toward internalization and universalization. See *The Philosophy of Moral Development: Moral Stages and the Idea of Justice* (San Francisco: Harper & Row, 1981). In feminist criticism of Kohlberg, the role of the other assumes even greater importance. Carol Gilligan made this point famously in *In a Different Voice: Psychological Theory and Women's Development* (Cambridge: Harvard University Press, 1982); and, with others, in *Mapping the Moral Domain: A Contribution of Women's Thinking to Psychological Theory and Education* (Cambridge, Mass.: Harvard University Press, 1988).

55. Whitehead, *Adventures of Ideas*, 157. Earlier (113), he applies this notion to understanding the topic of the laws of nature, writing of how laws are "immanent," for they describe the characters of the relevant things in nature and their interconnections. See also *Process and Reality*, 309, on how "the solidarity of the physical world" depends on "the fundamental internality of the relationships in question." See also chapter 2.

56. Jonathan P. Strandjord, "The Politics and Ethics of Beauty: A Theological Reconsideration of Conscience with the Aid of Whitehead and Levinas" (doctoral diss., Vanderbilt University, 1996), 159–60.

57. Levinas, *Totality and Infinity*, 291.

58. See the concern represented by Richard Kearney, "Others and Aliens: Between Good and Evil," in *Evil after Postmodernism: Histories, Narratives, and Ethics,* ed. Jennifer L. Geddes, 101–13 (London: Routledge, 2001), and our discussion in chapter 3, note 36.

59. Levinas, *Totality and Infinity*, 291. Similarly, another Jewish author, Michael Fishbane, writes of how "the fine attunements of relationships with one's neighbor—by strengthening the hand or treating it gently; by setting firm the foot or providing it with a crutch; by speaking the truth or not willfully dissembling in any way—all build up; the divine image in the world, the living divine image that appears to each person through the other." *Sacred Attunements*, 155.

60. Søren Kierkegaard, *Works of Love*, ed. and trans. Howard V. Hong and Edna H. Hong (Princeton: Princeton University Press, 1995), 56. See Amy Laura Hall, *Kierkegaard and the Treachery of Love* (Cambridge: Cambridge University Press, 2002), for a sustained reading of Kierkegaard that holds no hope for self-love.

61. Kierkegaard, *Works of Love*, 56.

62. Reinhold Niebuhr, *The Nature and Destiny of Man*, 2 vols. (New York: Charles Scribner's Sons, 1941–43). See especially 1:198–220.

63. Anders Nygren, *Agape and Eros*, trans. Philip S. Watson (London: SPCK, 1953), 217.

64. Ibid., 75–76. For a vivid contemporary statement of the "utterly gratuitous and therefore completely unconditional" character of God's love, see Miroslav Volf, "God Is Love," *The Christian Century* 127, no. 22 (November 2, 2010): 29–34. In *Defining Love: A Philosophical, Scientific, and Theological Engagement* (Grand Rapids: Brazos, 2010), 32–52, Thomas Jay Oord has a helpful discussion of the debate around Nygren's classic work. While I join the criticism of Nygren's disjunctive juxtaposing of agape and eros, I do note that Nygren introduces more relational themes in the third ("creative") and fourth ("initiator of fellowship with God") "features" of divine love.

65. Gene H. Outka, *Agape: An Ethical Analysis* (New Haven: Yale University Press, 1972), 277–79.

66. Ibid., 281.

67. Ibid. He nicely adds, "It is one thing to say that the agent is unable to love others without loving himself, another that loving them is simply a way of loving himself."

68. Ibid., 291. Don Browning sets this affirmation in relationship to other forms of love in writing, "Love as mutuality or equal-regard, with self-sacrifice serving as a transitional ethic designed to restore love as equal-regard, is an emerging dominant model of love in contemporary theological ethics." See his "Science and Religion on the Nature of Love," in *Altruism and Altruistic Love*, ed. Stephen G. Post, Lynn G. Underwood, Jeffrey P. Schloss, and William B. Hurlbut, 335–45 (New York: Oxford University Press, 2002), 339.

69. Marjorie Hewitt Suchocki, *The Fall to Violence: Original Sin in Relational Theology* (New York: Continuum, 1994), 152.

70. Catherine Keller, *From a Broken Web: Separation, Sexism and the Self* (Boston: Beacon, 1986), 12. The classic statement is, of course, Valerie Saiving's "The Human Situation: A Feminine View," in *Womanspirit Rising: A Feminist Reader in Religion*, ed. Carol Christ and Judith Plaskow (San Francisco: Harper & Row, 1979).

71. Kierkegaard, *Works of Love*, 18. In the discourse "The Woman Who Was a Sinner," Kierkegaard affirms the value of self-love in showing our need for God. See *Without Authority*, ed. and trans. Howard V. Hong and Edna H. Hong (Princeton: Princeton University Press, 1997), 149–60. Thus, the human need for God is our "highest

perfection." Cf. Stephen Evans, *Kierkegaard's Ethic of Love: Divine Command and Moral Obligations* (New York: Oxford University Press, 2004). Drawing on *The Sickness unto Death*, Wanda Warren Berry shows how one can sin "either by negating God in defiant 'strength' or by negating the self in weakly refusing to constitute a gathered will." See Wanda Warren Berry, "Images of Sin and Salvation in Feminist Theology," 25–54, *Anglican Theological Review* 60 (January 1978): 46. See also Celine Leon and Sylvia Walsh, eds., *Feminist Interpretations of Kierkegaard* (University Park: Pennsylvania State University Press, 1997).

72. Daniel Day Williams, *The Spirit and the Forms of Love* (New York: Harper & Row, 1968), 38. Geddes MacGregor, *He Who Lets Us Be: A Theology of Love* (New York: Seabury, 1975), 54, makes a comparable point in critiquing the classical notion that "He who 'sends' must be greater than he who is 'sent.'" Recognizing that the persons of the Trinity are truly equal in their eternality, one can appreciate there is the movement of love in both "directions." There is a remarkable convergence in recent theology on this point. To cite two otherwise very diverse theologians, see Robert W. Jenson's emphasis in *Christian Dogmatics*, ed. Carl Braaten and Robert W. Jenson (Philadelphia: Fortress Press, 1984), 1:156 ("The Spirit's witness to the Son is equally God-constituting with the traditional relations. And so is the Son's and the Spirit's joint reality as the openness into which the Father is freed from mere persistence in his pretemporal transcendence"); and Elizabeth Johnson's critique of "the structure of the processional model" in *She Who Is: The Mystery of God in Feminist Theological Discourse* (New York: Crossroad, 1992), 196, ("While affirming and promoting the equality of divine persons and their mutual interrelation, it nevertheless subverts this by its rigid hierarchical ordering").

73. Edward Vacek, *Love, Human and Divine: The Heart of Christian Ethics* (Washington, D.C.: Georgetown University Press, 1994), 201.

74. Browning, "Science and Religion on the Nature of Love," 339.

75. See Kierkegaard, *The Moment and late Writings*, 268, and our discussion in chapter 1, "God's Omnipotent Resolution" for Kierkegaard's prayer in *The Moment*.

76. Kierkegaard, *Works of Love*, 56.

77. Eberhard Jüngel, *God as the Mystery of the World*, trans. Darrell L. Guder (Grand Rapids: Eerdmans, 1983), 317.

78. Ibid., 318.

79. Ibid., where Jüngel appreciates Karl Barth's recognition of a "*common* place from which they both [agape and eros] come."

80. Michael Welker, *God the Spirit*, 313. Welker particularly draws on the work of Niklas Luhmann and the concept of how an organized social environment (a "domain of resonance") makes it possible for a self-referential center of action to become a person. Thomas Jay Oord in *Defining Love*, 89, draws on research by Samuel and Pearl Oliner (*The Altruistic Personality: Rescuers of Jews in Nazi Europe*), making the point that "those with an altruistic personality are typically both inclusive of and attached to others."

81. Welker, *God the Spirit*, 248–49.

82. Stephen Post, *Altruism and Altruistic Love*, 376, makes the point concisely: "It is a mistake to confuse the valid ideal of unselfishness with selflessness, its invalid exaggeration."

83. Harriet Goldhor Lerner, *The Dance of Anger: A Woman's Guide to Changing the Patterns of Intimate Relationships* (New York: Harper & Row, 1985), 123. Cf. Lerner's *The Dance of Intimacy* (New York: Harper & Row, 1989). She is working with the understanding of "self-differentiation" as that plays an essential role in the "eight concepts" forming the structure of Bowen family systems therapy theory. Here I am indebted to Rev. David Crum, who has particularly emphasized the connectedness between Bowen theory and Whiteheadian metaphysics.

84. Sarah Coakley, "Kenosis and Subversion," in *Swallowing a Fishbone: Feminist Theologians Debate Christianity*, ed. Daphne Hampson (London: SPCK, 1996), 108. Cf. Don Browning, "Love as Sacrifice, Love as Mutuality: A Response to Jeffrey Tillman," *Zygon* (September 2008): 541–62, on how "caritas" may include sacrifice but not as an end in itself.

85. Levinas, *Ethics and Infinity*, 56.

86. Levinas, *Totality and Infinity*, 236.

87. Thomas Ogletree, *Hospitality to the Stranger: Dimensions of Moral Understanding* (Philadelphia: Fortress Press, 1985), 3.

88. Dorothee Soelle, *Suffering*, trans. Everett R. Kalin (Philadelphia: Fortress Press, 1975), 75. Cf. Elaine Scarry, *The Body in Pain: The Making and Unmaking of the World* (New York: Oxford University Press, 1985), on the vital importance of "bringing pain to discourse." Sharon Betcher, a midcareer amputee, makes powerful use of such material in "Wisdom to Make the World Go On: On Disability and the Cultural Delegitimation of Suffering," in *God, Evil and Suffering, Essays in honor of Paul R. Sponhieim,* ed. Terence E. Fretheim and Curtis L. Thompson (St. Paul: Word and World, Luther Seminary, 2000), 87–98. Betcher offers a book-length development of this theme in *Spirit and the Politics of Disablement* (Minneapolis: Fortress Press, 2007).

89. Wolfhart Pannenberg, *Anthropology in Theological Perspective,* trans. Matthew J. O'Connell (Philadelphia: Westminster, 1985), 37.

90. Ibid., 39.

91. Ibid., 62.

92. Ibid., 371.

93. Ibid., 376.

94. Jürgen Habermas, *The Theory of Communicative Action,* trans. Thomas McCarthy (Boston: Beacon, 1984), 1:342. Earlier still, see his *Knowledge and Human Interests* (Boston: Beacon, 1971) on the very different categories of knowledge as that applies to genuine conversation.

95. James H. Burtness, *Consequences: Morality, Ethics, and the Future* (Minneapolis: Fortress Press, 1999), 46.

96. Thus, John B. Cobb Jr. titles his book on the conversation between the religions *Beyond Dialogue,* for he looks to mutual transformation.

97. Whitehead, *Process and Reality*, 111.

98. Mark D. Jordan, *Telling Truths in Church: Scandal, Flesh, and Christian Speech* (Boston: Beacon, 2003), 101.

99. Ted Peters, *God the World's Future* (Minneapolis: Fortress Press, 2000), 162, drawing on Letty Russell, *Human Liberation in a Feminist Perspective* (Philadelphia: Westminster, 1974).

100. I take this statement from an unpublished draft, "The Cross and Public Life in Pauline Theology." Cf. David Fredrickson, "Free Speech in Pauline Political Theology," *Word and World* 12, no. 4 (1992): 345–51.

101. Kierkegaard, *Works of Love*, 21.

102. Dietrich Bonhoeffer, *Life Together, Prayerbook of the Bible,* trans. Daniel W. Bloesch and James H. Burtness (Minneapolis: Fortress Press, 1996), 5.

103. Whitehead, *Process and Reality*, 338. Cf. *Adventures of Ideas,* 167, where the "message of peace, love and sympathy" and "the suffering, the agony, . . . the final despair" crowd into a single sentence.

104. Kierkegaard, *Works of Love*, 68.

105. Walter Wink, *Engaging the Powers: Discernment and Resistance in a World of Domination* (Minneapolis: Fortress Press, 1992), 263.

106. See "The Art of Power" in chapter 1, noting particularly the discussion of the passage in the journals cited there, 2:1251.

107. Gustaf Wingren, *Creation and Law*, trans. Ross Mackenzie (Philadelphia: Muhlenberg, 1961), 42–43.

108. See Outka, *Agape*, 302–3 for how agape may go "beyond a wide conception of justice." In effect, Outka is pointing out how agape cannot be commanded simply within a creational context (303).

109. Kierkegaard, *Concluding Unscientific Postscript*, 339.

110. Kierkegaard, *Works of Love*, 26, citing Prov. 4:23.

111. Ibid., 28.

112. Ibid., 12.

113. This is Marjorie Suchocki's formulation in the *The Fall to Violence*, ch. 9.

114. Post, *Altruism and Altruistic Love*, 8.

115. Catherine Keller, *God and Power: Counter-Apocalyptic Journeys* (Minneapolis: Fortress Press, 2005), 14.

116. Ibid.

117. Wink, *Engaging the Powers*, 267.

118. Physicist-theologian John Polkinghorne provides a helpful discussion of "motivated belief" in the fields of religion and science in *Theology in the Context of Science* (New Haven: Yale University Press, 2009). Of the motivation for religious belief, he writes, "There are two broad kinds of motivation for religious belief. One looks to certain general aspects of the human encounter with reality, while the other approach focuses on particularities of personal experience, including what are understood to have been specific acts of divine disclosure expressed through uniquely significant events and persons" (127). We can see Whitehead tending toward the former, and the latter being expressed by Kierkegaard.

119. I find particularly interesting Augustine's understanding of how in sin we use (*utor*) what in the order of being we should enjoy (*fruor*) and find our joy in what we should merely use. See *On Christian Doctrine*, trans. D. W. Robertson Jr. (Indianapolis: Bobbs-Merrill, 1958), book 1. Characteristically, Nygren remains critical: "Not even the ideas of 'Uti' and 'Frui' were able to deliver Augustine from the prevalent Hellenistic Eros theory. When he says we are to use the world in order to attain the enjoyment of God, he has the same idea as Plato had in urging us not to be captivated by the beautiful things in this world, but to use them as a ladder on which to ascend to the higher world." *Agape and Eros*, 512.

120. Catherine Keller, "Power Lines," 188–203, *Theology Today* 52, no. 2 (July, 1995): 203.

121. Catherine Keller, *On the Mystery: Discerning God in Process* (Minneapolis: Fortress Press, 2008), 84.

122. Langdon Gilkey, *Maker of Heaven and Earth: A Study of the Christian Doctrine of Creation* (Garden City, N.Y.: Doubleday, 1959, 1965), 22.

123. Wink, *Engaging the Powers*, 275.

124. Kierkegaard, *Concluding Unscientific Postscript*, 1:505. Indeed, there is a sense in which humor is not left behind in the decisively Christian. See *Practice in Christianity*, 125, for Anti-Climacus's presentation of the form of communication suitable for the contradiction involved in the God-man: a unity of jest and earnestness.

Chapter 5

1. *Webster's New World College Dictionary*, 4th ed. (Foster City, Calif.: IDG, 2001), 1221. For "recognize," see ibid., 1197.

2. At this point, theologians appealing to Luther's "theology of the cross" persistently refer us to Luther's twenty-first thesis for the Heidelberg Disputation: "A theologian of glory calls evil good and good evil. A theologian of the cross calls the thing

what it actually is." See *Martin Luther's Basic Theological Writings*, ed. Timothy Lull (Minneapolis: Fortress Press, 1989), 44.

3. Søren Kierkegaaard, *The Concept of Anxiety*, trans. Reidar Thomte (Princeton: Princeton University Press, 1980), 44–45.

4. Alfred North Whitehead, *Process and Reality*, corrected ed., ed. David Ray Griffin and Donald W. Sherburne (1929; New York: Free Press, 1978), 340.

5. Douglas John Hall, *God and Human Suffering: An Exercise in the Theology of the Cross* (Minneapolis: Augsburg Books, 1986), 54–56.

6. The Protestant Episcopal Church, *Book of Common Prayer* (New York: Seabury, 1976), 332.

7. Søren Kierkegaard, *The Sickness unto Death*, ed. and trans. Howard V. Hong and Edna H. Hong (Princeton: Princeton University Press, 1980), 14. The "forms of this sickness" are brilliantly detailed on pp. 29–74.

8. Whitehead, *Process and Reality*, 338.

9. Kierkegaard, *The Sickness unto Death*, 93.

10. Ibid., 29.

11. Kierkegaard, *The Concept of Anxiety*, 64–65. Cf. ibid., 47, 63, for the statement that women have more anxiety than men because they are "derived." The pseudonym Haufniensis does say "anxiety is by no means a sign of imperfection" (47).

12. Ibid., 66.

13. Ibid.

14. See the range of views represented in Céline Leon and Sylvia Walsh, *Feminist Interpretations of Kierkegaard* (University Park: Pennsylvania State University Press, 1997).

15. Kierkegaard, *The Concept of Anxiety*, 89.

16. Larry Rasmussen puts this succinctly in saying, "Nature and history are one." See his *Earth Community and Earth Ethics* (Maryknoll, N.Y.: Orbis, 1996), 259. The classic formulation is Claus Weizsäcker, *The History of Nature* (Chicago: University of Chicago Press, 1949).

17. Rita Nakashima Brock and Rebecca Ann Parker, *Saving Paradise: How Christianity Traded Love of This World for Crucifixion and Empire* (Boston: Beacon, 2008), 128.

18. A very helpful locating of freedom within the religion-and-science conversation is Joyce M. Cuff and Curtis L. Thompson, *Nature Alive: A Scientist and a Theologian Conversing on the Divine Promise of Possibility* (forthcoming). For an interesting biblical study on anthropology by an author knowledgeable about recent scientific findings, see Joel B. Green, *Body, Soul, and Human Life: The Nature of Humanity in the Bible* (Grand Rapids: Baker Academic, 2008). His "non-reductive physicalism" resembles Kierkegaard's emphasis on integration but adds a stronger place for body.

19. Whitehead, *Process and Reality*, 35.

20. Ibid., 108.

21. Whitehead, *Process and Reality*, 222. Cf. 255 on "the whole point of moral responsibility."

22. I have discussed this in *Faith and Process* (Minneapolis: Augsburg Publishing House, 1979), 303n54.

23. J. Gerald Janzen, "Modes of Presence and the Communion of Saints," in *Religious Experience and Process Theology*, ed. Harry James Cargas and Bernard Lee, 147–72 (New York: Paulist, 1976), 159.

24. Whitehead, *Process and Reality*, 308. A helpful secondary discussion is John Cobb's *A Christian Natural Theology* (Philadelphia: Westminster, 1965), 53, 78.

25. Alfred North Whitehead, *Religion in the Making* (New York: Fordham University Press, 1926, 1996), 111.

26. Charles Hartshorne and William Reese, eds., *Philosophers Speak of God* (Chicago: University of Chicago Press, 1953), 7.

27. Charles Hartshorne, *The Divine Relativity: A Social Conception of God* (New Haven: Yale University Press, 1948), 20. He writes, "This formula resolves the dilemma. For suppose the self-surpassing surpasser of all has the power of unfailingly enjoying as its own constituents whatever imperfect things come to exist. Then it will be bound to possess in its own unity all the values which the imperfect things severally and separately achieve, and therefore it is bound to surpass each and every one of them."

28. Kierkegaard, *The Sickness unto Death*, 126.

29. Ibid.

30. Ibid.

31. At least Christopher Hitchens will not grant us the first. See his *God Is Not Great* (New York: Warner, 2007).

32. Cf. David Blumenthal, "Theodicy: Dissonance in Theory and Praxis," in *The Fascination of Evil*, ed. David Tracy and Hermann Häring (Maryknoll, N.Y.: Orbis, 1998), for an eloquent protest against an abusive God.

33. I take this famous phrase from Maximus the Confessor, *Scholia "On the Divine Names" of Dionysius the Aeropagite*, 7.1 in *Patrologia Graeca* 4 (Paris: Garnier Fratres, 1889), col. 3412, as quoted in Jaroslav Pelikan, *The Christian Tradition, The Spirit of Eastern Christendom,* vol. 2, *(600–1700)* (Chicago: University of Chicago Press, 1974), 34.

34. Elizabeth A. Johnson, *She Who Is: The Mystery of God in Feminist Theological Discourse* (New York: Crossroad, 1992), 205.

35. Morris Cohen, "The Dark Side of Religion," in *Religion from Tolstoy to Camus*, ed. Walter Kaufmann (New York: Harper Torchbook, 1964), 289.

36. I have written of this in *Speaking of God: A Relational Theology* (St. Louis: Chalice, 2006), 150–55. A detailed engagement of the risks in faith's efficacy is available in my *God: The Question and the Quest* (Philadelphia: Fortress Press, 1985), ch. 4.

37. Rainer Maria Rilke, *Letters to a Young Poet*, trans. Stephen Mitchell (Boston: Shambhala, 1993), 34–35.

38. On Kierkegaard's appeal to Socrates, see *Søren Kierkegaard's Journals and Papers,* ed., Howard V. Hong and Edna H. Hong (Bloomington: Indiana University Press, 1970), 2:1251, and our discussion of the "art of power" in chapter one.

39. See Ted Peters, *God—The World's Future: Systematic Theology for a New Era,* 2nd ed. (Minneapolis: Fortress Press, 2000), 69–70.

40. Whitehead, *Religion in the Making*, 15.

41. Ibid.

42. Ibid., 18–19.

43. Ibid., 32.

44. Ibid., 54.

45. Ibid., 44.

46. Søren Kierkegaard, *Works of Love*, ed. and trans. Howard V. Hong and Edna H. Hong (Princeton: Princeton University Press, 1995), 379–80.

47. Søren Kierkegaard, *Concluding Unscientific Postscript*, ed. and trans. Howard V. Hong and Edna H. Hong (Princeton: Princeton University Press, 1992), 17.

48. Ibid., 201.

49. Ibid., 610.

50. Whitehead, *Religion in the Making*, 67.

51. This seems to be the direction Philip Clayton finds prevailing in postmodern faith. See his *Transforming Christian Theology: For Church and Society* (Minneapolis: Fortress Press, 2010), 39–42, where he stresses that "belonging comes first" in the triad "belonging, behaving, believing." An even more radical challenge is Tom Beaudoin, *Witness to Dispossession* (Maryknoll, N.Y.: Orbis, 2008), where we are called to recognize that "departure is the available and even necessary spiritual orientation for those who would try to deal with faith in the midst of the collapse of all attempts of religion to justify the truth of its claims by its exclusion of otherness" (140).

52. I particularly appreciate Douglas John Hall's emphasis at this point: "Faith that is *faith* and doesn't pretend to be 'sight' is modest enough to know (a) that it is one alternative among many, (b) that its public witness must be thoughtful and not just declaratory, and (c) that it may and must dialogue with other faiths." See his "Theology of the Cross: Challenge and Opportunity for the Post-Christendom Church," 252–63 in *Cross Examinations: Readings on the Meaning of the Cross Today,* ed. Marit Trelstad, (Minneapols: Fortress Press, 2006), 256.

53. Alfred North Whitehead, *The Concept of Nature* (Ann Arbor: University of Michigan Press, 1957), 163. The fuller reference is this: "Should we not distrust the jaunty assurance with which every age prides itself that it at last has hit upon the ultimate concepts in which all that happens can be formulated? The aim of science is to seek the simplest explanations of complex facts. We are apt to fall into the error of thinking that the facts are simple because simplicity is the goal of our quest."

54. In Whitehead's emphasis on the ultimate status of creativity, one certainly faces the stubborn fact that evil seems very creative. Thus, *Process and Reality,* 21: "Creativity is the universal of universals characterizing ultimate matter of fact. It is that ultimate principle by which the many, which are the universe disjunctively, become the one actual occasion, which is the universe conjunctively."

55. John Polkinghorne, *Science and the Trinity: The Christian Encounter with Reality* (London: SPCK, 2004), 150.

56. Jürgen Moltmann, *The Coming of God: Christian Eschatology,* trans. Margaret Kohl (Minneapolis: Fortress Press, 1996), 117–18. Helmut Peukert makes a comparable point about the connections between the generations in *Science, Action and Fundamental Theology: Toward a Theology of Communicative Action,* trans. James Bohman (Cambridge, Mass.: MIT Press, 1984), 69.

57. Kierkegaard, *The Concept of Anxiety,* 90. Cf. above, chapter 3, for our discussion of the "event-filled" character of creaturely life.

58. *Søren Kierkegaard's Journals and Papers,* 2:1123.

59. See especially 561–86 in the *Postscript.*

60. The Archimedean point image is Kierkegaard's own language about a key moment of disclosure in his own life, drawing on the image of a father's love as the key in the human experience of God. See the Hongs' discussion of this "fulcrum outside time and finitude whereby time and finitude can be moved" in *The Moment and other Late Writings,* ed. and trans. Howard V. Hong and Edna H. Hong (Princeton: Princeton University Press, 1998), xii.

61. See, for example, "The Moral" in *Practice in Christianity,* on grace as "the force" "from the other side" in the consciousness of sin. That God not only forgives sins but also forgets them is a vivid way of expressing divine decisiveness. See *Kierkegaard's Journals and Papers,* 2:1123. Cf. *The Sickness unto Death,* 100, for his critique of "speculation," which "cannot get it through its head that sin is to be completely forgotten." This decisiveness is what is at stake in the claim that "there is one way in which man could never in all eternity come to be like God: in forgiving sins." Ibid., 122.

62. Whitehead, *Process and Reality,* 91. Cf. the discussion in ch. two above.

63. Ibid., 92.

64. See the work of Catherine Keller and David Griffin regarding "*Creatio ex Chaosmos*" (creation out of chaos) in Thomas Jay Oord, *Defining Love: A Philosophical, Scientific, and Theological Engagement* (Grand Rapids: Brazos, 2010), 160–72.

65. I take this statement from Jonathan Strandjord's student essay "Do Not Go Gentle into That Good Night; Rage, Rage against the Dying of the Light," 32–49, in *Praxis: A Journal of Student Theology* (St. Paul: Luther Seminary, n.d.), 46. He makes the point that "there is no reason, therefore, that the present structure of the universe will continue forever. Indeed, it is more reasonable to suppose that a new cosmic epoch will evolve out of this one." This change would seem to offer the combination of continuity and

discontinuity entailed in Christian hope. Thus, in 2000, a group of scientists and theologians emerged from their three-year study process with the book *The End of the World and the Ends of God*, ed. J. Polkinghorne and M. Welker (Harrisburg, Pa.: Trinity Press International, 2000), writing that "the strongest theme to emerge from all our discussion . . . is the need to wrestle with the necessity for both continuity and discontinuity. . . . Too great an element of discontinuity would threaten the trust that it is 'Abraham, Isaac and Jacob' (and not some new persons bearing those names) who live with God. . . . Yet too great an element of continuity would threaten belief in the new creation, redeemed from the old creation's bondage to death and decay" (254).

66. Whitehead, *Process and Reality*, 346.

67. Ibid.

68. Ibid., 97.

69. Jay McDaniel has been particularly concerned to address the issue of ultimate hope for creatures other than humankind. In *Of God and Pelicans: A Theology of Reverence for Life* (Louisville: Westminster John Knox, 1989), he writes of the need for a "pelican heaven" for the backup chick that serves as insurance for the brood.

70. Marjorie Suchocki, *The End of Evil: Process Eschatology in Historical Context* (Albany: State University of New York Press, 1988). See also the remarkable debate between Suchocki and David Ray Griffin in *Process Studies* 18, no. 1 (Spring 1989): 57–68. A wide-ranging response to Professor Suchocki is Joseph Bracken, ed., *World without End: Christian Eschatology from a Process Perspective* (Grand Rapids: Eerdmans, 2005).

71. Suchocki, *The End of Evil*, 108.

72. Whitehead, *Process and Reality*, 340.

73. Ibid., 350.

74. In speaking of transitions large and small, it seems important to preserve the "arrow of time" as seems difficult to do in eschatological formulations speaking of God acting "from the future."

75. John Polkinghorne, *Science and Theology: An Introduction* (London: SPCK, 1998), 32.

76. John Polkinghorne, *Quarks, Chaos and Christianity* (New York: Crossroad, 1994, 2005), 101–2. Citing the "phase change" involved in something as ordinary as heating up water, he writes, "The laws of nature do not change, they are unfailingly consistent, yet the consequences of these laws can change spectacularly when one moves into a new regime."

77. The classic Christian eschatological formulation of that "next" life is that we will be *non posse peccare* ("not able to sin"), as distinguished from the Edenic state of *posse peccare* ("able to sin"). In between those boundary states lie two others, paradoxically mixed: "not able to not sin" and "able to not sin." Thus, the Christian diagram is not a circle. John Polkinghorne, *Theology in the Context of Science* (New Haven: Yale University Press, 2009), 157–58, seems to recognize this and offers an eschatology featuring "a new kind of matter" in which God's creativity redeems present matter "from the otherwise inevitable end in cosmic futility." For a fuller statement, see Polkinghorne's *Scientists as Theologians: A Comparison of the Writings of Ian Barbour, Arthur Peacocke, and John Polkinghorne* (London: SPCK, 1996), 54–55, where this new matter will have "new properties" by being "fully integrated with the divine life." Christopher Southgate offers a helpful summary of the options in *The Groaning of Creation: God, Evolution, and the Problem of Evil* (Louisville: Westminster John Knox, 2008), 87: "universal resurrection [Moltmann's own response to the need identified for us earlier], . . . objective immortality as outlined by Whitehead and taken up more recently by Haught; a modification of the latter to include subjective existence at the eschaton, . . . and 'material inscription,' a suggestion of the South African scholar Ernst Conradie."

78. Sharon Betcher, "Wisdom to Make the World Go On: On Disability and the Cultural Delegitimation of Suffering," in *God, Evil, and Suffering: Essays in Honor of Paul*

R. Sponheim, ed. T. E. Fretheim and C. L. Thompson (St. Paul: Word & World, 2000), 98. Dr. Betcher writes as a midlife amputee and may be presumed to know something about dependence on earth. See also Krista E. Hughes, "In the Flesh: A Feminist Vision of Hope," *Transformative Lutheran Theologies: Feminist, Womanist, and Mujerista Perspectives,* ed. Mary J. Streufert (Minneapolis: Fortress Press, 2010), 213–24.

79. Jürgen Moltmann, "Is There Life after Death?" in Polkinghorne and Welker, *The End of the World and the Ends of God,* 254. Cf. Moltmann's *The Coming of God: Christian Eschatology* (Minneapolis: Fortress Press, 1996).

80. See "Toward the Critique of Hegel's Philosophy of Law: Introduction," in *Writings of the Young Marx on Philosophy and Society,* ed. and trans. Loyd D. Easton and Kurt H. Guddat, 249–64 (Garden City, N.Y.: Doubleday Anchor, 1967), 250.

81. Alfred North Whitehead, *Adventures of Ideas* (1929; New York: Free Press, 1967), 296.

82. Ibid., 285.

83. In *Creation Untamed: The Bible, God, and Natural Disasters* (Grand Rapids, Mich: Baker Academic, 2010), 24, Terence Fretheim makes this point vividly, noting that in Genesis not only do humans share the sixth day with the animals, but also "in view of the genealogical reference in Genesis 2:4 . . . it could be claimed that the earth is understood to be an integral aspect of the human ancestral heritage."

84. See Arthur O. Lovejoy, *The Great Chain of Being: A Study in the History of an Idea* (New York: Harper, 1936).

85. Arthur Peacocke, *Paths from Science towards God* (Oxford: Oneworld, 2001), 72.

86. See above, notes 50 and 51 in chapter 1, on a debate among process thinkers as to whether some "interiority" goes "all the way down." In the contemporary religion-and-science conversation, Cuff and Thompson, *Nature Alive,* ch. 6, draw on Stuart Kauffman and reach back to Whitehead and Dewey to plead for a theological naturalism that recognizes humanity's embeddedness in the natural world.

87. Whitehead, *Process and Reality,* 348. Cf. the other parallels: permanent/fluent, one/many, immanence/transcendence.

88. Cf. above, ch. 2.

89. See Sharon Welch, *A Feminist Ethic of Risk* (Minneapolis: Fortress Press, 1990).

90. See above, ch. 2, the section on "Imagining God's World."

91. Kierkegaard, *Concluding Unscientific Postscript,* 341.

92. Ibid., 322–23. He is not at this point engaging the objective actuality of the paradox that the radically Christian "Religiousness B" entails. But this ethical stress on subjectivity is carried forward into that formulation of the "ethico-religious."

93. Cf. Kierekgaard, *Practice in Christianity,* 31.

94. Ibid.

95. Whitehead, *Process and Reality,* 346.

96. Sallie McFague, *A New Climate for Theology: God, the World, and Global Warming* (Minneapolis: Fortress Press, 2008), 15. A powerful literary apocalyptic is Cormac McCarthy's Pulitzer Prize–winning *The Road* (New York: Knopf, 2006). Disaster and hope are here held together.

97. Karen Baker-Fletcher, *My Sister, My Brother: Womanist and Xodus God-Talk,* Bishop Henry McNeal Turner/Sojourner Truth Series in Black Religion 12 (Maryknoll, N.Y.: Orbis, 1997), 84. She offers a full Trinitarian statement in *Dancing with God: The Trinity from a Womanist Perspective* (St. Louis: Chalice, 2006). Monica A. Coleman offers a very accessible discussion of a range of womanist theologies and pointedly summarizes Baker-Fletcher's emphasis: "We see Jesus not only in the faces of black women, but in the face of the earth, waters, wind and sun." *Making a Way Out of No Way: A Womanist Theology* (Minneapolis: Fortress Press, 2008), 29. An eloquent comparable effort drawing on Teilhard de Chardin is Alejandro Garcia-Rivera, *The Garden of God: A Theological Cosmology* (Minneapolis: Fortress Press, 2009).

98. Cf. above, ch. one, the section on "Despair: Sickness and Sin," and especially the reference to the *Journals*, 3:2513.

99. For specific examples from diverse cultures, see Rosemary Radford Reuther, "Ecofeminst Philosophy, Theology, and Ethics: A Comparative View," in *Ecospirit: Religions and Philosophies for the Earth*, ed. Laurel Kearns and Catherine Keller (New York: Fordham University Press, 2007).

100. John B. Cobb Jr., *Is It Too Late? A Theology of Ecology* (Beverly Hills, Calif.: Bruce, 1972). Jay McDaniel has been particularly active in developing the ecological imperative of a process-sensitive faith. See his *With Roots and Wings* (Maryknoll, N.Y.: Orbis, 1995).

101. Paul Santmire, *Nature Reborn: The Ecological and Cosmic Promise of Christian Theology* (Minneapolis: Fortress Press, 2000), 69–70. He goes on to wonder at the givenness, spontaneity, and beauty of the "other."

102. Holmes Rolston III, "Kenosis and Nature," in *The Work of Love: Creation as Kenosis*, ed. John Polkinghorne (Grand Rapids: Eedrmans, 2001), 56.

103. Ibid., 64.

104. Ibid. Taking the long view can become a sedative once again, of course. The "next millennium" has begun, and as I write this, we are anxiously lamenting the failed 2009 attempt in Copenhagen to write a meaningful global climate treaty. The agreement at Cancun in December 2010 for voluntary contributions to a Green fund represents inadequate progress. A current, thoroughly researched statement of the crisis is Al Gore's most recent book, *Our Choice: A Plan to Solve the Climate Crisis* (Emmaus, Pa.: Rodale, 2009). Looking ahead, Gore says that *if* we act responsibly in this critical time, it will have been for this reason: "Our way of thinking changed. The earth itself began to occupy our thoughts" (401).

Conclusion

1. *Webster's New World College Dictionary*, 4th ed. (Foster City, Calif.: IDG, 2001), 97.

2. William C. Placher, *The Domestication of Transcendence: How Modern Thinking about God Went Wrong* (Louisville: Westminster John Knox, 1996), 211.

3. Thus, Sarah Coakley writes, "God's causality is necessarily unique and sui generis. It is quite unlike any specific created causal act, because it operates on a completely different level." "Evolution and Sacrifice," *Christian Century*, October 20, 2009, 10–11. Coakley is discussing the contribution that "cooperation" in a technical, evolutionary sense makes to an understanding of God's action, linking the cross to God's creational activity and our calling to live with altruism on this imperiled planet. This admirable argument seems weakened by the mystifying special appeal on the matter of causality.

4. For a discussion of such double agency, see Robert H. King, *The Meaning of God* (Philadelphia: Fortress Press, 1973), 85–96. Cf. Alvin Plantinga, *God and Other Minds: A Study of the Rational Justification of Belief in God* (Ithaca: Cornell University Press, 1967); and *The Nature of Necessity* (Oxford: Clarendon, 1974) for his now classic rejection of the thesis that divine determinism and human freedom are compatible. Cf. Bruce R. Reichenbach, *Evil and the Good God* (New York: Fordham University Press, 1982), 74–76, for a critique of the attempt to distinguish between "causing" and "bringing it about."

5. See Heinrich Schmid, *Doctrinal Theology of the Evangelical Lutheran Church*, trans. Charles A. Hay and Henry E. Jacobs (Philadelphia: Lutheran Publication Society, 1889), 181, for how God "concurs" differently with good and evil actions, for "God is determined in employing different methods of directing the world for the accomplishment of his designs." The range is "permission, hinderance, [*sic*] direction and determination." Cf. ibid., 193.

6. Placher, *The Domestication of Transcendence*, 181.

7. John B. Cobb Jr. makes this point effectively by asking about the nature of true power: "This view [unlimited omnipotence] not only slanders the moral character of God, but also attributes to him very little power. He is seen as omnipotent in the sense of being the only power there is; but where there is no competing power, omnipotence means little. The power required to lead an army of tin soldiers is given to every child, since the soldiers have so little power to resist, but the power required to lead men [sic] is incomparably greater precisely because those who are led retain power of their own. To think of God as more like the potter or the child is to degrade his power. The power that counts is the power to influence the exercise of power by others." *God and the World* (Philadelphia: Westminster, 1969), 89,

8. Cf. Thomas Jay Oord, *Defining Love: A Philosophical, Scientific, and Theological Engagement* (Grand Rapids: Brazos, 2010), 187–89, for a comparable critique of "divine unilateralism," stressing the difficulties of "absolute determinism, divine predestination, and lack of intrinsic creaturely value."

9. Michael Peterson, *God and Evil: An Introduction to the Issues* (Boulder, Colo.: Westview, 1998), 102, citing Nancy Frankenberry, whose appreciative criticism is well known in the process community. Cf. *The Power of God: Readings on Omnipotence and Evil*, ed. Linwood Urban and Douglas N. Walton (New York: Oxford University Press, 1978), esp. 171–213, on "omnipotence and human freedom."

10. Søren Kierkegaard, *Either/Or*, ed. and trans. Howard V. Hong and Edna H. Hong (Princeton: Princeton University Press, 1987), 1:3. The concern for this distinction abides with Kierkegaard. Cf. the *Concluding Unscientific Postscript*, ed. and trans. Howard V. Hong and Edna H. Hong (Princeton: Princeton University Press, 1992), 1:138: "The longer life goes on and the longer the existing person through his action is woven into existence, the more difficult it is to separate the ethical from the external, and the easier it seems to corroborate the metaphysical tenet that the outer is the inner, the inner the outer, the one wholly commensurate with the other."

11. See Søren Kierkegaard, *The Sickness unto Death*, ed. and trans. Howard V. Hong and Edna H. Hong (Princeton: Princeton University Press, 1980), 13, for the full formulation: "The self is a relation that relates itself to itself or is the relation's relating itself to itself in the relation; the self is not the relation but is the relation's relating itself to itself."

12. Ronald L. Hall provides an instructive discussion of Kierkegaard on the value entailed in exercising human freedom in *The Human Embrace: The Love of Philosophy and the Philosophy of Love* (University Park: Pennsylvania State University Press, 2000).

13. "The Formula of Concord," in *Book of Concord*, ed. Robert Kolb and Timothy J. Wengert, trans. Charles Arand et al. (Minneapolis: Fortress Press, 2000), 488. It is true, of course, that the confessors also critique the opposite error of minimizing the gravity of human sin.

14. Terence E. Fretheim, *Nature Untamed: The Bible, God, and Natural Disasters* (Grand Rapids: Baker Academic, 2010), 15. He cites Isa 43:5 and Ps 8:5 as examples.

15. Edward Farley, provides a useful summary of this theme in twentieth-century philosophy in *Good and Evil: Interpreting a Human Condition* (Minneapolis: Fortress Press, 1990), 31–46.

16. I have offered a brief summary discussion in *Faith and the Other: A Relational Theology* (Minneapolis: Fortress Press, 1993), ch. 1. A fuller discussion is Lawrence Cahoone, *The Dilemma of Modernity: Philosophy, Culture and Anti-Culture* (Albany: State University of New York Press, 1988).

17. Alastair MacIntyre's classic analysis of this development in ethics is *After Virtue: A Study in Moral Theory* (Notre Dame: Notre Dame University Press, 1981). The parallel development in philosophy is well represented by Richard Rorty, *Philosophy and the Mirror of Nature* (Princeton: Princeton University Press, 1979). Robert Bellah's analysis

of the popular expression of this pole in "expressive individualism" and "utilitarian individualism" is *Habits of the Heart: Individualism and Commitment in American Life* (Berkeley: University of California Press, 1985).

18. Cahoone, *The Dilemma of Modernity*, 71–72.

19. Eberhard Jüngel, "The Truth of Life: Observations on Truth as the Interruption of the Continuity of Life," in *Creation, Christ and Culture*, ed. R. W. A. McKinney (Edinburgh: T & T Clark, 1976), 232–33.

20. Ted Peters, *God: The World's Future; Systematic Theology for a New Era*, 2nd ed. (Minneapolis: Fortress Press, 2000), 17.

21. Kierkegaard, *Either/Or*, 2:88–89. Consistently, Kierkegaard stresses that "a married man ought to be able to explain his marriage."

22. Ibid., 305.

23. Ibid., 263.

24. One associates that more disjunctive emphasis, as regards Creator and creature, with a dangerously selective reading of Karl Barth's references to Kierkegaard on the "infinite qualitative difference," especially in his *The Epistle to the Romans* (London: Oxford University Press, 1933). Less attention has been given to Barth's criticism of Kierkegaard for neglecting "the *joyous* message of God's YES to man." Karl Barth, "Mein Verhaltnis zu Søren Kierkegaard," *Orbis Litterarum* (1963): 69.

25. Søren Kierkegaard, *Concluding Unscientific Postscript*, 1:294.

26. Ibid., 555.

27. Søren Kierkegaard, *Fear and Trembling*, ed. and trans. Howard V. Hong and Edna H. Hong (Princeton: Princeton University Press, 1983).

28. Ibid., 70.

29. Alfred North Whitehead, *Adventures of Ideas* (1929; New York: Free Press, 1967), 157.

30. Charles Hartshorne, *The Divine Relativity: A Social Conception of God* (New Haven: Yale University Press, 1948), 60.

31. Were one to ponder the question of actual historical influence, a key would be to study the work of William James, who had read Kierkegaard with appreciation and whom Whitehead acknowledges as a major influence. See our discussion of "Ambiguity and Audacity" in chapter 3 above and particularly the passage cited there from *A Pluralistic Universe, William James' Writings 1902–1910* (New York: Library of America, 1961), 815.

32. Sallie McFague, *The Body of God* (Minneapolis: Augsburg Fortress, 1993), 16.

33. Philip Schultz, "The Music," in *Articulations: The Body and Illness in Poetry*, ed. Jon Mukand (Iowa City: University of Iowa Press, 1994), 3. I am grateful to Kirsten Mebust for this reference.

34. See the distinctions ("deconstructive," "liberationist," "conservative") suggested in David Ray Griffin, William A. Beardslee, and Joe Holland, *Varieties of Postmodern Theology* (Albany: State University of New York Press, 1989). In *Two Great Truths: A New Synthesis of Scientific Naturalism and Christian Faith* (Louisville: Westminster John Knox, 2004), Griffin details the "commonsense" notions about freedom and the role of mind in causation against sensationalist, atheistic, and materialistic views.

35. Kierkegaard, *The Sickness unto Death*, 79.

36. Ibid.

37. Dietrich Bonhoeffer, *Creation and Fall*, trans. Douglas Stephen Bax, ed. John W. de Gruchy (Minneapolis: Fortress Press, 1997), 63.

38. Kierkegaard, *The Sickness unto Death*, 13. My emphasis.

39. Kierkegaard, *Concluding Unscientific Postscript*, 1:118. It is true that he adds, "Existence itself is a system—for God." Yet one of the theses from Lessing that Kierkegaard claimed for himself was this: "If God held all truth enclosed in his right hand, and in his left hand the one and only ever-striving drive for truth, even with the corollary

of erring forever and ever, and if he were to say to me: Choose!—I would humbly fall down to him at his left hand and say: Father, give! Pure truth is indeed only for you alone!" (ibid., 1:106). Curtis Thompson has provided a very helpful discussion of the relationship between Kierkegaard and Lessing in "Gotthold Ephraim Lessing: Appropriating the Testimony of a Theological Naturalist," in *Kierkegaard and the Renaissance and Modern Traditions,* ed. Jon Stewart (Surrey, U.K.: Ashgate, 2009), 1:77–112. Here one treads on the ground of formulating the nature of God's qualitative difference from the creaturely. See our earlier discussion of this distinction, as found also in Whitehead, above, in "Imagining God's World" in chapter 2. But the qualitative difference is not to be formulated in a way that closes the future to the existing individual. See Patrick Sheil, *Kierkegaard and Levinas: The Subjunctive Mood* (Surrey, U.K.: Ashgate, 2010).

40. Alfred North Whitehead, *Process and Reality,* corrected ed., ed. David Ray Griffin and Donald W. Sherburne (New York: Free, 1978), 14. Recall also his emphasis on "A Deeper Experience" as discussed in chapter 2 above. Again here, as indicated in the previous note, one would need to place Whitehead's insistence that "God is not to be treated as an exception to all metaphysical principles, invoked to save their collapse" (343) in relation to the formulation of God's qualitative superiority, as suggested in Whitehead by the reversal of the poles of existence (36, 87).

41. They kept writing despite what had to be discouraging failures in communication. It is widely recognized that in 1846, Kierkegaard planned to stop writing because he believed his message had been conveyed. He would seek to do the work of a pastor in a rural parish. Hence, his final work was to be the *Concluding* [!] *Unscientific Postscript.* See the historical introduction in the *Postscript,* 2:xi–xii. See also his *Journals and Papers,* ed. and trans. Howard V. Hong and Edna H. Hong (Princeton: Princeton University Press, 1970), 5:5873. Deeply disappointed at the response to his writing, and aroused by the scurrilous attack on him by the popular magazine the *Corsair,* he could not ignore the "Christian collisions," so the *Postscript* is followed by the intensely religious works of Anti-Climacus, *The Sickness unto Death* and *Practice in Christianity.* Whitehead's discouragement may have emphasized oral communication. Victor Lowe, *Alfred North Whitehead: The Man and His Work* (Baltimore: Johns Hopkins University Press, 1985, 1990), 2:207–8, points to the failure of his 1927 lectures at the University of Virginia that became the book *Symbolism: Its Meaning and Effect* and reports (2:250) the dramatic dwindling of attendance at the Gifford lectures (1927–1928). His writing seemed to fare better, as notably with *Science and the Modern World* (1925).

42. Paul Ricoeur, *History and Truth,* trans. Charles Kelbley (Evanston, Ill.: Northwestern University Press, 2007), 5.

43. I particularly like Val Webb's early analytical book *In Defense of Doubt* (St. Louis: Chalice, 1995), as well as her more recent constructive effort, *Like Catching Water in a Net: Human Attempts to Describe the Divine* (New York: Continuum, 2007). A further statement can be found in Karen Armstrong, *The Case for God* (New York: Knopf, 2009).

44. Kierkegaard, *Concluding Unscientific Postscript,* 97.

45. Kierkegaaard, *The Sickness unto Death,* 87.

46. Kierkegaard, *Fear and Trembling,* 67. Cf. ibid., 121: "The highest passion in a person is faith." Cf. *Concluding Unscientific Postscript,* 1:610: "Being a Christian is defined not by the 'what' of Christianity but by the 'how' of the Christian. This 'how' can fit only one thing, the absolute paradox."

47. Dorothee Soelle, *Suffering,* trans. Everett R. Kalin (Philadelphia: Fortress Press, 1975), 107. She is fully clear about the creational basis for this affirmation, citing Simone Weil: "Not to accept an event which happens in the world is to wish that the world did not exist."

48. Jonathan P. Strandjord, "Suffering, Desire, Temptation, and Ecstatic Apologetics," in *God, Evil, and Suffering: Essays in Honor of Paul R. Sponheim,,* ed. Terence E. Fretheim and Curtis L. Thompson, 136–42 (St. Paul: Word & World, 2000), 141.

49. William P. Young, *The Shack: Where Tragedy Confronts Eternity* (Newberry Park, Calif.: Windblown Media, 2007), 95.

50. Ibid., 126. Cf. 132: "Freedom involves trust and obedience inside a relationship of love."

51. Ibid., 102. Cf. 163.

52. Søren Kierkegaard, *Christian Discourses*, ed. and trans. Howard V. Hong and Edna H. Hong (Princeton: Princeton University Press, 1997), 128.

53. Søren Kierkegaard, *Philosophical Fragments*, ed. and trans. Howard V. Hong and Edna H. Hong (Princeton: Princeton University Press, 1985), 55. See above, "God's Omnipotent Resolution" in chapter 1.

54. *Søren Kierkegaard's Journals and Papers*, ed, Howard V. Hong and Edna H. Hong (Bloomington: Indiana University Press, 1970), 3:2554. See also our discussion in chapter 1 of "God Willing One Thing." In *Jesus: Uncovering the Life, Teachings, and Relevance of a Religious Revolutionary* (New York: HarperCollins, 2006), 274, Marcus Borg has written vividly of how that decisive commitment is instantiated in the passion of Jesus: "His passion was God and the kingdom of God—and it led to his execution by the 'powers that be.'"

Borg helpfully distinguishes the notion of sacrifice from that of substitution (269), making the point that Jesus died "because of," not "for" the sins of the world (274). What is at stake in this is the very character of God. Let us not suggest that "God can forgive sins only if adequate payment is made" (270).

55. Whitehead, *Process and Reality*, 244.

56. Douglas John Hall, *God and Human Suffering: An Exercise in the Theology of the Cross* (Minneapolis: Augsburg Books, 1986), 99.

57. One recalls Jürgen Moltmann's distinctions in his bombshell book *The Crucified God* (London: SCM, 1974), 230: "There is unwilling suffering, there is accepted suffering and there is the suffering of love." For a sustained statement of the deleterious efficacy of the notion of impassibility, see Geddes MacGregor, *He Who Lets Us Be: A Theology of Love* (New York: Seabury, 1975).

58. Martha Nussbaum, *The Fragility of Goodness: Luck and Ethics in Greek Tragedy and Philosophy* (Cambridge: Cambridge University Press, 1986), 20. Ronald Hall brings Nussbaum and Kierkegaard together in an illuminating discussion in *The Human Embrace*.

59. Dietrich Bonhoeffer, *Letters and Papers from Prison*, ed. Eberhard Bethge, trans. Reginald Fuller and Frank Clarke (New York: SCM, 1967), 188 (letter of July 14, 1944). Thus Douglas John Hall can write that "love is the only power that to achieve its aim, must become weak." See his "Theology of the Cross: Challenge and Opportunity for the Post-Christendom Church," 252–58 in *Cross Examinations: Readings on the Meaning of the Cross Today*, ed. Marit Trelstad (Minneapolis: Fortress Press, 2006), 257. Comparably, Simone Weil talks of loving an "all-power*less* God." *The Notebooks of Simone Weil*, trans. A. Wills (New York: G. P. Putnam's Sons, 1956), 1:284. The recognition of genuine power may be compromised by an appeal to the hiddenness of God. See Alexander Nava, "The Mystery of Evil and the Hiddenness of God: Some Thoughts on Simone Weil," in *The Fascination of Evil*, ed. David Tracy and Hermann Häring, 74–84 (Maryknoll, N.Y.: Orbis, 1998).

60. Ibid. In "The Crucified God, Yesterday and Today: 1972–2002," 127–38, in *Cross Examinations,* 130–31, Jürgen Moltmann sees two reasons why patristic theology held fast to "the apathy axiom": distinguishing the Divine from suffering humans, and offering salvation to those humans through deification. He notes that these arguments fall short because they neglect "*active suffering,* which involves the willingness to open oneself to be touched, moved, affected by others—and that means the suffering of *passionate love,"* 130–31.

61. Walker Percy, *The Second Coming* (New York: Washington Square, 1980), 198. Recall from chapter 1 that Percy read Kierkegaard closely.

62. Burton Z. Cooper, *Why, God?* (Louisville: Westminster John Knox, 1988), 102.

63. Whitehead, *Process and Reality*, 343.

64. Ibid.

65. Bruce G. Epperly makes this point effectively: "Our creativity, even if it does not conform fully to God's ideals for a particular moment of experience, is not a fall from grace, but an opportunity for novel expressions of divine and creaturely creativity. Creaturely agency often leads to pain and suffering, but God is infinitely inventive in lovingly and non-coercively responding to both the negative and positive impact of creaturely agency." "Infinite Freedom, Creativity, and Love: The Adventures of a Non-competitive God," *Encounter* 71, no. 2 (2010), 45–54.

66. Whitehead, *Process and Reality*, 343.

67. Ibid., 351.

68. Cf. Marjorie Suchocki, *In God's Presence: Theological Reflections on Prayer* (St. Louis: Chalice, 1996), 24, as discussed above in the introduction.

69. In chapter 5 of *Why, God?* Burton Z. Cooper offers a detailed analysis of the power present in nonviolent resistance. Cf. Walter Wink, *Engaging the Powers: Discernment and Resistance in a World of Domination* (Minneapolis: Fortress Press, 1992).

70. Daniel Simundson nicely summarizes Bildad's counsel: "The only proper question for Job is to look deeply within himself and ask which sin precipitated all of this suffering and then to repent so he can move on to better things." "The Case of Job," in *God, Evil, and Suffering*, 75–84 , quoting from 81.

71. Carol Newsome, "Job," in *The Women's Bible Commentary*, ed. Carol A. Newsome and Sharon H. Ringe (Louisville: Westminster John Knox, 1992), 136.

72. William Brown, *Character in Crisis* (Grand Rapids: Eerdmans, 1996), 100. The translation of Job 42:6 is notoriously difficult. Terence Fretheim prefers J. Gerald Janzen's translation: "Therefore I recant and change my mind concerning dust and ashes." See Fretheim's *God and World in the Old Testament: A Relational Theology of Creation* (Nashville: Abingdon, 2005), 232. Perhaps Job came to know what Abraham believed in interceding for the righteous in Sodom: "Let me take it upon myself to speak to the Lord, I who am but dust and ashes" (Gen. 18:27).

73. The bibliography for these issues is vast. My basic effort is *Faith and the Other*. The pile of relevant books seems to grow exponentially. To mention simply three titles from the last couple of years: (for the first issue) Sallie McFague, *A New Climate for Theology: God, the World, and Global Warming* (Minneapolis: Fortress Press, 2008), (for the second) *The Embrace of Eros: Bodies, Desires, and Sexuality in Christianity*, ed. Margaret D. Kamitsuka (Minneapolis: Fortress Press, 2010), and (for the third) Werner G. Jeanrond, *A Theology of Love* (London: T & T Clark, 2010).

74. Cf. Frederick Sontag, "A Divine Response 'Now Hear This,'" in *Encountering Evil: Live Options in Theology*, ed. Stephen T. Davis, 204–9 (Louisville: Westminster John Knox, 1998), 206: "Since 'time before time' has meaning again in our evolutionary universe, so does 'time after time.'"

75. Cf. Scott Bader-Saye, *Following Jesus in a Culture of Fear* (Grand Rapids: Brazos, 2007). He is particularly helpful in warning against "fearlessness" as "a bad idea" and in calling us to the risks of hospitality, peacemaking, and generosity. In "In the Flesh: A Feminist Vision of Hope," in *Transformative Lutheran Theologies: Feminist, Womanist, and Mujerista Perspectives*, Mary J. Streufert, ed. (Minneapolis: Fortress Press, 2010), 213–23, Krista Hughes writes of how the rhetoric of fear on the airwaves and e-waves can cultivate "virtual fears," that take on a disproportionate life of their own. Such fears pose a triple danger: "distracting us from the real threats to livelihood and health that do deserve our attention, fostering a sense of our own helplessness, and projecting our fears onto others in the form of anger, hatred, and violence."

76. Miroslav Volf puts this beautifully: "Finally, the goal of God's love is—love." "God Is Love," 29–34, *Christian Century* 127, no. 22 (November 2, 2010): 34.

77. Kierkegaard, *The Moment and Late Writings*, 341.

78. Whitehead, in writing of many things that "constitute the ultimate religious evidence," remarks, "Mothers can ponder many things in their hearts which their lips cannot express." *Religion in the Making* (1926; New York: Fordham University Press, 1996), 67. This saying itself is worth pondering.

79. Thomas Jay Oord emphasizes how God's love may be expressed "indirectly" through "the impact of a localized creaturely body upon others." "A Process Wesleyan Theodicy: Freedom, Embodiment, and the Almighty God," in *Thy Nature and Thy Name Is Love: Wesleyan and Process Theologies in Dialogue*, ed. Bryan P. Stone and Thomas Jay Oord, 193–216 (Nashville: Abingdon, 2001), 214.

80. This formulation brings together the formulations of Anti-Climacus ("with God everything is possible"; *The Sickness unto Death,* 38–42) and Climacus (God is "obliged to continue" in the loving will known in the incarnate Christ; *Philosophical Fragments*, 55).

NAME/SUBJECT INDEX

SCRIPTURE INDEX